PIKE

An In-Fisherman
Handbook of Strategies

PIKE

An In-Fisherman Handbook of Strategies

Al Lindner
Fred Buller
Doug Stange
Dave Csanda
Ron Lindner
Bob Ripley
Jan Eggers

Published by
Al Lindner's Outdoors, Inc.

Book Compiled by Bob Ripley
Cover Art by Larry Tople
Artwork by Chuck Nelson and Dan Vickerman
Typesetting by Type/Graphics
Litho Prep by Nordell Graphic Communications
Printing by Bang
Copyright 1983 by Al Lindner
All rights reserved
Published by Al Lindner's Outdoors, Inc.
P.O. Box 999, Brainerd, Minnesota 56401
Printed in the United States of America
ISBN 0-9605254-2-4

First Edition, 1983

Library of Congress Catalogue
Card Number 83-83060

ISBN 0-9605254-2-4

ACKNOWLEDGEMENT

Most books on fishing contain very little that is truly new. At best, they may introduce one or two new concepts. However, not one concept—not two—but *most* of the information contained in this book is not only new—but of *breakthrough* status. The credit for this goes not only to the authors, but to the many knowledgeable folks the authors assembled this information from.

For example, we are very grateful to persons like former biologist Dick Sternberg (now project chief for a book company), who helped to initially crack the code of the pike's cold water nature as it grew to large size. We are also indebted to many state biologists, like Asa Wright (Michigan) and Lee Kernen (Wisconsin); and to Dr. E. J. Crossman, curator of the Department of Ichthyology and Herpetology at the Royal Ontario Museum; just to name a few, who contributed invaluable background information.

Then, too, there is the vast input gleaned from anglers themselves. Some of these folks have national reputation; others were lesser known—but just as knowledgeable. Men like Ron Kobes, for example, lent great help to us with his unique presentation tips. Fishing educator Tony Dean supplied much of the foundation knowledge for understanding reservoir pike behavior. And the list goes on.

We would especially like to thank our two European experts, Dutchman Jan Eggers and Englishman Fred Buller. Jan is a premier pike angler who speaks and translates a number of languages, and collects information from a broad array of sources. In fact, Jan knows more about worldwide pike records than any living man. Fred Buller, on the other hand, is an expert on refined fishing methods, which he feels are vital to catching the large, shy, heavily-fished, sophisticated pike of England and Ireland. Fred lent us great help in this regard.

Beyond this background material, each of the authors himself has shared in breakthroughs of major importance. Men like the legendary Bill Binkelman, who helped devise the Calendar Periods, and Ron Lindner, who developed the body of water classification system, aid us to more clearly visualize the pike's unique lifestyle. Through the authors' on-the-water experience, both individually and with great pike fishermen from all around the world, many secrets, tricks and tips are passed on to you in this original edition of PIKE: an *IN-FISHERMAN* HANDBOOK OF STRATEGIES.

VI

TABLE OF CONTENTS

INTRODUCTION

In many places (particularly North America), the pike is considered "the other fish"—a gamefish to go after in addition to a primary target like walleyes, bass or lake trout. It's often caught "by accident" while fishing for something else. However, many anglers go after pike "on purpose"—and not only catch pike consistently, but bag the big ones! Whether you're a big pike hunter, or just a "sometimes" pike angler, there's something in *Pike: An IN-FISHERMAN Handbook of Strategies* for you.

There is little need to praise the pike's fighting ability; it is a worldwide, legendary tackle buster. If North America did not have the musky to hang its myths and legends on, the pike's popularity would probably be much greater. Admittedly not as pretty as a trout, nor acrobatic as a musky, the pike, nonetheless, commands respect in each and every one of these categories. While the pike may take second place to these other fish for the aforementioned reasons, it takes no back seat for its wiliness.

Big pike (those fish in the 20 pound plus category) are perhaps the most elusive North American freshwater gamefish. We believe that, "numberswise," big pike are harder to catch than big brown trout—a fish known for its skittish nature.

While numbers of lunker pike can exist in a body of water, few are taken—especially during the open water season by rod and reel. Why? Well, after reading this book, you'll know not only why—but how to go about remedying the situation.

One of the major breakthroughs of this book is that, "a pike is not a pike, is not a pike." It quickly becomes apparent that small, medium and large-sized pike can and do exhibit markedly different behavior patterns—even within the same lake, river or reservoir. And, if you want to catch different-sized fish, you have to fish for them in very different manners. This is not necessarily true of other fish like bass, walleyes, muskies or trout. As you read each of the chapters, you will note that we treat different-sized pike almost as if they were different species of fish. It's vitally important to understand this all-important concept, because the material that follows hinges on this premise.

If you are not already acquainted with our Calendar Period and body of water identification formats, take the time to study them. Many of the chapters are designed around this basis. Further, we have coined many of our own terms—contained in the glossary at the end of the book. Take time to familiarize yourself with these *before* jumping into the book itself. It will help you better understand and appreciate the subtleties of pike fishing.

Over the years, the publishers, editors and contributors of the *IN-FISHERMAN* Magazine have pioneered the art of pike angling. Most major breakthroughs were either published first in the magazine, or spearheaded by one of its people. Therefore, no one, perhaps, was more qualified to compile a complete pike book than these folks. Because the subject is so broad—and spans such diverse regions of the world—no one person could have done justice to such an undertaking. Therefore, seven authors combined their experience, contacts and know-how to produce this comprehensive book.

Throughout the book, we use the *IN-FISHERMAN* classification system of lakes, rivers and reservoirs, and our Calendar Period format, to exactly explain specific circumstances. We detail when (what season, what time of day, etc.), and where (the exact structural locale) each condition occurs. Then, when we explain "presentation" (how to go about catching pike), you can visualize the *exact* circumstances to apply that specific method in. No guesswork here!

Pike: An IN-FISHERMAN Handbook of Strategies is at once a reference guide and a handbook. It is meant to be read for background material, and to act as a tutor for practical, on-the-water applications. The book is written in a "results-oriented" manner. After reading the book, you can weigh its worth by the fish you catch, and your ever-increasing ability to adapt to different pike waters and different seasons of the year.

Pike: An IN-FISHERMAN Handbook of Strategies is only one of a series of books produced by the *IN-FISHERMAN*. If you enjoy and learn from it, we suggest reading our companion titles *Bass: A Handbook of Strategies*, and *Walleye Wisdom: A Handbook of Strategies*.

Chapter 1
NATURE'S WATER WOLF... THE PIKE

"...From the days of Gesner (a 16th century chronicler) downward, more lies—to put it in very plain language—have been told about the pike than any other fish in the world; and the greater the improbability of the story, the more particularly it is sure to be quoted..."

(Frank Buckland, fishing writer circa 1880)

No species has inspired more fables than the evil-eyed marauder of inland waters, the pike. Even its Anglo Saxon name "pike" was derived not from nature, but from a "spear-like" slashing weapon of the Middle Ages.

Tales like this gave birth to the pike's scientific (Latin) name *Esox lucius*. If you compare the pike's sleek shape and sharp mouth with the weapon, and combine it with the fish's stalking and hunting habits, it's easy to see why Europeans likened it to a water wolf, "the luce," meaning a long, spear-like wolf of the water.

The pike has a long and hallowed history in mythology. For example, the famous Mannheim pike, which was supposedly stocked by Frederick the Great and prowled the moat around a medieval Germanic castle, reputedly lived 267 years and weighed 550 pounds. Normal pike life span, however, is about 10 to 12 years. Another fish, the Lake Kaiserwag pike (also of German extraction), was displayed in all its glory as a 350 pound mount for many years, but alas, was finally proven a hoax. Careful examination showed that the mounted specimen consisted of a number of pike skins sectionally reconstructed to make one huge fish, apparently by a prankster of yesteryear with an ageless sense of humor.

Imagination apparently played a large part in pike lore. It seems the monster pike of the 14th, 15th and 16th centuries not only attacked swans and dogs, but men and mules as well. But legend is only half the story. Medicine, too, played an important part. Alchemists used pike hearts and galls to cure pleurisy, the ashes of burned pike were used to dress wounds, and pike bones were worn as talismans against witchcraft. And to account for its presence in some unstocked waters, early-day naturalists believed that pike were bred from weeds and hatched by the sun's heat.

Mystery, of course, has always been an important ingredient in angling. Few fishing experiences excite the soul of a man more than the sudden appearance of a 20 pound pike, with steel-cold eyes and underslung jaw, taking a pass at a lure or bait.

Voracious is the word most commonly used to describe the pike's appetite,

and it's well deserved. We have all heard stories of pike attacking non-aquatic animals like small muskrats and baby ducks; and it does happen. On Lake Calhoun (in urban Minneapolis) during a 1976 bass tournament, a number of contestants witnessed at close range a small duckling grabbed, gashed and finally taken under by a big pike. The mother duck, after much consternation, finally committed junior to the deep, and swam away with the rest of her brood with a resignation found only in animals. Ducks Unlimited, a conservation organization, has documented the fact that pike prey on small ducklings, and the pike is listed as one of the duck's predators.

The jump from baby ducks to full grown 30 pound swans is really not too much to expect from man's natural exuberance or imagination. The tales abound and multiply, as Frank Buckland warned. Still, there is usually some truth to legend, and the fact is that European pike do grow to larger proportions (on the average) than their American cousins.

Fred Buller, one of England's foremost pike exponents and a co-author of this book, reports numerous European pike eclipsing North American growth potential. (See our chapter on Record Pike.) We will explore some of the reasons for this interesting phenomenon later.

About the only North American report of extraordinarily huge pike comes from Pierre Espirit Radisson, a French explorer who built a trading post near Ashland, Wisconsin, in 1660. He wrote in one of his journals concerning Chequamegon Bay of Lake Superior that, "In that bay there is a channel where we take stores of fishes, sturgeons of vast biggness, and Pycks seven feet long." "Pycks" seven feet long would weigh well over 150 pounds. Could he have meant muskies? Who knows?

Pierre Espirit Radisson

While European pike, in fact (as well as in lore), grow to massive proportions, North American pike (although the same species) seldom attain such
formidable size. They also apparently do not possess a jaded appetite that includes swans, mules and men. The fact of the matter is that North American
fish over 40 pounds are very, very rare, and pike over 30 pounds are truly exceptional fish. Maybe the musky, the American monster of the *Esox* family,
"copped" all the "tall tale" honors on the North American continent, and there
just ain't 'nuff left over for the old "speckled wolf."

Although wild pike folklore has remained chiefly on the other side of the
ocean, Americans and Canadians have spawned pike tales and misconceptions
that are uniquely their own—myths this book will both explore and dispel.

Chapter 2

THE PIKE IS WORLDWIDE

The northern pike is the only species of the five member *Esox* family which has a broad geographical and environmental range (see maps). Pike are found on all the continents fringing the North Pole. Such diverse cultures as Mongols, Lapps, Eskimos, Cree Indians and Europeans have recorded encounters with old tooth mouth. On the other hand, other members of the pike family like the redfin, grass and chain pickerels, as well as the musky and amur pike, have very limited ranges. Pickerel and muskies are confined to specific areas of North America, while the amur is limited to a small portion of Asia.

Northern pike are found in many diverse waters, reflecting their ability to adapt to a wide variety of environmental conditions. On the other hand, the specialized make-up of its other cousins in the *Esox* family apparently limits them to certain types of environments. Northern pike, however, appear to be able to "hack it" just about anywhere—anywhere, that is, where the alkalinity and water temperatures do not rise too high. In fact, few freshwater fish have such an extensive range.

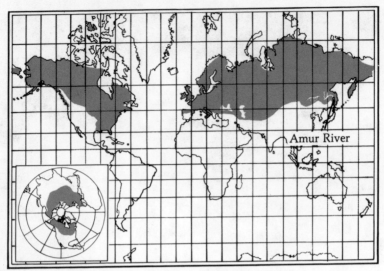

Worldwide range of the Esox family.

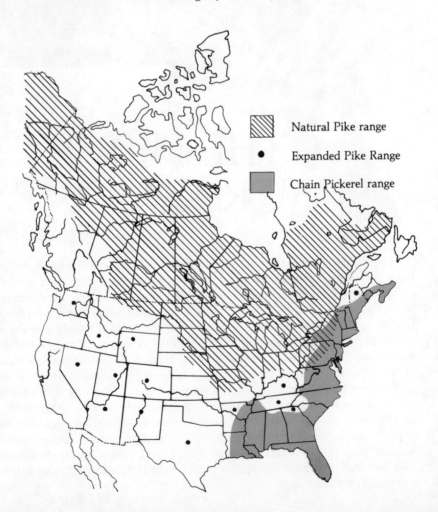

Natural Pike range

Expanded Pike Range

Chain Pickerel range

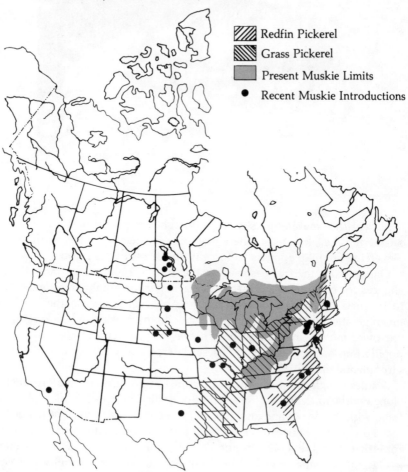

E.J. Crossman; Taxonomy and Distribution of North American Esocids; Am. Fish Soc. Spec. Pub. 11:13-26, 1978

Legend:
- Redfin Pickerel
- Grass Pickerel
- Present Muskie Limits
- ● Recent Muskie Introductions

Known the world over by many names—pike, northern, snake (U.S.); jackfish, pickerel (English Canada); grand brochet (French Canada); hauki (Finland); wasserwolf (Germany); lance (France); luce (Italy); and shuka (Russia)—the pike is a universal brawler. Pike probably supply *more* action for the average sport angler, worldwide, than any other gamefish.

The northern pike's jaws boast large, sharp, pointed teeth flanked by razor-sharp cutting edges, while the roof of the mouth is covered with short, backward-pointing teeth. This allows the pike to mortally slash and wound its prey, and at the same time hold it fast in its vice-like jaws.

As a predator, the pike is king of the pond, pit, stream, lake or impound-ment. In fact, in waters where it co-exists with the musky, the northern pike's wider range of adaptability usually, in the long run, forces the musky out of the system—or at least limits its numbers. Pike spawn in much the same waters

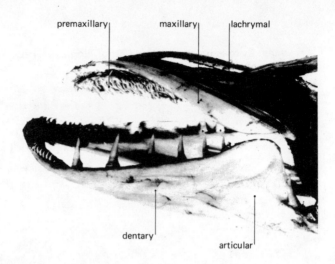

premaxillary   maxillary   lachrymal

dentary   articular

—but *earlier*—making musky fry vulnerable to predation by newly-hatched northern pike. In areas where the pike's range overlaps with the chain pickerel's, the pike appears to force it out of the system, too.

One popular theory reasons that the more specialized a fish is, the less its chances for survival are if the particular environmental conditions conducive to its survival change too drastically. Apparently, the northern pike has a much greater latitude in adaptability, while the musky and pickerel fill much narrower niches. In some waters, however, pike tend to co-exist with other populations of the pike family. These waters usually have a long history of environmental stability.

Besides the glaring teeth, other prominent northern pike features include an elongated head depressed forward into a pair of duck-like jaws. The body is long, with the dorsal and anal fins set far back on the body. The pelvic fins are located midway between the pectoral fins and the anal fin—a shape designed for efficient and diverse foraging. Yes, the pike is a veritable eating machine.

Due to its shape, speed and coloration, (as well as its ability to tolerate a wide temperature range), the northern pike is able to survive in both open water and in the cover of the shallows. The long body, with large dorsal and anal fins near a muscular tail, enables the pike to take off very quickly. When a pike lines up an intended victim, it lunges from an S-shaped position, and most targeted prey are caught. In weeds, the pike's torpedo-like shape allows it to use ambush tactics. In open water, however, the shape also lends itself to efficient, effective, fast pursuit—if even only in short bursts.

Because the northern pike is primarily a sight feeder, the eyes are located on top of the head so the fish can see ahead and upward. The northern has very good vision, and tests indicate that it can distinguish as many as 20 or more hues. However, the fish also has a sensitive smell apparatus as well. With its razor sharp, large mouth, good eyes and ability to smell, it can and does forage on just about anything—even dead things. (A fact of great importance, as you will see later.)

A study of the pike's physical makeup shows that the cheek covers on the northern pike are totally scaled, while the gill covers are scaled on only the upper half. This provides a very easy and accurate clue for identifying pike from other species like the musky, amur or the pickerels. There are usually five pores on each side of the pike's lower jaw. The redfin pickerel, on the other hand, has four pores, while the grass pickerel has three on one side and five on the other. By the same token, the musky usually has six or more pores. Amur pike also have six or more.

Results of crossing esocid species and their fertility.

	Northern pike	Muskel-lunge	Amur pike	Chain pickerel	Redfin pickerel	Grass pickerel
Northern pike	XXF	XXS	XXF	—	—	X?
Muskellunge	XXS	XXF	XX?	XS	XS	XX*
Amur pike	XX?	XX?	XXF	—	—	—
Chain pickerel	XS	XS	X?	XXF	XXF	XXF
Redfin pickerel	XS	X*	O?	XXF	XXF	XXF
Grass pickerel	XXS	XX?	X?	XXF	XXF	XXF

Key:

Hybridizing
XX = Good hatch and fry survival.
 X = Some survivors but poor egg fertility or fry survival.
 — = Unsuccessful cross.
 O = Cross not made
 * = Fry hatched and died.

Fertility
S = Hybrid sterile.
F = Hybrid fertile.
? = Hybrid fertility not determined.

Numerous natural and man-induced hybrids have resulted from cross-breeding various members and strains of the pike family. These crosses also exhibit cross characteristics. (See the accompanying illustrations.)

The pike's color, as well as body shape, can vary greatly. However, it is usually a greenish or bluish gray fish with a white or yellow belly. Some European pike (from Finland) have markings which cross the belly. The upper portion of the head is generally brilliant dark green to olive green, or even green brown. The background color of the sides is lighter.

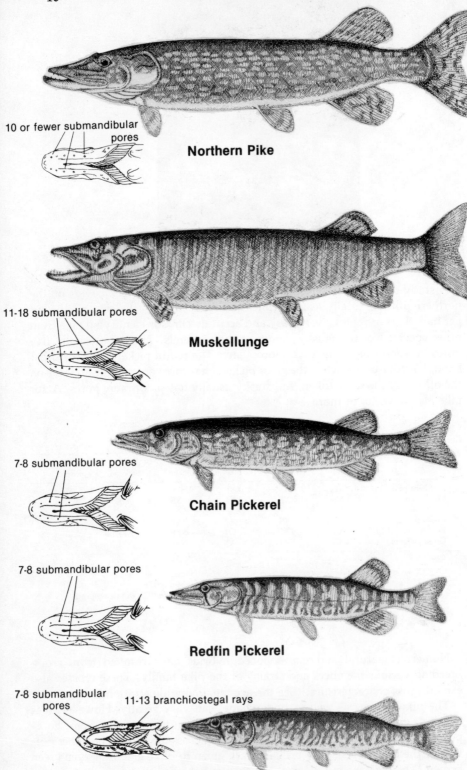

10 or fewer submandibular pores

Northern Pike

11-18 submandibular pores

Muskellunge

7-8 submandibular pores

Chain Pickerel

7-8 submandibular pores

Redfin Pickerel

7-8 submandibular pores   11-13 branchiostegal rays

Grass Pickerel

Young pike, because of their light-colored bars which have not yet broken up into white spots, are sometimes mistaken for muskies. At other times they're confused with small grass or redfin pickerel. These bars gradually break up into lighter spots as the fish grow to about six inches in length, becoming the rows of spots seen in the adult pike.

Anatomical Features of the Northern Pike

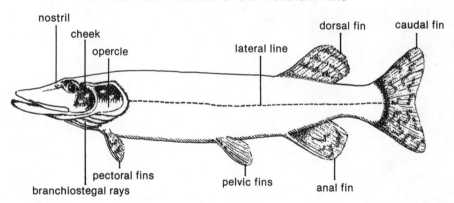

The caudal, anal and dorsal fins are greenish yellow, sometimes pale orange to red, and blotched with irregular black markings. The eyes are bright yellow. The eye-bars are not noticeable, as they are in pickerel.

In Canada, Minnesota and parts of northern Iowa, a mutant form of pike termed "the silver" or silver pike occurs. Although anatomically the same (except for a few characteristics), a recessive pigmentation gene apparently affects some local populations. Some of the authors have caught silver pike and were not impressed with the fish beyond its oddity value. Silver pike seldom exceed 10 pounds, and most are two to four pounds. While not an especially great fighter, it does, however, appear more prone to jump than many of its normally-colored cousins.

Northern pike are commercially fished in North America—more so in

Canada than in the United States. The total U.S. catch is usually under 500,000 pounds annually. The Canadian catch averages about five million pounds or so annually, much of which is sold in New York and processed with carp to make gefilte fish (a Jewish delicacy). While a good tasting fish, (its flesh is white and flaky), its culinary qualities are usually not acclaimed. Several factors come into play here.

First off, the pike's bony skeleton makes quick and easy boneless filleting a little tedious. The pike also has a heavy mucus covering which, if not handled properly, smells strong. The pike in some lakes are also subject to two troublesome parasites, high levels of which can make fish (by law) unmarketable for human consumption. When you add these facts up, fish like walleyes, whitefish and lake trout are a much easier commodity to handle, process and market commercially. In fact, pike are usually sold headed and gutted, rather than filleted. (See our boneless fillet method.)

To date, there have not been any controversies between sportsman's groups and commercial pike harvesters as there are with walleyes and lake trout. The total yield is relatively low, and most netting is accomplished in winter under the ice (and thus not witnessed by anglers). In some areas (particularly in Canada), the pike has not (yet) achieved full gamefish status. Because of reasons like these, and because few studies have been done, the extent to which commercial fishing affects pike growth is not known.

Amur Pike

Chapter 3

THE PIKE'S PERSONALITY

"THE COOLEST OF THE COOL"

To understand how pike adapt and respond to differing environments, it's important to realize that pike do best (in terms of overall growth performance) in environments which are very cool—as opposed to ones which are predominantly warm or very cold. In fact, we contend that of the various freshwater gamefish, pike could be described at the "coolest of the cool water fish."

Any experienced pike fisherman knows big pike become scarce when water temperatures get into the high 60°F's. Numerous studies indicate that once the surface water temperature rises above 65°F, angling success drops. Oh, sure, you can still catch young, small pike, or the so-called stunted "hammer handles" which operate like young fish, in any weedy patch or along any fish-attracting drop-off. But the big fish? Well, everyone agrees that they are very hard to come by in summer.

Fish contests show few big fish weighed in during summer, and guides will tell you that big pike fishing is tough at this time. Facts like these give us some clues about the larger adult pike's nature.

First, young pike (or stunted fish which operate like small fish) react differently and live in different environmental niches than large, mature fish—or even average-sized pike. Furthermore, if you call various baitshops, resorts and guides, and poll them as to when you have the best chance to catch large pike (those trophy fish over 15 pounds), in almost all cases the answer is early and late in the season—times when cool water is evenly distributed, or when big pike are drawn (by nature) to shallower water, as during the Pre-spawn and Spawn Periods.

Apparently, juvenile, young pike and stunted fish tend to stay relatively active and feed all summer long, regardless of water temperature. By all indications, young (or stunted) pike are quite warm water tolerant, which accounts for their widespread distribution in shallow, warmer lakes. It also appears that large, mature fish are more affected and/or adversely stressed by warm water, and the larger the fish, the more the stress. They appear to like cool water, which accounts for their more numerous appearance in cool water lakes.

We know that large, landlocked stripers absolutely require much cooler water, with an adequate oxygen supply, than small fish do. Although a body of water may easily support young stripers, it must have deep, cold water options if the fish are to grow past a certain stage. And it appears that much the same thing happens with pike as well.

In scrutinizing the pike's lifestyle, we checked with many winter spearfishermen in Minnesota (where this activity is legal). Spearfishing for pike (from a dark house with a decoy) has long been a point of contention between the spearing fraternity and hook-and-line anglers. The most common charge is that the "harpooners" (as spearfishermen are sometimes referred to) take all the big fish—those 15-25 pound plus trophies—not to mention countless 8-14 pound fish. In retort, the spearfisherman's defense is that hook-and-line, open water anglers never really catch that many big pike anyway, so why let them go to waste?

While there are no figures to substantiate it, there is a widely-held belief in Minnesota that spearfishermen (numbering no more than 40,000 or so) take more big pike than the 2 million or so open water anglers. While we don't feel this proportion (because of the sheer numbers involved) is correct, we definitely *do know* that spearfishermen do proportionately take many times more *big* pike than hook-and-line anglers.

Regardless of the numbers, fisheries biologists and spearfishermen *know* and agree that big pike actively feed in cold water. In fact, there is strong evidence (in some lakes) that they actually do grow in length during the winter months. Conversely, where waters occasionally warm too high, big pike can become so stressed that eating actually stops in the summer months, growth ceases and weight loss may occur. Indeed, we feel this stress factor in waters that warm far above optimum pike levels is probably the prime reason why few big fish are taken during the warm months.

Preliminary research on this subject shows that the cooler a body of water, the longer big pike remain actively feeding into the summer season, and the earlier active feeding commences in late summer. For example, in the far Canadian north, water temperatures on some lakes rarely exceed 50°F in open water and 60°F in shallow water. Consequently, the average catch in June is only slightly better than in July or August. But as you move further south and encounter higher water temperatures, big pike fishing (or even fishing for moderate-sized fish) becomes less consistent.

All fish march to their own internal drummers, and apparently big pike, as the coolest of the cool water fish, are more prone to be active in water temperatures from 39°F to 65°F, than in waters 65°F and up. This may explain why winter anglers take more big fish than summer fishermen, and why more big pike are taken in summer in the cool waters of the far north than in more southerly waters.

Numerous recurring incidents also tend to reinforce the contention that the pike is "the coolest of the cool." Let's look at a few.

COLD WATER PIKE

On a blue gem wilderness Canadian lake, a young guide watches a big arched hook form on the graph paper—then another—then still another—then more yet. "The jackpot . . . ," he muses. Turning his boat around in a slow, wide circle, the lad makes another trolling pass across the deep water point, but this time a little closer to shore. As the boat glides out of the turn and straightens, the guide smugly tells his customers to ". . . Hang on, we're gonna have a laker on right quick . . ." In a subtle vote of confidence, one of the old gents' hands firm on the rod handle. The wire line hum-cuts the water, while 55 feet down at the other end of the wire a paper-thin silver spoon, attached to a three-way swivel and weighted down with six ounces of lead, dances over the bottom. Then, almost as if on cue, the man stands, arches and sets the hook. Excited, the man calls to his companion, "Hey Sam, this kid knows his business!"

About halfway in, however, the old-timer loses a little of his enthusiasm. Looking at the young guide, he spits ". . . Must be a small one . . . Ain't fightin' too good . . . But he sure hit it hard at the beginning . . . Thought I had a good one . . ." A few seconds later, the fish momentarily flashes into view in the gin-clear water, and then disappears. "Hey, it is a big one; longest trout I ever saw," the old-timer yells.

The young guide, however, got a better look at the fish, and from past experience knew what the old fellow had. All the guide said was, "Heck, it's a pike . . . But a good one; looked to be maybe 10-12 pounds."

While the young guide removes the hooks from the pike's mouth, and the old-timer mutters in wonderment about pike coming out of 50 feet of water in mid-summer, a biologist 400 miles south conducts some offbeat research fishing on the Mississippi River. An electroshocking crew had reported collecting numerous large northern pike from ice-cold spring holes and from the mouths of cold water streams. The biologist is following up these leads.

He casts a six-inch sucker, rigged on a slip bobber, into a cold water pocket formed by the incoming water of a frigid brook. The water temperature registers 49°F here, while most of the other parts of the river are a warm 72°F. Moments after the bobber hits the water it disappears, and the biologist soon lands a 14 pound pike. Repeating the operation, he eventually lands eight more fish. He then moves to another area, where a cold spring hole bubbles up from the bottom, and accomplishes much the same thing.

While these two incidents are occurring, a puzzled salmon fisherman near Washington Island in Wisconsin's Door County peninsula inspects an 18 pound northern pike he just caught on a J-plug. The salmon fisherman had his downrigger lines set 60 feet deep, and trolled along a very sharp drop-off bordering an immense, shallow-water flat containing weeds. The water temperature down at 60 feet registers 52°F—cold enough to harbor salmon and lake trout, but obviously also accommodating enough for big pike.

Occurrences like these are recorded in summer in many areas of the pike's range. While not everyday events, reports of pike catches in cold or very cool water areas still happen with enough frequency to indicate that pike (especially big pike) love cold water, or at least exhibit a definite willingness to lay in it. They imply that mature, non-stunted pike will retreat from waters that are too warm, if available.

ADAPTATION

While lake type pretty much determines how pike can respond to warm water stress, lake type is no guarantee of a given kind of productivity. You can find small, shallow lakes that produce only small pike. But you can also find (a few) small, shallow lakes which grow decent or even large-sized fish. By the same token, there are cool mesotrophic and cold oligotrophic bodies of water which also produce only small pike. So, while cool water environments are ordinarily advantageous for pike success, other factors must be present and come into play for pike to truly thrive. Thus it is important to realize that pike growth (or a body of water's productivity) *is not* solely a question of water temperature, but overall environmental conditions, of which water temperature is only one factor.

In general, in highly eutrophic (fertile) bodies of water which are very warm, and most probably shallow, pike do not seem to do too well. In fact, if conditions become harsh enough, pike are actually purged out of these kinds of systems. On the other hand, in certain highly oligotrophic bodies of water which are ultra-cold and devoid of almost all weeds, pike also do not do well. Again, if the going gets too tough, they are again purged out of the system.

In between these two extremes, we find lakes with a vast array of environmental situations, most of which sustain pike in the northern hemisphere. The pike's response in these varied watery environments (in terms of the kind of food available, the type of habitat it must adjust to, and the water temperatures it must deal with) decides how big or small pike will grow. The specific kind of environment also determines the number of pounds of pike an acre of water will support, and the numbers of fish those pounds will encompass. It also determines what color variations pike can take on and what body forms they develop.

In the past, some biologists have speculated and suggested that pike could be separated into various sub-species categories by body proportions, maximum size growth or color variations. However, today, a comparison of proteins in pike taken from the Volga River in Russia and Minnesota, as well as a comparison of chromosomes of English fish with Canadian pike, show *no* disparity which might reflect genetic divergence. While there are superficial differences from continent to continent, there are no distinct taxonomic deviations that warrant a separate species or even sub-species designation. Unless new extensive tests by a process called electrophoresis suddenly tell us something different, what we are probably dealing with is simply a widely-distributed, very adaptive species which develops certain localized body forms, color patterns and growth characteristics.

The fact that the pike's basic nature allows it to exist in so many diverse environments has great impact on a pike's possible adaptation to varied situations. It answers the questions as to why certain growth rates develop, and also why differing head and body forms and color variations are produced. Similarly, there are certain environmental conditions which allow pike to grow to maximum size potential, and there are those which severely restrict or retard that growth.

What this all boils down to is that certain kinds of waters produce only small, stunted, sickly, "snakey" pike. Yes, they produce numbers of fish, but no size. Then there are environmental conditions which allow pike to multiply to good numbers, attain a good moderate size, but never grow to large proportions. Then again, a body of water might produce monsters—but very few pike. On the other hand, an environment might be so optimum (in terms of everything being right) that you might catch numbers of very large pike (15 to 20 pound fish). You can also encounter waters which have the potential to produce huge trophy pike, but maximum size is kept down by heavy fishing pressure.

Yes, many factors can come into play. Now that we are aware that they exist, we can better size up any potential pike fishing situation. Importantly, we now know that not all bodies of water are capable of producing big fish—or even lots of moderate-size pike.

NICHE

This brings us to the factor of *niche*. A niche is an organism's specific place within an environment. First, it's important to realize that fish *are not* born into the niche that they can ultimately grow to and exist in. Most other animals, like birds and mammals, are born in a niche, and even if they're reared for awhile by parents, they operate within that niche most of their lives.

For example, horses live on prairies and graze on grass. They do this regardless if they're a colt or a big old stallion. Eagles live in high nests and prey on rodents and fish, whether they're a fledgling or a big old bald eagle. On the other hand, a fish must graduate from one niche to another, or find itself stranded at a particular level of habitat and food usage. Yes, fish can become locked into a given pattern of hunting, in a certain lake zone, and into foraging on a given size of prey. Once they do, growth usually either slows or ceases.

For example, walleye fry move to the surface levels of open water and feed on microscopic organisms called zooplankton. Then, when they reach the fingerling stage, they move back to shallow water and feed on tiny fish and insects, as well as some plankton. What happens is that they sort of wean themselves from one kind of food type and size to another.

If they are to continue to mature and grow, the walleyes' diet becomes more exclusively small fish, like young-of-the-year perch. This kind of prey primarily lies at the edges of weedlines. So again, the walleyes make a change in the lake zone they use. Then, as the walleyes graduate to larger and larger-sized perch, which happen to operate on deep sunken islands, they make another move to another zone of the lake. Finally, as walleyes grow to lunker proportions, they might start foraging on larger-sized ciscoes, and again move out and start utilizing open water. At each stage of their growth, walleyes switch their prey source and lake zone (habitat) usage.

However, if one of the links in this chain is missing from the lake—say, for instance, the large-sized perch which operate on deep sunken islands—the walleyes of the lake would most likely be *frozen* at the size level they attained just before encountering this missing link. Even if the lake holds large-sized ciscoes, the fish (because of this missing link) can never get large enough in the first place to start successfully preying on the ciscoes. Even if the lake has large panfish like bluegills, the walleyes won't be able to prey on them, because the walleyes' mouth size and teeth, etc., can't effectively and efficiently handle them. In a body of water like this, the top-out walleye size might stop at about four pounds or so.

Oh, sure, an occasional seven or nine pounder might pop up, but it is one of those rare fish which for some reason manages to get a head start (growth-wise) on their brothers and sisters at one of the previous growth levels. This rare fish is able to get "on top of" the food chain and forage on bluegills and ciscoes. However, with a vital link missing in the overall food chain, no significant number of fish will graduate to the larger size range.

And so it is with pike—*except more so!* The steps in the food chain not only must be available in the body of water, but have to be present at each stage of the pike's growth, and be there at the right time, seasonally.

For example, different-sized shad might be available in a body of water, but shad have a generalized water temperature preference much higher than pike. So this food source, although plentiful, of high fat content, and of differing sizes, is not available to the pike all through the year. Thus the pike cannot make optimum use of it. In the face of what looks like plenty, a pike might stay small.

SIZE OF PIKE AND PREY

Pike Length	Sucker Length	Perch Length
10 in.	4 in.	4in.
15 in.	5 in.	4½ in.
20 in.	5½ in.	5 in.
25 in.	8½ in.	8 in.
30 in.	9½ in.	—

4-Inch Bait: All sizes of northerns but usually those of five pounds and less.
6-Inch Bait: Usually northern pike between 3 and 8 pounds.
8-Inch Bait: Usually northern pike between 5 and 15 pounds.
12-Inch Bait: Usually pike over 8 pounds. This also will take lunker northerns.
Over 12 Inches: Such baits generally are too large to use easily, but they will take the true lunker northerns.

If pike are to attain their maximum growth potential, it's apparent that a food source not only has to be the right type and right size, but must also be in harmony with the pike's lifestyle and be available in the corresponding different lake zones pike use as they grow from one size to another. Yes, for pike to continue to grow, they must pass the threshold from one niche to another.

Incidentally, the niche thresholds between, say, a ½ pound crappie and one that weighs 1½ pounds are not as great, as numerous, nor as distinct as between a ½ pound pike and a 30 pound lunker. The ½ pound pike absolutely cannot survive in the conditions necessary to sustain the 30 pound lunker, and the 30 pound lunker cannot long function within the ½ pound pike's domain. But the ½ pound and 1½ pound crappie can operate in the same areas—indeed, within the same school. While this niche threshold factor applies for all fish, it becomes much more critical where there is great size differential between the smaller and the ultimate sizes.

With pike, each growth stage demands an almost unique set of environmental conditions. To attain maximum growth, they must *all* be present within a given body of water, or pike will become frozen at a given level of growth. We can briefly divide these niche thresholds into four broad, but very distinct, stages:

1) A shallow water existence.
2) An edge of a weedline/slightly down the drop-off stage.
3) An edge of the weedline, deep sunken island and some open water lifestyle.
4) A deep, open water existence except for spring spawning time.

A shallow water environment only allows growth to a certain stage. If environmental conditions don't exist to jump the next threshold, that's it for growth—except for those rare exceptions.

Most likely, these kinds of waters have conditions ripe for spawning and rearing small pike. But the rest of the lake is *not* conducive to continued pike growth nor longevity. Something in the environment—a step past the next step threshold level—is lacking.

When conditions like these exist, life becomes a constant hassle for food, and few fish make it to the top of the food chain. Cannibalism is rife and competition is keen. The pike in these waters live fast and die young. Reports from some waters show that these fish don't live much longer than four or five years.

Environments like these are the breeding grounds for what are disparagingly called "snake" pike. This physical expression of a local environment produces skinny fish, which have a sickly yellowish color (and are many times covered with grubs, or infected with other parasites) and which never seem to grow beyond a couple of pounds. At times they appear to be more head than body. Even their teeth (although sharp) never fully develop. They also appear to live a constant shallow water existence and prey on anything they can—usually small fish like bluegills, perch, or other hard-scaled, spiny-rayed species—which means they must burn more energy capturing and digesting their food.

If a lake provides a jump past the next environmental threshold—to weedline edges where medium-sized perch can develop—then the next stage of pike

This is an example of a recently caught European pike. Notice the deep body, large jaws and over-whelming size. Total weight, 44 pounds.

European Pike

growth and existence can occur. In environments like these, pike can grow up to 6 or 8 pounds.

Continuing on, if a lake has some deep sunken islands, and extensive flats with short sandgrass, and perch can grow to even larger sizes, the next threshold jump can occur, and the next pike growth stage can take place. These conditions allow fish to grow to the 8 to 12 pound bracket.

At the end of the threshold spectrum, we find the large, block-shaped pike specimens similar to some European fish. These fish usually have deep, vivid

A salt and pepper "snake" type pike that is infected with grubs.

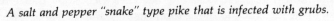

hues and are brilliantly mottled. The fish have prominent neck muscles, and big jaws that sport a vice-like bottom lip. These pikes' teeth are big, many, glaring and sharp. They are usually the product of big, deep, clear, cool environments like those of certain lakes in the Canadian midlands of Manitoba and Saskatchewan—with deep, oxygen-rich, prey-packed, cool/cold water zones. In waters of this type, high-fat, soft-finned prey of various types provide lunker fish the "good and easy" life. At this stage, big pike (except for the spring spawn) may lead a continual deep or open water existence. In fact, some big female pike may even cease to come in for spawning, and seldom move into the other lake zones.

These cool waters are also favorable for longevity—an important factor allowing maximum growth potential. Fishing pressure, too, is often miminal. In other words, when this niche is available, pike can grow to their maximum potential.

The longevity factor is vitally important if fish are consistently being cropped off before they reach their growth potential. Otherwise, lunker class fish simply don't develop. As a pike continues to grow larger, the chances of it being caught also increase. In waters where there is intense, effective fishing pressure, numbers of big fish simply do not develop—even if the body of water is capable of producing them.

Cool and cold water environments are also more conducive to pike aging than warm water environments. Research in some warm lakes, where fish never attain any real size, showed that most fish die at four or five years of age. In these warm environments, it appears that with their increased metabolic rate, the fish simply "burn themselves out" by the fourth or fifth year.

On the other hand, there are environments (usually cool or cold) where pike do not have to expend much energy to survive, and where ages up to 25 years have been recorded. While age (of fish) is no guarantee of continued growth, it is conducive to growth if the other optimum factors are also present.

GROWTH POTENTIAL

Assuming that the correct pike spawning and rearing areas are present, let's explore some of the conditions to look for to determine the potential for maximum pike growth.

Basically, we feel the following factors are the most advantageous:

1) Generalized cool water temperatures are available somewhere throughout all seasons.
2) Adequate prey of the right size and type are available for pike at each stage and season of growth.
3) Prey of a high-fat content, soft-finned, soft-bodied variety are available.
4) There is room within the environment for pounds of pike flesh to be expressed in larger fish, instead of numbers of smaller fish.
5) There is limited competition from other species which use much the same water, like bass and muskies.
6) There is low fishing pressure.

We feel these are the optimum conditions for rearing big, healthy northern pike in respectable numbers. The less of these a body of water has, the less likely it is to produce numbers of large, healthy pike.

It should now be clear that pike activity can differ depending upon which of the broad niche stages they operate in. How much and when do the fish move around—or remain sedentary? How much and when do they feed a lot, or a little—or not at all? Each case is different.

Because of the diversity of niches and their usage, fish operating in a shallow water environment may be feeding quite heavily, while (at the very same time) those using one of the other niches may be feeding less—or not at all. The situation could be the reverse as well. Keep in mind that, most times, fish making use of the different environments are usually separated by size.

For example, in summer on an oligotrophic lake, small fish will usually be

shallower. The intermediate-sized fish (up to 6 or 8 pounds or so) might make use of the edges of weedlines and drop-offs. The 8 to 12 pound, moderate-sized fish might be on deep sunken islands, and the lunkers (15 to 20 pound fish) might be suspended and feeding on large ciscoes, smelt or even small trout. So, while large pike in oligotrophic lakes might continue to be prone to strike baits and lures in summer, the larger-sized and lunker class fish (if they exist) in meso and eutrophic lakes would most probably be tough to catch.

Fish that are reared generation after generation in conditions far below optimum, or even mediocre, develop what can be termed poor pike characteristics. Those that are reared in better conditions, however, usually develop outward physical qualities which can be described as good pike characteristics.

For example, on English waters called broads (channelized flooded marshes), the pike's primary prey is a stout, thick-bodied fish called the European bream. In these waters, we find very long, moderately-built pike with huge heads (from the back of the gills to the tip of the snout), and big, rounded alligator jaws—apparently a very worthwhile weapon to hunt European bream with.

On the other hand, 200 miles or so across the Irish Sea in the land of shamrocks, big, cool, deep lakes called "loughs" also have big pike. But these fish have small heads and shorter, but stockier, deep, block-like bodies. Interestingly, these fish utilize more elongated, soft-bodied, soft-finned prey. Both environmental conditions grow big fish, but the fish's shapes are different, which probably reflects their adaptation to a particular situation.

Another lake in Ireland produces what are called pug-nosed pike—fish with a "deformed" upper lip. One of the authors knows a small lake in Minnesota that produces humpback pike—fish with a distinct bulge directly in the back of the head. All of this brings us to the questions of "breed."

"Breed" can develop in closed environments (lakes which are totally isolated for long periods of time), and certain inherited superficial characteristics (like the previous examples) can develop. In Canada and the United States, however, things like "wild cat" stocking, stocking in general, pike rescue programs, flooding and interconnecting of waterways by raising water levels with dams, etc., pretty much preclude such selective breeding from taking place in any significant way.

While it's true that small "snake" pike transferred to more opportune lake environments seldom grow to maximum potential, they nonetheless exhibit growth. The only reason that growth maximums are not attained is that the fish burned up some of their potential earlier, and just can't catch up.

What about different color variations and body proportions in the same lake? Well, again, they are primarily a product of habitat and food usage, and not a question of "breed."

While a pike is a pike, the environment they live in has a great bearing on not only which lake zones the pike use, and the kind of prey they most probably relate to, but also how big we can expect them to get, and maybe even what relative body proportions will develop. Therefore, let's take a close look at the different kinds of lakes pike inhabit and see how their different environments affect pike growth, location and behavior.

BODY OF WATER TYPE
CAN DETERMINE PIKE RESPONSE

Basically, our findings indicate that there are various generalized ways mature pike can try to escape warm water stress, depending upon body of water type.

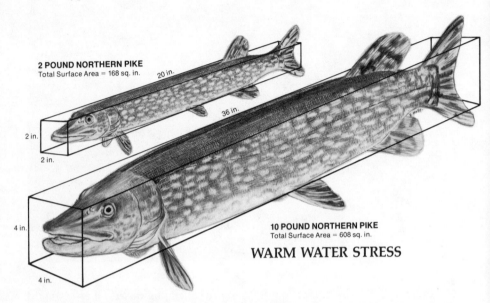

2 POUND NORTHERN PIKE
Total Surface Area = 168 sq. in.

20 in.

36 in.

2 in.

2 in.

4 in.

10 POUND NORTHERN PIKE
Total Surface Area = 608 sq. in.

WARM WATER STRESS

4 in.

In oligotrophic lakes, which are well oxygenated in the depths, larger pike usually move deeper in summer to reduce warm water stress. When they enter the colder water realm, we believe their activity slows dramatically compared

OLIGOTROPHIC ENVIRONMENT

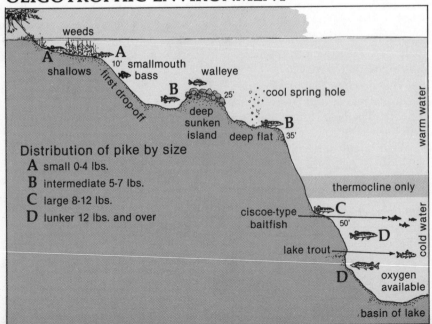

weeds

A

A
shallows

10' smallmouth
bass

walleye

first drop-off

B

25'

cool spring hole

deep
sunken
island   deep flat   35'

B

warm water

Distribution of pike by size
A small 0-4 lbs.
B intermediate 5-7 lbs.
C large 8-12 lbs.
D lunker 12 lbs. and over

thermocline only

ciscoe-type
baitfish

C

50'

cold water

D

lake trout

D   oxygen
available

basin of lake

to that of shallow water fish. It's very probable that temperature *alone* is not necessarily the sole motivating force here. Apparently, season has a bearing in some fashion, as well as the available food/oxygen levels, pH (acidity) and the like.

Interestingly, burbot (eelpout)—a deep-running, cold-water fish which exists in many of the same waters pike do—*do not* feed much during the summer months. Just as bass reduce food consumption greatly in winter, burbot appear to become very lethargic during the summer months. This activity mode occurs even though summer water temperature and oxygen levels *do not* preclude it from feeding. Instead, it appears that the summer months are simply a natural lull in the burbot's activity cycle. This seasonal lull in activity also seems to affect big northern pike in some manner. Or, perhaps the summer lull in activity may simply be attributed to where big pike are: a huge expanse of deep water that makes it difficult for anglers to contact them.

At any rate, once pike are pushed out of the upper layers of an oligotrophic lake in summer, their food options change. In shallow water, anything (of the correct size) that swims is a target. But in summer, in the cool/cold depths, whitefish, ciscoes, or smelt—all a pelagic (open water) type of prey—are available.

In these types of waters, some pike, usually caught from great depths, have flesh of an orangeish color, indicating they are feeding on a prey with a keratin-rich diet. It just may be that these pike also feed on lake trout. So, some feeding might take place, even if on a very reduced scale.

In lakes of the mesotrophic variety, pike usually respond in a different manner. These bodies of water usually both thermocline and oxycline in summer. While it has not been fully researched or documented, we theorize that big pike may be able to lay in an oxygen-poor hypolimnion layer if and when pH levels remain opportune. In other words, the theory suggests that pike might be able to inhabit oxygen-poor water if the pH remains constant, in perhaps

MESOTROPHIC ENVIRONMENT

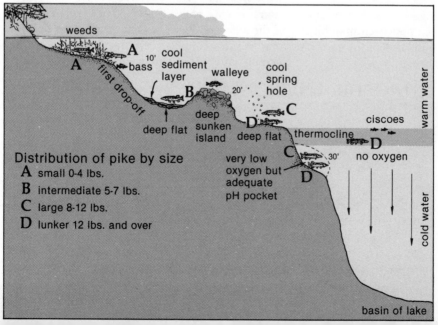

the 6.0 to 8.0 range. They would vacate such areas based primarily on pH, and secondarily on oxygen levels. If this is the case, however, the fish would still be extremely lethargic, and active feeding would be highly doubtful.

On the other hand, if oxygen is removed from the depths and the pH levels are not accommodating, big pike would be forced out of the depths. If they are, they probably hover suspended over deep water areas near the thermocline, and we again feel they greatly limit their activities. They might also move to mid-depth cover, like a cleft among boulders, or lay quite dormant in cover like deep weeds.

Even when pike are unquestionably forced out of the deep water by lack of oxygen and poor pH levels, and pushed into a zone that is accessible and heavily-fished by sport anglers, few huge pike are caught during the warm months. This tends to reinforce our view that big pike restrict their activities during this period. It may be that pH plays a role here, too, but we have not yet fully documented this phenomenon. Evidence suggests that pike may go through an inactive period of pH acclimation. Pike activity usually commences on mesotrophic waters during the end of the Post-summer Period—a time when the surface waters begin to cool.

Recently, fisheries biologists have used trawler nets in a few meso lakes in areas where suspended fish have been marked on graphs, and have found northern pike mixed in with preyfish like ciscoes. However, all of the pike (most of them large) had empty stomachs and exhibited the tell-tale shrunken, flabby, "V-shaped" bellies indicative of long periods of fasting. While the pike were in the same areas as the baitfish, there is little evidence that they are actually preying upon them. It is very possible that the pike are at that locale for temperature or pH reasons, and not for feeding purposes.

We may add that we have tried fishing for what we are almost sure are suspended pike—with practically no success. We've tried to vertically jig them; we've tried using reaction baits like Sonars; we've used jigging spoons; trolled over them with plugs; and even hung live suckers at the proper level—all to no avail! There very well may be an effective and efficient way to trigger these fish on meso waters, but we haven't discovered it yet. The dead bait approach may be one of the answers. (See the chapter on dead bait.)

In lakes of the eutrophic type, numbers of pike rarely reach the lunker category. Still, what few big pike come out of these waters are also conspicuous by

EUTROPHIC ENVIRONMENT

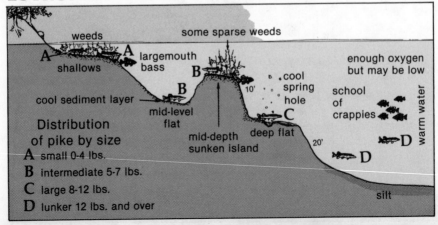

their absence during summer. Many of these lakes neither thermocline nor oxycline, and some fish have been known to lay on the bottom in cool, deep sediment layers for protracted periods of time.

In rivers and reservoirs, as well as all of the aforementioned lake types, cold springs and cold water pockets formed by incoming streams provide an ideal summer refuge for big pike. In fact, in large bodies of water which boast a variety of environmental conditions, pike can relate (depending upon what is locally available) to any or all of the options previously mentioned, with the cool sediment layers on deeper flats being particularly attractive to pike and equally difficult for anglers to fish effectively.

Divers will tell you, and any adventurous swimmer will confirm the fact, that sediment layers on the bottom are much cooler than the surrounding water. In some bodies of water, a milky, fog-like layer veils the tops of these areas. With oxygen levels still adequate, but light penetration cut and temperature low, these sediment areas provide an ideal summertime big pike retreat. Here, with visibility cut to a minimum and temperatures cool, plus the fish's metabolism reduced, the chances of an angler's offering being taken by a big pike are extremely low.

While very little substantiated scientific evidence exists on the subject of the northern pike's water temperature modes, and their summertime responses to it, our observations lead us to believe that while the adult pike is *not* technically a cold water fish, it is "the coolest of the cool." If we have any corroborative clues as to how to take big pike in summer with *any* regularity, it would be utilizing live or (better yet) dead bait in cold water pockets or on cool, muddy flats, or fishing in open water zones. It just may be that these fish are scavenging during this period, and are picking dead fish off the bottom in the cool/cold water areas of the lake. We've had some reports from the Dakota reservoirs and Canada in this regard, but not enough of them to make any positive conclusions.

At this juncture, we bequeath what knowledge we do have to the inventive, inquisitive members of the angling fraternity, and to the research staffs of the scientific community. We hope they can find the next piece in the complex but intriguing pike puzzle.

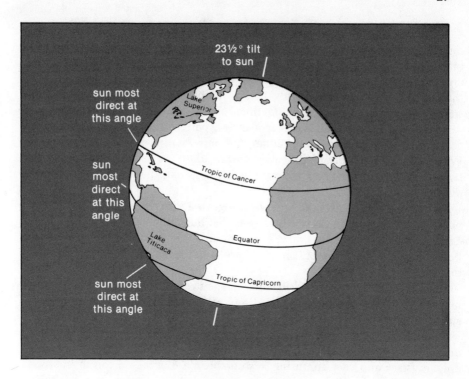

Chapter 4

Introduction to the CALENDAR PERIODS

Spring, summer, winter and fall are events common only to the temperate world. The tropics, on the other hand, display alternating cycles of rain and wind that signal to the various life forms that the earth's angle to the sun is changing. In the inhospitable polar world, spring, summer and fall are but a brief pause in an otherwise harsh, constant gloom and cold. Only the middle (temperate) zones of the earth experience the four separate and distinct seasons. And it's here the pendulum swings noticeably enough between periods of darkness and brightness that we can easily recognize definable patterns emerging within nature.

We know that light (or length of daylight) plays a major role in the day-to-day feeding, movement and activities of pike and other fish. We also know that light seasonally controls or regulates migrations and plays an important part in the spawning process.

The basic nature of some species of fish dictates that they are principally diurnal (most of their activity takes place during the daytime). Others are mainly circadian (most of their activity takes place at night). Still others are crepuscular (major activities occur at or around twilight). However, it is not that cut-and-dried, because many species adapt to local or seasonal circumstances, and sometimes become daytime, nighttime, or twilight activists.

Despite this, there are general tendencies, patterns and trends that should concern us. The bullhead is circadian, and moves and feeds mainly at night. Walleyes have a mainly crepuscular rhythm; they are usually most active at twilight. On the other hand, pike are usually diurnal; they live, loaf and feed during the daylight hours.

It's common for anglers to fish a weed edge or a rocky point during the early hours, and catch a pike every once in a while. But come 9:00 AM, all of a sudden the fish start biting like crazy. Yet an hour earlier there might be no indication of any concentration of fish. In all probability, the pike were there all the time.

What triggered them? In all likelihood, the degree of light intensity (plus a number of still unknown factors). At any rate, light is the signal; it acts as a synchronizer!

On land, the many seasonal changes are quite evident, but underwater it's difficult to see nature's forces at work. Consequently, aquatic seasonal cycles are a mystery and very confusing to some people. But it is in this mysterious and constantly-changing environment that fish live. Thus you must be in touch with the aquatic environment to catch pike with any consistency.

While most other freshwater fish (regardless of year class and/or size) more or less respond to the seasonal changes in an environment in pretty much the same way, this is not true of pike. For all practical calendar response purposes, big pike and small pike could be two different species. For example, a two pound pike in a warm, eutrophic lake may remain active, move around a lot and feed all summer long. But a 25 pound lunker may greatly curtail not only its feeding, but its movement activities as well for long periods of time. So, while the Summer Calendar Period may be a "time of plenty" for small pike, it could be a "time of stress" for large pike because of their adverse reaction to warm water.

While there can be some disparity in behavioral response between, say, a small walleye and a more mature eight pound fish, or between a one pound largemouth bass and a five pound fish, or little difference between an eight pound lake trout and a 20-pounder, it is nowhere near as great, nor as distinctive, as between the various size classes of pike.

The bass is a warm water fish at all stages of growth. A walleye is a cool water fish regardless of size. And a lake trout is a cold water critter, whether a peewee or a monster. But early in life, a pike can function as a warm water fish, at middle age as a cool water fish, and when it becomes huge, as a cold water fish. Therefore, a pike's response to the changing seasons, and the seasonal impact on an environment, depends if it is a big, medium or small-sized fish.

A fish's movements, actions and attitudes are not arbitrary. There are valid reasons for each and every activity. The most obvious of the myriad of forces that control the aquatic world is the intensity and duration of light. This is related to the earth's yearly orbit around the sun.

THE AQUATIC CALENDAR

In the northern hemisphere, the sun is most direct and the day longest on June 21-22. The sun is least direct and the day shortest on December 21-22. Water temperatures warm or cool accordingly, and this affects each organism from the lowest form of algae to the highest form of fish. Insect eggs hatch to larvae, and larvae in turn become insects. Snails and aquatic worms move seasonally from zone to zone. Plankton periodically blooms, is consumed, and dissipates in a complicated, interrelated web of life.

Our Calendar Periods divide the year into cycles of fish response. There are no such things as weeks or months—only seasonal periods. Periods (depending on weather) which might last nine days one year, could run sixteen days the next year. Since our Calendar Periods depend upon climate conditions from year-to-year, they are elastic in duration. Calendar Periods do not last a fixed number of days, nor do they occur on given dates each year.

Further, some of our Calendar Periods relate primarily to the pike's biological demands: Pre-spawn, Spawn and Post-spawn. So, in one region of the continent, a period (for example, the Spawn Period) might arrive months earlier than in another part of North America. The later Periods—Pre-summer, Summer Peak, Summer and Post-summer—are based more on the condition of the total environment and the condition of a body of water. In areas of northern Canada, a Calendar Period like Summer might be a brief five weeks long—while in Nebraska it might be three or more months in duration. Finally, some periods are determined mainly by water temperature levels, like the Turnover and the Cold Water Period.

There is another fine point that you must understand to view the Calendar Periods in their proper perspective. You might assume that the best time to fish would be a Calendar Period when the water temperature is at an optimum for the pike's metabolism, causing it to feed the most. But it doesn't always work that way. Water temperatures in oligotrophic environments, for example, allow different size pike to utilize different water temperatures, in different zones of the lake, at the same time.

On the other hand, an adverse water temperature does not always mean fish are hardest to catch. In fact, this is particularly true with small-sized pike. The available food supply, the timing of feeding movements, overall population levels and competition, as well as the differing response by different sizes of pike, all play an important role in angling success. These are the kinds of factors we took into account when we developed the Calendar Periods.

The Calendar Periods are not, as some think, simply the seasonal conditions of a body of water. A lake, river or reservoir may be in a seasonal time frame (spring, summer, fall or winter), but pike response to that environment determines the Calendar Period. Different species of fish, as well as different sizes of pike in any given body of water, can be in different Calendar Periods at the same time.

For example, the majority of largemouth bass are in their Pre-spawn or Spawn Calendar Period in mid-spring. They will usually be shallow and quite easy to catch. But, at the very same time, pike, which spawn earlier than bass, would be in their Post-spawn or Pre-summer Period, and fishing for them would be slow. And in oligotrophic lakes, large fish may move into cold water in summer—while the small fish remain shallow.

Once you learn to "read the signs," you'll have little difficulty identifying one period from another and discerning when different species are in different Calendar Periods. The difference between the unsuccessful angler and the truly successful one often boils down to two things: recognizing the seasonal movements and probable response patterns of pike.

MOTHER NATURE'S CLUES

If we lived underwater, the pike's seasonal movements would become much easier to understand. As the food chain developed and moved through its cycles, we would see signs of it everywhere: emerging vegetation, schools of minnows and baitfish relating to their food sources, and growing numbers of developing insect larvae and crustacea. But since the surface of a body of water is all that most of us ever see, we need to be aware of other clues that indicate these changes.

There are other natural cycles corresponding to the Calendar Periods that are quite visible. Lilacs in bloom usually mean that pike are in their Pre-summer Period, and fishing will only be so-so. When the water is warm enough for comfortable swimming, pike will be in their Summer Period. In one kind of lake, the big pike might be lying in cool, deep sediment layers in an inactive state. But in another kind of lake, the lunkers might be suspended under ciscoes in deep water, and feed on them from time to time. Then, as the water begins to cool, you'll know that the Post-summer Period has commenced, and you can expect some fast-action pike fishing on shallow, weedy flats. The fall arrival of massive flocks of coots (mud hens) on some lakes is a sure sign that the Cold Water Period is here. On certain waters, deep, slow jigging with big minnows would be an appropriate presentation.

While these signs may vary from region to region, the perceptive angler learns to recognize nature's clues, and changes his location and presentation accordingly. Here is where a log book proves invaluable.

The next time you observe a "peak time" on your lake, river or reservoir, take a look around the surrounding countryside. What is going on that can give you a clue? Is a particular plant just coming into bloom? Have you just seen the first robin of the year? How about an insect hatch or the budding of some kind of aquatic weedgrowth? Since these events occur regionally, the signs are many and varied. However, it is amazing how consistent these patterns are once you learn to identify and recognize them.

Water temperature, of course, is one major key, since it partially controls weed growth and dissipation. Water temperature also triggers insect hatches (or their dissipation), etc. Taking constant temperature readings will keep you in touch with many of the Calendar Periods. The patterns you see developing on land are also a function of the same weather conditions that determine some of the underwater patterns.

Astute old-timers are well aware of these cycles, and this is one source of folk wisdom that is usually right on target. Old, experienced hands are instinctively able to see, smell and feel a Calendar Period arriving, leaving or holding. But, this is where we also pick up many old tales or folklore that are not always true.

It's important to be aware how weather conditions affect a lake, river or reservoir. Flowage (impoundment) lakes connected to a river system can warm up incredibly fast as the result of a heavy, warm rain. Yet a self-contained, big, deep lake a few miles away will remain cooler and take longer to warm up. The fish in both bodies of water could be in vastly different Calendar Periods and react much differently.

There are vast numbers of good technical fishermen who have mastered a variety of presentations, but who still fail to understand how the predator/prey link relates to the Calendar Periods. So they run into recurrent problems at various times of the year. Our experience shows that understanding baitfish movements, and patterns of other forms of prey, is another key to successful angling.

So, not only do different lake conditions dictate different lure presentations and techniques, but gamefish demonstrate marked preferences for certain kinds of lures and baits throughout the various Calendar Periods.

In the final analysis, the only way to understand how the different Calendar Periods function on your particular body of water, or any other for that matter, is to spend enough time there to begin identifying these patterns. Comparing notes with other anglers will help you get a grasp of the Calendar Periods. Keeping a daily log of weather and water conditions, as well as fish feeding patterns, also helps considerably. A review of last year's fishing log during a cold winter night often provides not only a glimmer of past fishing glories, but also an insight into seasonal fishing patterns you never noticed before. In this way, you can learn the seasonal circumstances that trigger fish response, and the locational patterns that result from them.

As we cover the Calendar Periods, we'll also include some clues on pike behavior and activity. The activity mood levels are broken into three basic groups: negative, neutral and positive. These are defined as appetite moods, and are further described in our glossary!

THE TEN CALENDAR PERIODS

1. Pre-spawn	6. Summer
2. Spawn	7. Post-summer
3. Post-spawn	8. Fall Turnover
4. Pre-summer	9. Cold Water
5. Summer Peak	10. Frozen Water*

*Ice cover is actually a phase of cold water, but is used to differentiate conditions.

Normal Calendar	1	2	3	4	5	6	7	8	9	10
Pike	1	2	3	4	5	6	7	8	9	10

Chapter 5

THE
CALENDAR PERIODS

THE PRE-SPAWN PERIOD

A Time of Anticipation

Generalized Environmental Conditions
Surface Water Temperature Range: 32°F
(from just before first ice melt to actual ice melt)
General Fish Mood: Neutral

Apparently, the pike's metabolism requires a time period in which the water cools to a point where some ice forms (even if for a short time). If a body of water does not go through a cooling cycle like this, the females' eggs will probably not develop and spawning cannot take place. Even in "put and take" fisheries (where natural spawning is not a concern), pike do not do well in waters which do not seasonally cool to near-ice levels.

At any rate, after a long winter of regularity (in most areas of the pike's North American range), an inbred urge begins to stir the pike. Even before the ice is off the lake and the first trickle of ice melt begins to run, the fish begin abandoning their winter haunts and start migrating toward and staging near their prospective spawning sites. The journey could be short, as in the case of small lakes, or many miles, as on some large rivers, lakes and reservoirs—or in lakes fed by long rivers. Pike have been known to move 30 miles or more to a spawning site.

Even near their spawning grounds, pike will relate to some element of the food chain, and perhaps grab very easy targets of opportunity. While the fish are not chiefly interested in food during the staging process, they do pick up dead bait and will (although more reluctantly) strike lures or live bait—especially in the earlier phases of the Pre-spawn Period. Males usually exhibit more aggressive behavior, and consequently more males can be caught than females. Nonetheless, both sexes, while not biting everything in sight, are heavily grouped, so you can expect action once you locate fish. This is especially true in some far-flung Canadian wilderness waters.

Various pike groups will start making a pre-spawn movement in relation to the distance they are from their spawning grounds. All fish on a lake or reservoir do not make the move at the same time. Even on smaller bodies of water, all the pike do not begin making a pre-spawn movement at the same time. It also appears that there is a homing instinct which draws fish back to the areas they were hatched in, or sites that they used in previous years.

For example, fish which spawn in the backwaters of an incoming river or creek arm may stay at the mouth, or actually run up the river or creek, while the main lake or main reservoir is still ice-covered. Yet fish groups which spawn in the cold, main lake may remain in their winter haunts for longer periods of time, until the conditions along a cattail-lined bank or backwater slough are more opportune.

On large bodies of water, pike groups may stage in proximity to the main-lake spawning grounds while the water is still covered by ice, although they usually do this slightly later than the river- or creek-run fish.

While some pike groups might also winter in various sections of a lake or reservoir, each mid-winter movement brings them closer and closer to the spawning grounds. These are gradual movements, as opposed to specific spawning migrations.

During the end of this stage, pike move directly onto the spawning sites. The bigger female pike (if they spawn) appear to come in earliest, while the smaller females come in later. We believe that some bigger and older female lunker pike (the biggest of the big) might be past the reproduction stage; with their ovaries non-functional, they might simply never come in shallow.

Basically, the Pre-Spawn Period is a time of anticipation—a period when the pike's interests are primarily focused on the coming reproduction ritual.

THE SPAWN PERIOD
A Time of Tension

Generalized Environmental Conditions
Surface Water Temperature Range: 39°F-52°F
General Fish Mood: Negative

This is a brief, variable period usually lasting from one to three days for individual female pike and a bit longer for individual males. The Spawn Period includes the peak spawning temperature range for pike (approximately 39°F-46°F). Pike may begin spawning at temperatures as low as 39°F, and have been recorded spawning up to temperatures in the low 50°F's. So temperature is not the only factor. Other environmental conditions, weather, light intensity, etc., can also have an effect.

While a fish that has not spawned is still technically in the Pre-spawn Period, the reality is that the closer the fish comes to actually spawning, the less likely it is to strike a bait, or exhibit other pre-spawn traits. Feeding activity during actual spawning is practically nonexistent. However, cantankerous males, cruising around waiting for a female, will make reflex strikes at baits, lures or other intruders in staging areas—but not during the actual spawn. By and large, it is a very, very poor time for pike fishing.

Remember, while actual spawning is taking place in one area, there can be groups of pike waiting to spawn in different areas, and groups which have completed the spawning ritual in still others. The Spawn Period must therefore be considered a local activity. Yet within most bodies of water, the great majority of the pike population will usually spawn in a two-week period or less. In huge bodies of water like giant reservoirs or the Great Lakes, however, it can last a bit longer.

Most fish will arrive at a spawn site from dusk to about midnight. Yet even if the fish arrive at the spawning site at night, spawning usually takes place in the daylight hours. The height of the activity appears to occur in early afternoon. In fact, still, calm, sunny days seem to be the most advantageous mating time.

Most females will deposit their eggs within 24-48 hours. But females will keep making false runs, usually toward evening, until their eggs are ripe. Their actual spawning period is very short-lived. And again, some females may not spawn at all.

Interestingly, when a female accepts the approach of a male pike, both move forward together and the spawning act is achieved while the fish are in motion. The male pike's position in relation to the female is achieved through an eye-to-eye orientation. The water displaced by a fish moving forward causes a current to flow in the opposite direction. This being the case, the induced current sweeps the milt cloud "through" the heavier falling eggs.

Should an attendant male pike happen to be longer in body than its mate—so that the vent is to the rear of the female vent when he is moving forward eye-to-eye with her—the milt cloud would be released to the rear of the falling eggs. In this case, the current would tend to separate the milt and the eggs, resulting in no fertilization. Therefore, for pike hatches to be successful, the majority of the male pike are normally quite a bit shorter than the females.

While the spawning process itself takes a short period of time for an individual fish, a group of pike in a generally ripe condition may spend a week or more in a spawning area. This is what we term the Spawn Period, even if the fish have not actually spawned yet.

Conversely, after a female drops her eggs or a male milts out, the fish is technically in its Post-spawn Period. However, they may "hang" in a spawning area for a short period of time and exhibit attitudes like spawning fish. Yet if there is a food source in or adjacent to the spawning site, pike may even remain there to feed for a few days. However, this only occurs under ideal conditions, and it is far more typical for the fish to begin dispersing out of the area very quickly.

Basically, the Spawn Period is a time of tension—a period when the pike are subjected to great stress, and their reactions correspond with this mood.

THE POST-SPAWN PERIOD
A Time of Recuperation

Generalized Environmental Conditions
Surface Water Temperature Range: High 40°F's to Low 50°F's
General Fish Mood: Negative to Neutral

Post-spawn is a complex period and difficult to portray in simple terms. Any characterization in "definite" terms is misleading. This remains a somewhat mysterious period, largely because of the lack of concentrated pike and our limited knowledge of exactly what they are doing.

For example, while we can generalize and suggest that the water temperature will usually be in the low 50°F's, water temperature is not the only factor influencing this period. We are dealing with a "recuperation period," so time is also of the essence. Logically, how long it takes individual pike, and thereby the entire pike population, to recover from the "time of tension" can vary.

So, it is very important to keep both time and temperature in mind when considering Post-spawn. We've found that a week or two is usually long enough for the fish to recuperate and move into their Pre-summer Period (characterized by a more aggressive mood). We've also fished enough waters to know that surface temperatures of about 56°F in bays and other spawning areas often distinguish the resumption of active feeding, thus signalling the end of Post-spawn.

Post-spawn is usually characterized by inconsistent fishing, but there are exceptions. For example, small male pike, or small pike in general, seem easier to locate and catch near spawning areas, and they are often active. While big females usually have extreme cases of "lockjaw," they are sometimes caught (admittedly in smaller numbers) in a multitude of ways. However, it would be poor advice to plan your annual fishing vacation to coincide with the Post-spawn Period.

Just as there is a pre-spawn assembly of pike, so too is there a post-spawn dispersal. How fast this occurs depends on a number of factors. Experience shows that a body of water's physical make-up affects pike dispersal. In oligotrophic waters, small and large pike do different things. In mesotrophic and eutrophic waters, they can and will do different things—and things different from pike in oligotrophic environments.

Forage can also influence post-spawn pike dispersal. At some point during the recuperation process, a pike's basic needs return to normal; the fish becomes concerned with food and comfort! If there is forage on or near a spawning area, many pike (especially in oligotrophic waters) have the option to remain shallow in slowly-warming bays. Some big pike, however, may move immediately to the deeper water, feed on ciscoes, and never come back in shallow again until next year. And there are conditions in these "oli" waters where there is a slow retreat to the deeper water, where big pike might stop for awhile along sharp-dropping rock points.

Thus, Post-spawn is a recuperation period. Pike behavior is determined primarily by the lake type a pike is in, and the niche it fills in that body of water.

Recognizing a general post-spawn pike dispersal pattern is probably most important in reservoirs and lakes where pike leave the main body of water to spawn in large creek arms or in large, weedy, flat bays. In these situations, pike leave the spawning grounds, stopping to rest and maybe even feed a bit along the way. If you can visualize the route back to the main lake or reservoir, or to a summer holding area, you can usually pick out areas where the fish could hold—and catch some. By this time, however, the fish are beginning to cross over that thin line distinguishing the Post-spawn Period from the Pre-summer Period.

Interestingly, an old myth (originally spawned in Europe) used to be that the reason fishing slows so dramatically after spawning is that the big female turns and eats the smaller male once spawning is complete; the smaller mate not only provides the seed for the egg, but food for the big female until she is better equipped to resume hunting. While it's possible, we can find no substantiating facts for this "fancy."

Basically, the Post-spawn Period is a time of recuperation when the pike's hormone levels change. The pike's biological emphasis switches from that of a fish primarily involved with reproduction to one of a fish primarily interested in satisfying its needs for food and comfort.

THE PRE-SUMMER PERIOD
A Time of Transition

Generalized Environmental Conditions
Surface Water Temperature Range: Mid 50°F's to Low 60°F's
General Fish Mood: Neutral to Positive

While the Post-spawn Period is characterized as a resting stage when fish scatter and feed little, a change is imminent. The pikes' bodies need nourishment, and the resumption of regular feeding activities indicates the beginning of a new pattern we call the Pre-summer Period. This period can be one of the fish's prime growth times of the entire year. This is especially true for small and medium-sized fish which use the shallow water and mid-depth zones. During this and the Summer Peak Period which follows, small and medium-sized pike can grow the most in length, though not necessarily in weight.

During the Post-spawn recuperation period, pike change from being primarily preoccupied with the reproduction ritual (and its various aftereffects) to being primarily interested in satisfying their everyday needs of food and comfort. While no set temperature level indicates when pike enter the Pre-summer stage, the surface waters will nonetheless have warmed to a point where the pike's metabolism demands more food to sustain their energy levels. When surface water temperatures reach the high 50°F's or low 60°F's, you can usually assume that the small and medium-sized pike are "back on the bite." Once again, keep in mind that different-sized pike can all behave and operate in different manners, depending on what is available in an environment.

Pre-summer is a time of emerging weedgrowth and a developing food chain. Generally, surface water temperatures vary less from section to section of a lake compared to the earlier spring periods, although certain sections of lakes and reservoirs can be warmer than others.

Prior to this, and depending upon the area of the lake, different groups of pike could have been in a pre-spawn, spawn or post-spawn attitude within the same broad time frame. But during the Pre-summer Period, most of the pike population will have completed the spawning ritual and the aftereffects phase. They begin to scatter to and operate in their respective niches.

For example, big females which return to a deep and/or open water existence during the post-spawn dispersal continue to function in these same zones—the only difference being that they begin to feed more regularly. While the large-sized pike may not feed voraciously, they do take nourishment on a more predictable basis. Other pike groups (usually of the intermediate size range) might not move deep right away, but will eventually go down as the surface warms. These fish can be found on shoreline points near fast drop-offs, relating to various food sources. On the other hand, the smaller fish (which operate in shallow water most of the year) will relate to weeds and the food sources there.

In Pre-summer, a body of water itself can offer the most pertinent clues to possible pike behavior. Pre-summer is a time when fish are hard to pinpoint; they are often here today and gone tomorrow. Indeed, a prime characteristic of the Pre-summer Period is the variety of different fishing patterns. You may catch several pike rigging live bait in deep water, several more fish trolling mid-depth flats, and then take some fish casting extremely shallow water.

It has been our experience that most of the big pike taken after the Spawn Period will be taken now. This is particularly true in the slowly-warming waters of the Canadian North. Apparently, a lull in big pike action takes place after this period, and the next time any number of big fish are caught is the Post-summer Period. However, small and medium-sized fish will not only continue to be taken, but the action can even get a little better in the next (Summer Peak) period.

The pike is primarily a diurnal (daylight) feeder. Very generally, you can expect more action in the morning and afternoon hours as opposed to twilight or dark. Dark, overcast days with a chop on the water are usually better than very bright, calm, flat days.

Slowly, as surface water temperatures continue climbing upwards, the various-sized pike move to the respective niches they will occupy for the next two Calendar Periods. There is also a gradual tendency for pike to start keying in on more specific food sources—food sources most available within the various environmental niches.

Basically, the Pre-summer Period is a time of transition when a lake's or reservoir's warming surface waters transform it from the cooler environment of spring to the warmer environment of summer. Fish begin regrouping (primarily by size), and definite patterns begin to emerge.

THE SUMMER PEAK PERIOD
A Time of Separation

Generalized Environmental Conditions
Surface Water Temperature Range: Mid 60°F's to Low 70°F's
General Fish Mood: Positive (Small Fish)
Positive to Neutral (Intermediate Size Fish)
Neutral (Large Fish)
Unknown (Lunker Fish)

As summer progresses, the Pre-summer Period develops into what we term the Summer Peak—a short period of fast-action fishing for pike in the small and intermediate size ranges (fish up to eight pounds or so). At this time it is impossible to walk in the woods, along a beach, or down a country road and not feel nature's increased rhythm. Nature is alive, conscious and moving.

The final trigger that pushes the two smaller-sized ranges of pike from the Pre-summer Period into the short-lived period of feeding we term the Summer Peak always appears to be the same: namely, a span of relatively calm, very warm weather. In many cases this is the first really hot, summer weather of the season—and more importantly, the first hot nights of early summer. It's also a time when the larger and trophy-sized pike seem to disappear.

The Summer Peak, although not one of the best times of the year for lunker pike fishing, is nonetheless a period when you can take numbers of small and moderate-sized fish. Not only do you encounter groups of fish, but groups of feeding pike.

Most of a lake's ecosystem reaches its maximum fruition during this cycle. All the cool and warm water species (in most cases) will have spawned. The transformation from a colder to a cooler to a warmer water environment is complete. Insect hatches explode. Most major rooted weedgrowth begins to mature. Most distinct weedlines and edges are perceptible, and plankton are multiplying. Almost everything is reaching its peak of production. Fishing is generally excellent for cool and warm water fish like walleyes and bass.

Here are some basic rules of thumb to go by for recognizing the onset of the Summer Peak. First, the surface temperature of meso (middle-aged) lakes usually hovers around 72°F-74°F. It may eventually climb into the upper 70°F's or even low 80°F's, but this typically happens very slowly. Thus, the Summer Peak Period—for pike—seems to begin with the end of the rapid, early-summer rise in water temperature. In cooler Canadian lakes the water temperature might only reach the mid-60°F's, yet the principle is the same.

In effect, this period (as the saying goes) "separates the men from the boys." More precisely, it separates the big gals (large and lunker-sized pike) from the smaller gals (the not fully grown females) and guys (the males which never attain any real size in the first place).

Whatever lakes (oli, meso or eutrophic) large or lunker-sized pike are in, they now must deal with warm water stress by using whatever is available to them in the environment. However, the small fish are not that stressed, nor are the intermediate size fish stressed to the extent that the bigger fish are. Thus these fish can stay shallow and continue to move about and feed. The big fish, however, now make their move to whatever retreats are available, and set up a pattern of usage that will continue throughout the remainder of the summer.

The Summer Peak Period is basically a time of preparation for the long, hot summer. This is the time when the different niches for different-sized pike develop for the summer. Large pike move to avoid or minimize warm water stress, while the smaller and intermediate size pike cope with their increased metabolic rate by feeding (and burning it off) and feeding some more. While the Summer Peak is a time of fulfillment for bass and walleyes, it's a "time of separation" for various-sized pike.

THE SUMMER PERIOD

A Time of Stress (Larger Fish)
A Time of Plenty (Smaller Fish)

Generalized Environmental Conditions
Surface Water Temperature Range: Maximum Temperatures of the Year
General Fish Mood: Positive to Neutral (Smaller Fish)
Neutral to Unknown (Larger Fish)

The Romans believed the dog star Sirius rose with the sun, giving the days of July and August a double measure of heat. Thus, the term "dog days" was thrust into angling. While a misnomer that implied lethargy for most other species of gamefish, it appears appropriate for big pike. Now, more than at any other time of the year, nature is converting the sun's energy into living matter in full gear. We call this interval the Summer Period.

Abundant prey is now available in the form of fry and fingerlings for the smaller, shallower niches of pike. The lake has blossomed with food, and fish can become more selective in their choice of meals. Controlling factors like thermoclines, sunlight, increased metabolism and presence of prey all demand order. For the larger pike, this also contributes to a stressful situation. Plus, there are a host of other factors. Nature responds by regulating feeding times. For some fish it is a time of plenty; for others, it's a time of stress.

Summer pike fishing can be perplexing. While the smaller fish feed, the abundance of food and the density of cover can make fishing for pike of any size tougher, especially on lakes where the fish penetrate weedlines. Feeding activity may be short and fire off at short intervals. Movements may be of short duration, yet very intense.

On the other hand, large and lunker pike are conspicuous by their absence. It's as if, all of a sudden, big pike don't exist. On lakes where numbers of big fish are caught (usually in the period following this one and to some extent in the earlier ones), anglers can't buy a big pike now.

Some bigger pike, however, are taken in cold water pockets of rivers. Occasionally, big fish are captured in cold water zones of oligotrophic bodies of water. But on waters of the mesotrophic and eutrophic variety, the big pike appear to have shut down completely.

While the Summer Period is a time of plenty for small and intermediate-sized fish—plenty of food, plenty of cover and plenty of distraction in terms of increased traffic, sun penetration, cold fronts and the like—it's a time of stress for big pike. This period is the warmest cycle of an environment for the year.

THE POST-SUMMER PERIOD
A Time of Impending Change (Smaller Fish)
A Time of Refreshing (Larger Fish)
Generalized Environmental Conditions
Surface Water Temperature Range: The Water Begins Cooling Quite Rapidly
From Its Highest Temperature Range
General Fish Mood: Neutral to Positive

Post-summer, in effect, is the reversal of the Pre-summer process. It is a time when a body of water starts changing back from a warmer to a cooler water environment. This period takes place during the tail end of summer. Hot days with dead-calm periods, followed by cool nights, are typical. The days grow shorter, and this becomes the cosmic signal to the ecosystem that things are slowing down.

Most of the food in any lake, river or reservoir has already been produced for the year, and summer's time of plenty slowly gives way to reduced food stocks (at least for the smaller-sized pike). The density of weeds, too, begins noticeably diminishing. Insect hatches dwindle, and, in some cases, water levels can be quite low. Last, but not least, baitfish start shifting position as they mature, are lessened in numbers by predators, or as cover diminishes. In fact, during Post-summer, everything shifts as the water cools to about 65°F.

Pike can respond to these environmental changes in a variety of ways, and a variety of patterns can emerge. Interestingly, even the most marginal anglers manage to start catching a few fish—just as they did during the Pre-summer Period—and for much the same reasons.

In most waters, some of the best pike fishing, especially for trophy pike, occurs during this cycle. In mesotrophic waters, big pike may have been lying in cold water spring holes, in cool sediment layers or suspended in the thermocline in order to "beat the summer heat." But now, with the generalized cooling of the surface waters, they are free to start changing zones and foraging shallow again. The small fish scatter.

In eutrophic waters, the process (although not identical) works much the same way. In oligotrophic waters, the big pike may or may not make a shallow water feeding foray, depending upon the positions and the amount of food available. In some "oli" waters, they never face stress in the first place, so there is little need to "make up" by going on a feeding binge. Thus, in some cold "oli" waters which provide food in the depths through all seasons, the fish just might stay down. If the prey, however, is not lying in the depths, pike will move to whatever level they can best feed at. Sometimes there may be a very short burst of activity in some weedy bay which saw little big pike action since spring.

Interestingly, many times smaller pike activity slows up as the lunkers "come in"—or more precisely "start biting." In fact, from this point on, small pike fishing will slowly fade until the onset of the Cold Water Period (after the Turnover), when it resumes on a regular, but not necessarily ferocious, basis.

Just prior to this (in the Summer Period), the various-sized pike groups might have been doing a lot of different things. Thus, the angler had to be very specific in his presentation, and many times your approach had to be quite refined. But now, in Post-summer, these very defined patterns break down, and fish of various niches start moving about more. In many cases, fish from one area mingle with other groups, forming loose, short-lived concentrations. Pike also now tend to hold in feeding periods longer. When you add all these factors up, pike fishing is easier; in fact, it can be fantastic.

The internal workings of the environment trigger these changes in a pike's pattern of operation. Summer pike (depending upon the kind of lake, river or reservoir they live in, and the size group they are in) were restricted from intermingling because of water temperature. But when Post-summer comes, most of these environmental niche partitions disappear.

With the cooler water temperatures and the breaking up of niche partitions, the pike start mingling with other size fish. As the food supply becomes generally less plentiful, it takes longer to satisfy the fish's appetite. So, in this case, we vividly see how the environment affects fish activity—and, of course, "catchability."

Basically, the Post-summer Period is a time of impending change for small fish, and a period of refreshment for larger ones. It's a time when a body of water (and the aquatic life in it) goes through the transition from a warmer to a cooler enrivonment.

THE TURNOVER PERIOD
A Time of Turmoil

Generalized Environmental Conditions
Water Temperature Range: Variable
General Fish Mood: Very Negative

As a time of turmoil, the Turnover Period is relative. First, all bodies of water do not stratify during summer, so they do not "turn over" as such. Most rivers are a case in point. Lakes and reservoirs, too, may or may not stratify. Usually, shallow bodies of water—which the wind periodically stirs up—or ones with a lot of current flowing through them, are fairly immune to the stratifying process. Consequently, the fish in these waters are not subjected to the amount of stress as fish in waters where the transition from a warm to a cold water environment is an explosive event. Nonetheless, the change from a warmer to a cooler to a colder water environment demands some adjustment.

The most classic (drastic) turnover situation occurs in bodies of water which set up (stratify) in distinct temperature layers during summer. Since cold water is heavier than warm water, the warmer water stays on top and the colder water sinks and builds up on the bottom; in between lies a narrqw band of rapid temperature change from warm to cold called the thermocline.

In these waters, a thermocline condition usually remains in effect throughout most of the Summer Peak, Summer and Post-summer Periods. But during the tail end of the Post-summer Period, as the sun grows less direct, seasonal hard, driving, cold winds and rain begin chilling the surface temperature of the water very quickly. As the heavier (colder) water begins sinking, it comes in contact with the warmer water below. This action forces the lighter, yet warmer, deeper water back to the surface. Eventually, the narrow thermocline layer ruptures and a mixing or "turning over" process takes place. As the wind beats the water, the mixing action continues until it thoroughly homogenizes the water to a point where the whole body of water is the same temperature. This process also reoxygenates the deep water.

Turnover usually occurs after several days to a week of the first late-summer cold snap characterized by a succession of dark, cold, wind-driven rainy days. This is a signal that the Cold Water Period is about to arrive. At times, you can actually smell the stagnant bottom water as it rises to the surface. You might even see dead weeds, decomposed fish and other bottom debris floating on the surface or washed ashore.

The actual Turnover process itself takes place once the thermocline layer ruptures. But the turmoil that takes place usually adversely affects the fish for a period of time after this event actually occurs. Fishing doesn't pick up again until these conditions stabilize. In general, once the water temperature drops to about 55°F and the water clears perceptibly, cold water fishing patterns emerge.

Fishing during the Turnover Period on bodies of water that actually thermocline is tough, to say the least. However, since all bodies of water do not turn over at the same time, it is usually best to switch to waters which have already turned over—or bodies of water which have not yet begun to—or to waters which don't actually thermocline and turn over so drastically.

Exactly what happens to fish, and pike in particular during Turnover, has yet to be documented. In fact, anglers are some of the best sources of information about this turbulent time. No fish like unstable conditions, so the best fishing usually occurs in areas where the Turnover effect is minimal. Shallow waters are usually best, or perhaps the shallowest areas of a lake that are least affected by the main lake Turnover.

Basically, the Turnover Period is a time of turmoil when fish activity grinds to a halt, although action will pick up as conditions gradually stabilize.

THE COLD WATER PERIOD
A Time of Stability

Generalized Environmental Conditions
Surface Water Temperature Range: 55°F and Down to the Lowest Temperature
of the Year
General Fish Mood: Neutral

We term the entire time span from the end of the Turnover to freeze-up as one singular period (Cold Water). Generally, the pike's metabolism slows a little in response to the changing ecosystem. However, being the coolest of the cool, pike can be quite active. Cold water unlocks many barriers and frees the really big pike to do their thing as king of the predators.

Pike will hit a moving crankbait sharply in the early Cold Water Period, yet slow to prefer a jig-and-minnow or jig-and-waterdog "teasing" presentation by the end of the period. Thus, as the water cools, you should slow down your approach. The pike angler must view this entire period within these parameters.

The Cold Water Period is a gradual slowing down and stabilization of the entire ecosystem. The water temperature regresses to the lowest of the year, and the pike's metabolism follows. As the days grow steadily shorter, weed-growth, insect hatches and plankton blooms slow down. The big female pike's eggs are already fairly well developed (but still developing), and pike will occasionally feed quite heavily to strengthen themselves.

In lakes where small and intermediate-sized pike inhabit weedy flats in summer, the fish may now drop down and concentrate on steep drop-offs or move to deep flats. These areas are usually located near the deepest depths of the lake. In reservoirs, pike can gather around points. Drop-offs with forage hold the key to fish location.

The generalized exodus from the shallows in the early stages of the Cold Water Period often results in tighter concentrations of big fish. Feeding intensity, however, can vary, ranging anywhere from intense to lockjaw, depending upon a host of circumstances.

The mixing process and reoxygenation of deeper water opens up formerly uninhabitable areas to groups of shallow water fish, which otherwise would perish with the coming of ice cover. Understanding this process is important, because the fall cold water season can offer some of the finest pike fishing of the year—if you understand fish location.

The Cold Water Period, however, is a time of stability. Though pike may bite well, everything seems to move at a slower pace. However, the more stable the environment, the better the fishing. The combination of stability and cool water temperature make this the most consistent period of the entire year for catching big pike.

THE FROZEN WATER PERIOD
A Time of Consistency

Generalized Environmental Conditions
Surface Water Temperature Range: When a Body of Water is at its Coldest For an Extended Period of Time
General Fish Mood: Neutral

On some southern reservoirs, ice cover may briefly occur in coves and wind-protected bays, while the main lake never freezes. The point is, the Frozen Water Period occurs when a body of water is at its coldest range for an extended period.

Because all lakes do not ice over, we thus define the Frozen Water Period as the longest period of the coldest water of the year. However, most bodies of water which contain reproducing populations of pike experience ice cover at some time during the year. Pike must spend a protracted period of time in water decreasing in temperature for their eggs to develop properly. This is similar to walleyes, for which studies have shown that the water temperatures must drop below 50°F for their eggs to develop properly. In fact, this period can last the longest over the greatest part of the northern pike's natural range —in some areas five months or more. It is also the period when environmental conditions remain consistent for the longest period of time.

During this time span, the entire ecosystem of a lake, river or reservoir slows. Yet pike feeding takes place on a very regular basis. Female fish must feed regularly to maintain their eggs and bodies, and male fish feed to sustain life. In fact, some pike growth has been recorded during this period. While the entire ecosystem seems to move at a slower pace than during other Calendar Periods—at least for warm and even some cool water species—pike actually seem to enjoy it and thrive.

Because of the breaking down of niche partitions—caused by summer water temperature differences in the different lake zones—pike of all sizes are free to roam anywhere in the Frozen Water Period. However, they tend to relate to prey of the proper size. In one study, good-sized pike (six to nine pounds) fitted with radio transmitters exhibited a great wandering spirit, slowly roaming over good parts of the lake. By the same token, ice and spear fishermen have observed definite feeding patterns (times and depths) that held up for long periods of time.

In winter, pike (especially the big ones) forage on dead (but non-decayed) bait which falls to the bottom or gets caught in the bottom layers of the ice. Yes, big pike have been spied grabbing small fish which get caught in surface ice. There is no question that big pike are scavengers.

During the Frozen Water Period, ice anglers take some of the biggest pike of the year.

The Cold Water Period is a time of consistency when pike continue to roam and feed. Pike behavior remains fairly stable all the way up until the spring thaw.

When viewing the Calendar Periods, keep in mind that these time frames are elastic. Each year the weather varies, and so too will each Calendar Period. Some of these periods may be shorter than a month; others might last two or more months. The timing and length of each period depends on water temperature, light intensity and duration, and other natural influences that affect the various species' hormones—and consequently their behavior.

Beyond the differences that can occur in a specific body of water, regions of the country also play a big role. For instance, in northern Canada, the first nine periods of the yearly cycle can take place in four months or less. Yet in the deep South, the Presummer, Summer Peak, Summer, Post-summer and Turnover Periods might last nine months.

The lake type has a great bearing on when these periods take place. Small, dark lakes warm faster than large, clear ones, so lakes across the road from each other will not necessarily find the same species of fish in the same Calendar Periods.

Calendar Summary

A VEST POCKET GUIDE TO THE CALENDAR PERIODS

Period	Description	Key Factors
Pre-spawn	Length varies between lakes, rivers or reservoirs. Main movement toward spawning areas. Heavy numbers of fish on a "light bite." Some trophies.	Ice melt. Water temperature. Hormone level. Length of daylight. Bottom conditions.
Spawn	Timewise a very short period. But all spawning does not take place at the same time. Fishing poor.	Water temperature. Hormone level. Bottom condition.
Post-spawn	Recuperation period for females. Males may be more aggressive than females. Fishing usually slow.	Dispersal from spawning area.
Pre-summer	Peak movement for all sizes of pike. Pike are actively feeding. Many fishing patterns.	Water temperature. Food chain.
Summer Peak	Pike niches form for summer season. Shallow water niche fish are active. Larger fish become more difficult to locate.	Food chain. Prey size. Water temperature.
Summer	The bulk of the fishing season for most anglers. Niches remain separate. Natural food chain at its peak.	Food chain and weed-growth fully developed. Oxygen becomes a factor. Water temperature.
Post-summer	Water begins cooling rapidly. Different niches come together as pike switch locations. Pike activity increases as the water temperature drops to 65°F.	Food chain slows. Water temperature.
Fall Turnover	A classic situation on bodies of water that stratify during the summer. Surface water cools and sinks. A general mixing of the water.	Oxygen. Mixing water. Temperature.
Cold Water	Excellent time for trophy pike. Good movements.	Location of available food.
Frozen Water	The coolest of the cool. Pike continue feeding and movements can be very good.	Location of available food.

Chapter 6

THE WATERS PIKE LIVE IN

Because pike possess such an adaptive nature, they can be found in just about any kind of lake, river, reservoir, pit or pond in the northern hemisphere that does not warm for an extended period during the year, nor contain highly alkaline water. However, bodies of water that simply have pike in them, and prime pike waters, are two different stories. In this chapter, we concern ourselves mainly with those waters (and environments) which can produce large (8 to 14 pound) and lunker (14 pound and over) pike.

Few North American river stretches, and fewer still reservoir types, have this capability. Therefore, we will zero in on particular lakes, and note special river, stream and reservoir types where pike not only survive, but thrive. We'll also look at special Asian and European waters which produce lunkers. We'll even examine Great Lakes pike in a separate chapter. But first, a basic understanding of the different types of lakes, rivers and reservoirs, and the environments they offer, provides the basis for becoming a consistent pike angler.

Every time a new lure or system gets popular, people naturally want to get in on the action. But few folks stop to consider the kinds of waters these tactics are designed for. To complicate matters even more, many anglers are in various stages of the learning process, and have difficulty putting the whole picture together.

For example, an angler hears about and buys a big, weighted bucktail spinner designed to be trolled very fast over the tops of weeds. This system is just clobbering pike in another part of the country. On a fine post-summer's day, our hero motors out to *his* lake (which is a different lake type from those where the bucktail/fast-trolling system has worked so well). He expects to clean up on ol' iron jaw. But, he strikes out! What happened? Naturally, he figures he either did things completely wrong, or was sold a bill of goods.

Confused, he ponders the problem. He's heard the stories about the magnificent catches of pike taken by the lure and trolling system, but is dumbfounded to know why the method doesn't work on *his* lake. But if he understood the basic differences in the bodies of water, his questions would have been answered.

A horse is a creature of the plains, and a mountain goat one of the peaks and ledges. Each functions extremely well within its own niche, but is at a distinct disadvantage out of it. So it is with pike. Small fish can make do in small, shallow, warm, silty, weedy lakes, or in timbered impoundments with tremendous water level fluctuations. You may even find them surviving in narrow, rock-strewn, cold, fast-running streams. But in the long run, pike do much better and grow to a larger potential in large, deep, cool, mesotrophic and oligotrophic natural lakes, plateau and hill-land reservoirs, or middle-aged river stretches. These bodies of water provide more ideal pike conditions than any other.

On the other hand, where the total environment is not that suited to the pike's basic nature, you can find waters which produce numbers of small fish, but few big ones, or waters which occasionally produce big pike, but few of other sizes. Therefore, when you fish for pike, first study the body of water type. Then, and only then, can the ramifications of niche partitions, location, feeding times and presentation methods be viewed in the correct light.

In the following sections, we'll examine some of the prime types of lakes, rivers and resevoirs that house pike and explain how to identify each of them. We will begin with our Natural Lake Classification System. Then we will analyze the various river categories, and lastly, investigate the different kinds of reservoirs. Each type of lake, river or reservoir is more or less inviting to pike, and you will learn how to recognize one from the other.

Before we zero in on any of these in particular, it is important to understand how we categorize bodies of water. They are broken into "age stages" that start at the youngest stage (which primarily provides cold water environments), advance to the middle-aged stage (which are primarily cool water environments), and finally proceed to the oldest stage (which primarily offers warm water environments). In between these major categories lie a number of lakes in *transition* stages: For instance, from a stable, cold water environment to a less stable, cold/cool water environment. Thus there are many different lake types, and each category often has a distinct bearing on pike location and behavior. This is true for rivers and reservoirs as well.

Chapter 7

CLASSIFICATION OF NATURAL LAKES

A basic understanding of the different types of natural lakes is essential to becoming a consistent pike angler. Most natural lakes in North America were created by the retreat of glaciers northward during the last ice age. The earth was first subjected to a great variety of natural forces, and when the glaciers receded, the myriad cuts and gouges in the landscape filled with melt water, forming lakes.

All lakes go through a natural aging process called eutrophication. The initial stages can take thousands of years, but the final ones may happen quickly —especially with the addition of man-made causes. Throughout this process, the total environment of a lake—its structural condition, food chains, vegetation levels and dominant fish species—change considerably. Man-caused eutrophication, or aging, is due to the expanding human population and disposal of waste products. These have caused changes in lakes so quickly that man has accomplished in a generation what it would have taken nature hundreds or thousands of years to do.

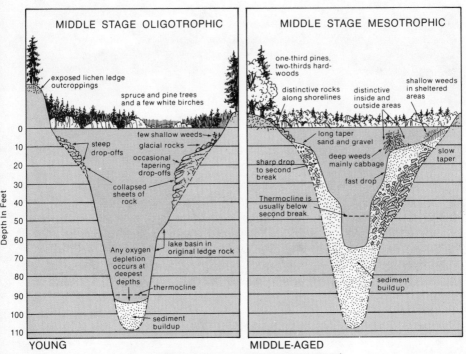

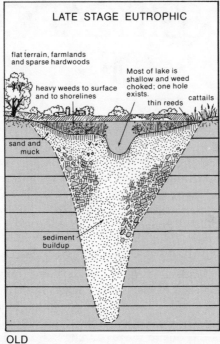

Consequently, we view and classify natural lakes according to their condition, and not necessarily their chronological age. A lake is basically either young, middle-aged or old. Since some lakes are in between these broad types and almost defy classification, our classifications should not be taken as absolutes. Instead, each category is meant to be a convenient point of reference—a definition we can start to learn from.

As lakes "age," their character changes. Generally speaking, geologically "young" lakes are deep and clean; older ones are shallow and murky.

The natural order is such that on one end of the aging scale we find young lakes (with oxygen-rich deep water) which can support fish like lake trout and whitefish. At the other end, we find lakes with another kind of makeup which can only support fish such as carp and bullheads.

Obviously, a lake trout cannot live in a shallow, murky, weedy, low-oxygen lake of the midwestern prairies. And carp have a tough time making it in the rocky, ice-cold, weedless environment of a trout lake. But between these two extremes fall lakes of all sorts—each of which are more or less hospitable to certain species of fish.

Pike, for example, have a lot of latitude in their genetic makeup, and can at least exist in varying degrees in all but very young or extremely old bodies of water. Sometimes this aging is determined by fertility—the youngest lakes being infertile while the oldest are very fertile. We categorize natural lakes in the following nine states:

THE STABLE, YOUNG, INFERTILE, COLD WATER ENVIRONMENT STATES
   1. Early stage oligotrophic
   2. Mid-stage oligotrophic
THE TRANSITION FROM COLD TO COOL WATER ENVIRONMENT STATES
   3. Late stage oligotrophic
   4. Early stage mesotrophic
THE STABLE, MIDDLE-AGED, MODERATELY FERTILE, COOL WATER ENVIRONMENT STATE
   5. Mid-stage mesotrophic
THE TRANSITION FROM COOL TO WARM WATER ENVIRONMENT STATES
   6. Late stage mesotrophic
   7. Early stage eutrophic
THE STABLE, OLD, FERTILE, WARM WATER ENVIRONMENT STATE
   8. Mid-stage eutrophic
THE TRANSITION FROM WARM TO VERY WARM WATER ENVIRONMENT STATE
   9. Late stage eutrophic

When you analyze a particular lake, remember that these categories are simply points of reference to work from. However, as you become familiar with the system, you will be able to easily recognize a lake as being early stage eutrophic—instead of late stage meso.

The youngest type of lakes—oligotrophic—typically have rock basins and are found almost exclusively in the upper portions of the North American continent. They usually have steep, sharp drop-offs, few weeds, pine-studded shorelines, and a fish population composed of cold water fish like lake trout and members of the whitefish family. The nutrient level of the water is usually low, and oxygen is available in deep water at all times. Thus, the lake is termed infertile.

As this type of lake ages, the shorelines become less gorge-like, and the drop-offs less abrupt and steep. Big boulders turn to smaller rock, and more sand and gravel become apparent. Weedgrowth develops. The trees that bound the lake also tend to change. Since the surrounding terrain changes, the water quality takes on a new character (more nutrients). These are the first signs of the transitory process between the oligotrophic and mesotrophic categories.

Little by little, the lake changes and eventually develops characteristics typical of a middle-aged, mesotrophic lake. When a lake reaches its mid-mesotrophic stage, much of the exposed rock, except right along the shoreline, is gone. Sand and some gravel now prevail in the lake's basin. The shoreline tapers become more gradual, more weeds appear in the shallows, and the trees that surround the lake begin changing from evergreens to hardwoods. A distinct thermocline and oxycline usually form.

By the time the next transition (mesotrophic to eutrophic) stage occurs, a lake, by geological aging standards, is getting old. First, it is getting shallower. Sand begins turning to muck or clay in certain sections, and the erosion process results in less extensive shoreline tapers than in the mid-meso classification. Secondary drop-offs in deep water are obliterated or less defined.

Marshy areas usually dot certain adjacent sections. Hardwood trees and flat shorelines rim the lakeshore, rather than steep cliffs or high hills. The lake is changing from a cool to a warm water environment.

When a lake moves into its mid-eutrophic stage, it becomes a true warm water environment. In its oligotrophic stage this body of water was a cold water environment; in its "meso" stage a cool water environment; and now in its eutrophic stage a warm water environment.

By geological standards, this lake is now quite old. It has become very shallow, and the erosion process is near completion. Farmlands usually surround these waters. Thermoclines generally don't develop or last a long time. Weedgrowth is thick, and sandy areas become quite soft. Water color becomes darker, so weeds grow to lesser depths, and the shoreline just sort of blends into the basin of the lake.

In a nutshell, this is the aging process all natural lakes go through. Study the accompanying drawings carefully, so you understand the different types of natural lakes. Most importantly, as you learn to recognize lake types, you'll learn what to expect in terms of pike size and probably population density. In the final analysis, this will help you fish smarter—not harder!

NATURAL LAKE CLASSIFICATION SUMMARY

It has been our observation that pike in the large and lunker size groups (8 to 25 pounds) occur most frequently in the following lake types:

LATE STAGE OLIGOTROPHIC
EARLY STAGE MESOTROPHIC
MID-STAGE MESOTROPHIC

Now this *does not* mean that late stage mesotrophic, early stage eutrophic or even mid-stage oligotrophic environments do not or cannot produce any big pike. It's just that these environments are generally *not* that capable of putting out significant numbers of lunker-sized fish on a consistent basis.

Each of the prime pike lake types, while a bit different, has a number of factors in common. To be a good body of water, it must have adequate pike spawning and rearing areas. These waters are usually good-sized and have various levels (or lake zones) where the four different niches of pike (small, intermediate, large and lunker) can function efficiently for most of the year.

To be "pike provident," a body of water must at least be a cool or cold water environment, as opposed to a warm one. If the oxygen is depleted in the depths in summer, it must only be for a slight period of time (usually 5 weeks or shorter in duration), and during this period must offer bigger pike some sort of refuge from warm water stress in the form of deep cool sediment layers, cold water springs, etc. Remember, the cooler the water, the greater the longevity—and longevity is a key to large growth.

To produce numbers of good-sized pike, a lake must have sufficient prey for pike at each level of growth. One significant factor for growing big pike is the presence of deep and/or open water prey in the form of a soft-finned, soft-bodied species like ciscoes or smelt.

Bays of the Great Lakes, and some sections of the Great Lakes themselves, fall into these lake classifications as well. Because of their unique status, we'll discuss the Great Lakes in a separate chapter. Chapter 17 covers the Great Lakes' oftentime untapped, yet phenomenal, pike potential.

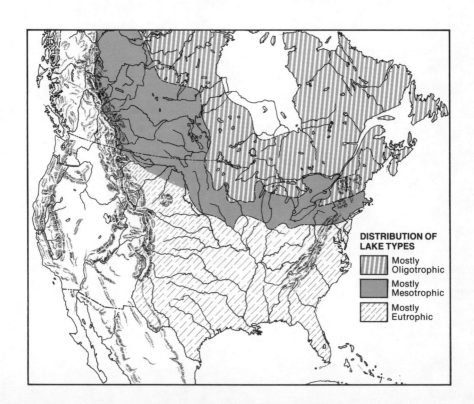

DISTRIBUTION OF
LAKE TYPES

Mostly
Oligotrophic

Mostly
Mesotrophic

Mostly
Eutrophic

Chapter 8

CLASSIFICATION OF RIVERS

Just as lakes are formed through the forces of nature over long periods of time, so are rivers. Therein lies the clue to our classification approach. Like lakes, rivers follow a natural development pattern from young to old.

Geologists refer to rivers as being "young," "middle-aged," or "old." Since rivers do not thermocline, terms like oligotrophic, mesotrophic and eutrophic (although having some application) do not really describe a stretch of river's condition or nature. Instead, "young," "middle-aged" or "old" better describe the condition of the landscape carved by the river, more so than the actual age of the river itself or its primary environmental condition.

On some big rivers like the Mississippi, Missouri, Ohio and Arkansas, there are sections of huge, well-developed flood plains—evidence of an old river. Here, the original banks are miles away and hundreds of feet higher than to-day's existing stream bed. That's what we mean when we say the surrounding geography and generalized shape of the riverbed are the main clues to a stream's age.

In its flow, a young river plunges rapidly downhill, cutting through narrow valleys. As a river matures, it moves downhill more slowly and meanders a little more gently through broad valleys bounded by smoothly rounded hills. In "old age," a river curves widely across level flood plains surrounded by worn-down hills.

For a stream, the major catalyst to aging is erosion. In general, the longer a stream extends in length, the more aging occurs in the form of erosion. The process of erosion actually carries the aging process upstream. So, as time goes on, older geological conditions which form at a river's delta continue to move further and further upstream.

Since there are variations in the aging progression in successive sections of a stream, as well as some overlap between the abundance and presence of the cold, cool and warm water fish species, the only way to view a stream is by stretches. In this sense, a particular stretch can be young, old or somewhere in between in terms of geological makeup.

For instance, a stream might be quite shallow, have a slow taper for several miles, and possess a number of backwater areas with soft bottom and aquatic weedgrowth. Here, largemouth bass and/or northern pike might find adequate habitat. But all of a sudden, this same stream might break into a sharp gradient as it shoots through a rocky, cliff-like area, creating a rapids and finally pouring into a boulder-based pool. This younger stretch, although further downstream, could house smallmouth bass and possibly stocked rainbow trout.

Different stretches of the same stream can have different personalities and different fish species. Rarely is a stream the same from beginning to end, because few regions are geographically consistent.

Because of these limitless variations, we devised the following method of classifying streams. With these categories, we can identify and recognize most river stretches found in North America. Of course, there will be exceptions: usually those parts in transition between types, much like a natural lake that has eutrophic bays, while the main body of the lake is mesotrophic in character.

These classes are best viewed as guidelines to a better understanding of the rivers you fish, and the quantity and types of predominant fish you could expect to find in them.

(1) VERY YOUNG	—Brook trout and/or grayling
(2) YOUNG	—Stocked trout
(3) ADULT	—Appearance of cool water fish (pike)
(4) MATURE	—Good populations of pike
(5) MIDDLE-AGED	—Large pike
(6) OLD	—Small pike or pickerel
(7) VERY OLD	—Mostly rough fish
(8) TIDAL	—Backwaters of the ocean (European pike)

Within this context, we can isolate stretches which are "pike prime." These conditions usually occur in river stretches we term Adult, Mature, Middle-Aged and Tidal (Europe).

The following charts give us the generalized makeup of each river type:

Tidal rivers have brackish water and do hold pike—and some pretty good ones! But these seem to be found chiefly on the European Continent around the Baltic Sea. You'll catch an occasional good fish in tidal rivers like the Connecticut River. However, we do not know of many rivers in the western hemisphere which are truly brackish and put up any number of big pike.

	ADULT	MATURE	MIDDLE-AGED
SHAPE OF CROSS-SECTION	Prominent Vegetation Gravel Deposits Begin to Build Erosion really flattens out the stream bed.	Flood Plain Sand and Gravel Deposits	Channel Bottom is Completely Smooth — Broadened Flood Plain Sand and Mud Deposits
SOURCE AND GEOGRAPHICAL DRAINAGE AREA	This stretch can be of highland or pastoral origin and will drain an expansive area, like marginal hardwood forests that contain mixed pine, and fringe agricultural areas. At this stage, the river has its maximum number of tributaries and will drain generally infertile, sparse areas. The source is usually a young river, but could be a lake or spring in the lower foothills or in a sand or gravel locale. Sometimes adult streams drain "meso" lakes or highland reservoirs. There are almost no intermittent streams acting as feeders.	This stretch may either emerge from or cut through a pastoral landscape, usually composed of sandstone and other soil types. The drainage area can include farmland as well as major urban and industrial areas, which can have a major impact on pollution levels. The number of tributaries start to decrease at this stage.	This stage often has a farmland origin. The drainage area is very large with high weedgrowth adjacent to agricultural areas. Tributaries consist mainly of adult rivers.
WATER QUALITY	The water is semi-clear but can become very murky during heavy rains, particularly in farm areas or small urban areas. Premature aging may occur in areas of intense agricultural activity when nutrient levels are high or where pollution is substantial.	The water will be semi-clear to semi-murky. During high water periods, it will be very turbid, especially around agricultural areas, usually taking four to five days to clear up after a rain. Slower-running water will make the temperature higher. Aging will accelerate because of agricultural and industrial pollutants.	The water is murky to quite turbid most of the time due to the suspended mineral and soil particles and increased organic nutrients. Turbidity is a constant factor because of the large size of the watershed, a situation that makes angling difficult. Where this river broadens into a large lake, settling will occur and water quality will temporarily improve.

	ADULT	MATURE	MIDDLE-AGED
PROBABLE SPECIES PRESENT	Generally cool water fish such as small-mouth bass, northern pike, some walleyes, and maybe some carp. Possibly a few muskies.	Walleyes, sauger, some smallmouths, northern pike, muskies, catfish, white bass, sturgeon, a few largemouths, perch, crappies, carp, suckers, buffalo, and rock bass.	Northerns, sauger, walleyes, a few muskies, silver bass, good largemouths, and catfish. Certain sections of a middle-aged stretch will be more hospitable to one species because of structural make-up, even though they cut through the same terrain.
TYPICAL ILLUSTRATIONS	These stretches are found in western Pennsylvania (in the Appalachians), Arkansas (the Buffalo), the St. Croix in Minnesota, the upper stretches of the Mississippi, the upper Potomac River and stretches of the Shenandoah.	These stretches can be found in major drainage areas in any part of the country. For example, large stretches of the Mississippi and the lower Allegheny River in Pennsylvania.	The St. Lawrence River bordering the U.S. and Canada has middle-aged stretches, as does the Detroit River, and, of course, a good part of the Mississippi and Ohio Rivers.
KEY I.D. FEATURE	Trout can no longer survive or reproduce naturally. The appearance of coolwater fish. (walleyes, smallmouths)	The ability to produce quantities of preferred game species such as walleyes, sauger, and northern pike. Deep pools provide refuge, and marshy backwaters provide pike spawning grounds. A mature stream can produce good populations of several kinds of gamefish; sandy, rocky sections with fast water will hold smallmouths while the deeper, slower sections or pools will contain walleyes.	The presence of naturally-reproducing walleyes and sauger mixed with fair levels of largemouth bass plus northern pike. This is the river of large pike. There is a diversity of habitat for just about any kind of fish. This is the last stage for quantities of naturally-reproducing coolwater fish. (northern pike)
GRADIENT AND DEPTH	Gradient: Two to three foot drop per mile. Depth: Six to ten feet average with intermittent deep and shallow stretches based on the amount	Gradient: 1.5 to two foot drop per mile. Depth: Depth will vary. Some stretches will be four to five feet deep, while deeper holes can be fifteen to	Gradient: One to 1.5 foot drop per mile. Depth: Depth will vary from shallow, one foot deep weedy backwater pockets to forty foot pools. Runs of twelve

	ADULT	MATURE	MIDDLE-AGED
GRADIENT AND DEPTH	of sand and gravel present. Most pools following rapids are eight to ten feet with occasional isolated holes of fifteen to twenty feet.	twenty feet. There is a lot of eight to ten foot water.	feet are common. Under dams, gouges of fifty feet can occur.
GEOGRAPHICAL MAKE-UP AND BOTTOM CONTENT	The stream bed is alternating sections of gravel, sand, and fist-sized rocks with sporadic boulders and no silt. There will be shallower sections and some rocks dressed with moss. Weedgrowth is sparse. Shoreline banks composed of fist-sized rocks, trees, and brush. Occasional wing dams will be present.	The main channel is composed mostly of sand. Siltation is now a significant factor; wing dams are sometimes constructed to control this. There are some rock outcroppings. Aquatic growth is common, along with a higher nutrient level.	Flows mostly through soft sedimentary rock and sandy subsoils. Sand is the dominant riverbed material. Time and erosion have pulverized the rocks and gravel. There will be a few rock outcrops along the banks of the river. This stage will exhibit well-developed flood plains; flooding is common.
COMMON TRAITS	This stretch contains a higher nutrient level, and warmer and slower moving water than the very young or young stretches. Typical of this stretch are alternating "riffle" or "slick" sections. Gone are the roaring, cascading rapids—replaced by mini-rapids that are not dangerous. There is increased fertilizer runoff and sewage input. Damming is more frequent, and occasional islands will be found. Sand and gravel bars have become a prominent feature.	Rapids nonexistent; at best a few shallow "riffles" will occur. Mature rivers can and do overflow. They will begin to meander and develop flood plains. On this river stage, dams actually create miniature impoundments. Although they are called "pools," they function much like reservoirs. At certain times of the year, usually spring or fall, all the gamefish species could be stacked up against the dam! This stream is an *IN-FISHERMAN* paradise and is the first stage that produces multiple quantities of preferred gamefish.	This stretch usually flows by river towns and metropolitan areas where pollution can be a severe problem. It is at this stage that the river really starts to show the buildup of nutrients, erosion, and pollution. Except for trout and salmon, just about any type of fish can survive. This stream will offer the most pounds of gamefish per acre provided it is unpolluted. Flood plains can create backwater sloughs or flat, high, fertile fields. A dredged, mid-ship channel is usually maintained for barges, and dams with locks are common.

PIKE AND MOVING WATER

Most rivers allow small and medium-sized pike (which are primarily warm or cool water fish) to exist. However, most large-sized rivers do not remain cool or cold enough (nor offer enough of the right kind of prey) for big and lunker-sized pike to develop unless they're fed by cold brooks or streams with enough of a gradient. For this reason, numbers of big pike generally do not develop in these systems.

In most cases where numbers of big pike are reported from rivers, investigation showed the big pike came from stream mouth areas, where the river joined a lake, from a widening of the river (which functioned like a lake), or where the river met a larger body of water and the pike were only there seasonally for one reason or another. This is the case in the famed Canadian Churchill River chains. Big pike are also taken from the Thousand Islands area of the St. Lawrence River—although an impoundment situation and not a true river. Apparently, a river must have some unique features to produce big pike.

Alaska is one place which offers some of these unique, moving water environments, and big pike can be found in such waters during all seasons. Rivers like the Notak, Middle Yukon and the Tanana all produce big pike. Interestingly, these waters are cool or cold most of the year, quite isolated (and thus subject to little fishing pressure), and apparently offer enough forage of the correct size (for all pike niches) all year long, and big pike can develop.

While a river like the Yukon River, which is a mile wide in some places and provides backwaters, might fall into a middle-aged category, it has stretches intersected by other streams which fall into young, adult, and middle-aged classifications. These places support the big pike. In other stretches of these rivers which do not have the proper environment, pike are either small, medium-sized or absent.

SUMMARY

River fishermen face more sudden, dramatic changes in water conditions than lake fishermen can ever imagine. Most lakes are "a piece of cake" when compared structurally with rivers. Water levels in natural lakes remain relatively stable over long periods of time. It usually takes a long-term drought or heavy rainfall to bring about severe high or low water levels in a lake. Yet river anglers are always fighting rising or falling water levels. More than just contending with water level "flux," they must adjust to bottom structure that is here today and gone tomorrow. Sandbars come and go. Flow patterns can change in a subtle manner with a shift of the stream's course or an increase in current speed.

Changing bottom conditions obviously also affect fish location. As rapidly as water levels rise or fall, a key fish-attracting current break like an eddy near a deep washout hole can suddenly appear or completely vanish, and affect fish location accordingly. A backwater slough that might hold pike during the high water of spring might be high and dry a week later. Remember, the ability to read current is the key to successful river fishing. Take the time to learn how it functions with rising or falling water levels, creating or eliminating fish-holding areas in the process.

Fish like pike relate to structural elements one way during high water, and another way when the water is low. It must be realized that of all the various freshwater gamefish, the pike is a relatively poor swimmer. Sure, it can exhibit a fast burst of speed to grab a meal; however, it has a tough time swimming and fighting current, and is not a particularly efficient current predator. So, objects producing those all-important "current breaks," which produce sections of slack water where food accumulates, will attract pike. Pike hold and set up feeding stations at these points.

A list of some of the major structural elements found in streams would surely include most of the following:

(1) MAIN, FEEDER AND SIDE CHANNELS
(2) POINT BARS ON THE INSIDE BENDS OF RIVER CURVES
(3) MAN-MADE STRUCTURAL ELEMENTS
(4) SLOUGHS OF DEAD WATER
(5) NATURAL LEVEES OF HARD MATERIAL LEFT BY FLOODS
(6) BACKWATER AREAS
(7) SANDBARS
(8) POOLS
(9) RIFFLES
(10) EDDIES
(11) CURRENT BREAKS
(12) THE INTERSECTION OF A TRIBUTARY STREAM
(13) AREAS BELOW A DAM

Most streams contain these various components in differing combinations.

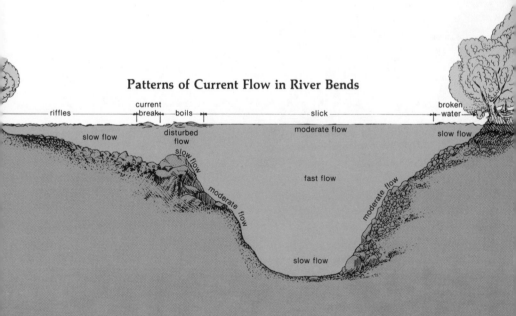

Patterns of Current Flow in River Bends

riffles — current break — boils — slick — broken water

slow flow — disturbed flow — moderate flow — slow flow

slow flow — moderate flow — fast flow — moderate flow

slow flow

Chapter 9
CLASSIFICATION OF RESERVOIRS

Just as lakes and rivers fall into distinct, descriptive categories, reservoirs, too, fall into various classifications by way of makeup and function. A reservoir is, after all, simply an impounded body of water held back by a dam. The artificially-impounded water floods natural terrain such as marshes, plains, hills, plateaus or canyons.

Taking a cross-section of North America, you would see that some areas might be low, sort of swampy or marshy, or rather flat like an old flood-plain region. In other places, the terrain is hilly. Still others have mountains and highland ridges rising up to form foothills. These are usually low mountain ranges like the Boston or Ouachita ranges in Arkansas, the Appalachian chain in the east, the Cumberland highlands of Kentucky and Tennessee, or the low coastal ranges of the West Coast.

In the plains west of the Mississippi, you encounter what are termed "high plains." Just west of them is an immense plateau that lifts step-like up across the mid-section of the continent. This plateau area is adjacent to the rugged Rocky Mountains. Reservoirs built in the canyons of the mountains take on long, snake-like shapes, and their cross-sections have towering, sharp, almost vertical walls.

A mind-boggling array, isn't it? Yet it's not as awesome as it first appears, because fish within similar types of reservoirs respond in much the same manner. In other words, pike in various shallow, dark water, wetland (flowage) reservoirs tend to exhibit typical movement and response patterns. Pike in deep, cool, plateau reservoirs respond somewhat differently. In short, reservoirs constructed in similar land forms—even if they're in different parts of the country—are enough alike that we can fit them, for identification purposes, into six basic groups. These groups are:

(1) CANYON
(2) HIGHLAND
(3) PLATEAU
(4) HILL-LAND
(5) FLATLAND
(6) WETLAND

While certain regions of the country have had their state pike records caught from reservoirs, many are not true trophy pike waters, as the following records indicate:

TENNESSEE	10 lbs. 13 oz.
KENTUCKY	9 lbs. 8 oz.
TEXAS	14 lbs. 4 oz.
MISSOURI	18 lbs. 9 oz.
ARKANSAS	16 lbs. 1 oz.

These *are not* waters you would *go* to to catch big pike. In most cases, the fish are incidental catches. In the following areas, however, occasional big pike are caught in reservoirs, as the following records show:

ARIZONA	24 lbs. 2 oz.
OKLAHOMA	36 lbs. 8 oz.
NEW MEXICO	36 lbs. 1 oz.

But even in these cases, the low numbers of available pike make them poor choices to fish with the sole intention of trophy pike fishing. The action would be too inconsistent, because of the low numbers of pike. What, then, is the answer?

Although pike occur in many types of reservoirs, we have found that worthwhile numbers of pike in the big or lunker-sized range are most likely found in cool-water, *plateau* or *hill-land* impoundments. You might assume that numbers of big pike would also thrive in canyon or highland impoundments, but we cannot find any incidence of this in North America, other than a few cases in the Western U.S. Apparently, pike have not been stocked in more than a handful of favorable trophy waters, and suitable spawning areas are often lacking to develop numbers of big pike. By the same token, we know of numerous flatland and wetland impoundments which have pike, but most of these do not host appreciable numbers of big fish. They often have plenty of marshy spawning water, but lack the cool water or proper food sources necessary to produce lunkers. Interestingly, some of these waters put out big muskies—but few big pike.

Apparently, the canyon and highland impoundment environment offers potential for big and lunker-sized pike, but the niches for small and medium-sized fish are simply not there. The necessary factors for the preliminary growth stages are missing. While a 12 or 20 pound pike can survive—and perhaps even thrive—the fish have little or no opportunity to grow to that size in the first place. On the other hand, flatland and wetland reservoirs—while apparently producing conditions for small and medium-sized fish to develop—lack the next niche partition in the environment for big pike to blossom.

Of the various impoundment categories, the two which offer the best potential for prime pike development are plateau and hill-land reservoirs. A description of these types of impoundments follows.

Remember that all hill-land or plateau reservoirs do not necessarily house pike. Indeed, across North America, the greater number don't. However, if pike exist, and the system is in a part of the country where the water stays cool or cold, the environmental conditions are such that there is a good chance for pike to mature in both numbers and size.

Examples of pike-productive plateau reservoirs are:

Lake Sharpe	South Dakota
Oahe Reservoir	South Dakota
Lake Sakakawea	North Dakota
Tongue River Reservoir	Montana

Examples of pike-productive hill-land reservoirs are:

Kinzua Reservoir	Pennsylvania
Council Grove Reservoir	Kansas
Bond Falls Flowage	Michigan (U.P.)
Keyhole Reservoir	Wyoming

Plateau Impoundment

Certain plateau reservoirs have good populations of northern pike. Big fish often run 20 pounds and more. Given adequate spawning conditions, the cool/cold water and suitable food sources provide a favorable environment for growing lunker pike. The Missouri River impoundments fall into this classification.

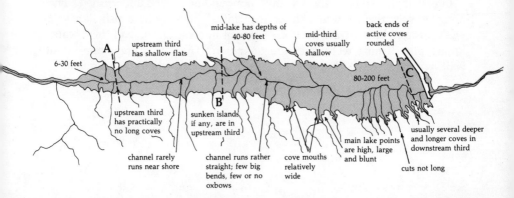

Hill-Land Impoundment

Some hill-land impoundments grow large pike, even though the pike population seldom blossoms to immense proportions. A big pike might run 14-15 pounds, with an outside shot at 20 pounds. In general, the less water fluctuation, the more weedgrowth, and the better the pike spawning conditions.

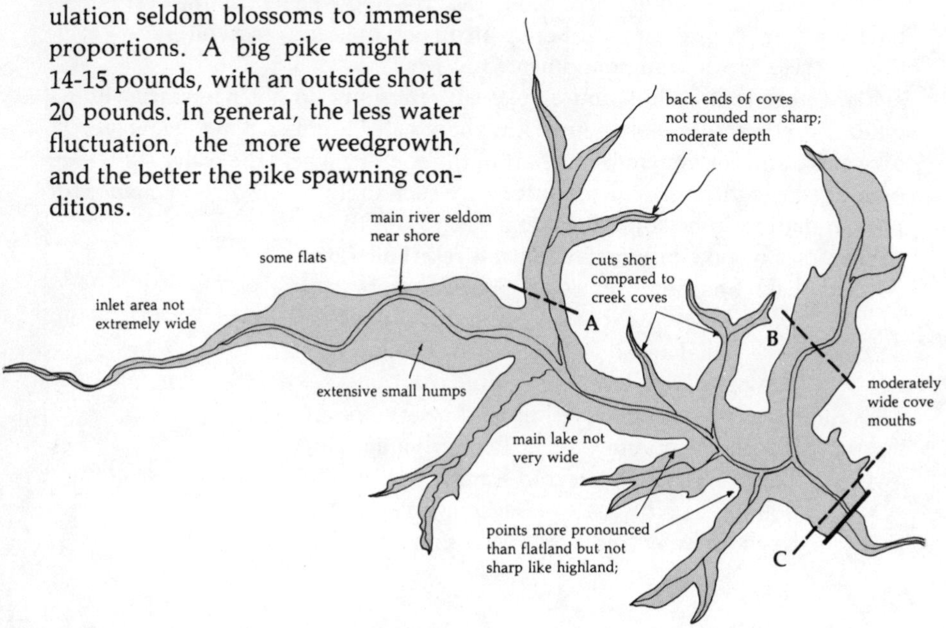

back ends of coves
not rounded nor sharp;
moderate depth

main river seldom
near shore

some flats

cuts short
compared to
creek coves

inlet area not
extremely wide

A

B

extensive small humps

moderately
wide cove
mouths

main lake not
very wide

points more pronounced
than flatland but not
sharp like highland;

C

SUMMARY

When selecting a reservoir to fish for pike, the first thing to establish is whether or not the body of water has pike in it, and then judge—by the environmental guidelines established in this book—if it has the potential for big fish.

Interestingly, some "pike worthy" impoundments are underfished. There are places in the western half of the United States where fish like trout, walleyes, and bass attract the lion's share of interest. In some of these waters, lunker pike fishing techniques are unknown. There is a great opportunity waiting for those who know the how's, where's and when's of pike fishing.

Chapter 10

THE PRE-SPAWN PERIOD

"A Time of Anticipation"

This is one of the top Calendar Periods for trophy northern pike. However, many northern states and Canadian provinces have closed pike seasons at this time of the year. Be sure to check local fishing regulations.

For our purposes, the pike's Pre-spawn Period begins before ice-out. The actual timing varies due to latitude and local climate conditions. Pre-spawn may start as early as February in Ireland, April in Minnesota, or as late as July in northern Canada.

Females are usually first to stage near, or move closer to, spawning areas. Since surface temperature is still very cold, pike activity will be slow. Their general mood can be regarded as neutral.

The following are our location and presentation guidelines for key pike waters during the Pre-spawn Period.

Pre-Spawn Reservoir Pike

Not surprisingly, most of the really big fish are taken during the spring Pre-spawn Period. Even then, fishing pressure is very light and nearly all of the big fish are taken by a small fraternity of anglers. The combination of light fishing pressure and large numbers of readily accessible fish (and some true trophies) makes for great fishing.

During most years the Pre-spawn Period starts in early April. The fall Cold Water Period begins in about early October and offers nearly the same opportunity. In the spring, however, the fish are more concentrated. You'll find this true in most reservoir pike situations.

Excellent fishing begins early—when there's still ice cover on the main reservoir except for small open water patches near shore. Move inside a large bay and you'll find big pike lying just under the protective ice cover at the edges of open water areas. The boat ramps are still iced in, so the fishing is best done from shore. Even if you could launch a boat, it'd be downright dangerous because the massive ice floes have a way of moving with the ever-present winds.

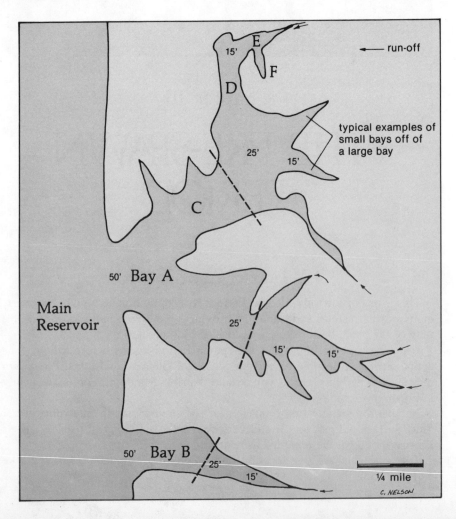

run-off

typical examples of
small bays off of
a large bay

25'

15'

15'

E

F

D

15'

C

50' Bay A

Main
Reservoir

25'

15'

15'

50' Bay B

25'

15'

¼ mile

C. NELSON

Nearly all feeder cuts or bays with a bit of water color usually attract some pre-spawn pike. Normally, the water color is due to the small, intermittent feeder creeks. Because Bays A and B both have these feeder creeks, they would probably both have the proper water color and temperatures to attract fish. Remember, the water should be slightly murky, but not muddy!

Water color aside, Bay A will usually attract more fish than Bay B simply because of the size and number of feeder cuts inside it. Normally, the more diverse the inside of a bay is (or the more feeder cuts there are), the more fish it will hold. For example, a feeder cut by itself is good (C); a feeder cut off of a feeder cut is better (D); and still more cuts off of a second cut, like E and F, make the area even better.

Most pre-spawn pike fishing occurs in the back ends of the bays beyond the areas indicated by the dotted lines. Under optimum conditions, the fish proceed as far up into a feeder cut as possible. Under frontal conditions, however, they drop back into slightly deeper water. Thus Area E, and especially Area F, would probably host plenty of fish under optimum conditions, while a cold front would probably push the pike back out to Area D.

Trophy pike hunters have a favorite tactic for fish lying just under the edge of the ice cover. They cast a spoon right up on top of the ice, slowly drag it to the edge, and let it fall off into the water. Allow the spoon to drop vertically. Many times it never hits the bottom!

When the ice goes, it goes quickly. Once you're able to launch your boat, concentrate on the fairly large bays. Specifically, look for large bays with many small bays inside them. The most consistent producers have an active creek flowing into them. The pike typically move well back into the small bays, virtually as far back as possible, right to where the bay dwindles to become simply a small creek. Also look for slightly murky, off-colored water and try to stay away from bays with very clear water. If you follow these simple guidelines, you'll be on the fish.

PRESENTATION

Let's take a close look at a typical reservoir situation such as Lake Oahe, South Dakota.

Moderately-heavy spinning tackle is adequate for handling Oahe pike, since there are few snags in most of the bays. We do recommend a fairly stiff rod, one with backbone for a good hook set. Light bait casting tackle will also do nicely.

Cold water fishing also calls for a quality monofilament line. Eight, 10 or 12 pound test line is sufficient. Most anglers seem to prefer 10 pound test.

According to our records, water temperature can tell you a lot about fish location and the subsequent methods used to catch them. Thus, we'd recommend some type of temperature-taking device. You'll also need a needle-nose pliers to assist in removing hooks, and a really large, musky-size landing net.

You do not need a wide variety of baits to handle the different pike fishing situations you're going to encounter. When weather conditions are perfect and the fish move right up into the back ends of bays or feeder cuts, or right along shorelines within these areas, 4 or 5 inch minnow-imitating plugs such as the Rapala, Rebel, Cordell Red Fin, Bomber, Heddon Hellcat or Lindy/Little Joe Baitfish are consistent producers. There's nothing very technical involved with fishing the bait; just cast it up shallow and retrieve it very slowly. Color does not seem to be a big factor either, but we've had our best success with patterns that most nearly duplicate smelt and spottail shiners. In other words, the standard silver minnow pattern works well.

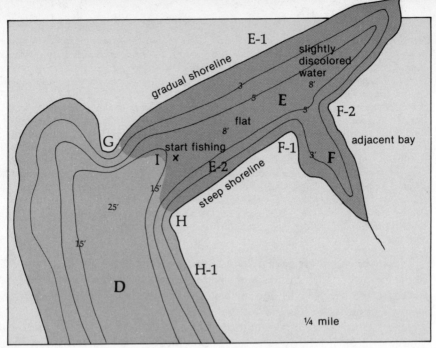

Begin your search for pre-spawn pike by either locating bay areas on a lake map, or, better yet, by asking local anglers for information. If there's still ice present, you may be forced to fish from shore. Once the ice goes out, however, you can launch your boat and motor along the shoreline until you locate a bay—preferably a large bay with a small bay or two inside it.

Although the back end of a slightly discolored bay is usually a key spot, don't immediately motor all the way into it; you may spook the fish! Instead, start your fishing on the flat near the mouth of the bay (X marks the spot). Use your trolling motor to slowly cruise along, fancasting your way to the back end of the bay. Active spring pike tend to favor a gradually-sloping shoreline (E-1), over a steeper one (E-2), so concentrate on the more gradual side of the bay.

After working your way to the back end of the bay, position the boat a cast's length from the shoreline and work your way along the back end. In this instance, of course, you should also spend some time covering the small adjacent bay (F). First fish the mouth of the bay, and then the interior. Then, depending on the size of the bay (E) and how thoroughly you worked it during your approach, you might also want to spend more time working the 8 foot flat at the mouth of the bay (I).

Under mild cold front conditions, the fish will drop back from the shallow end of Bay E and away from the gradually-sloping shoreline. If they do not vacate the bay altogether, you could expect to find them suspended slightly out from the steeper shoreline (E-2). The fish also exhibit a distinct tendency to favor quicker-breaking points under cold front conditions, so points F-1 and F-2 might be key areas.

Under severe cold front conditions the fish will definitely vacate the shallow 1-8 foot water in the bay and probably suspend 10-18 feet down over 15-25 feet of water. Now, steep-breaking shorelines (like H-1), points G and H and the deep flat (area I) out at the mouth of the bay will hold most of the fish.

When weather conditions are stable and the fish are actively feeding in the back ends of bays and along gradually-sloping shorelines, you can expect to find them very close to shore. Cast right up to the shore with a minnow-imitating bait or light spoon, and work it back to the boat. Fishing suspended fish on shallow 8 foot flats calls for the same baits, but with a fancasting approach. When severe cold fronts drop the fish into 10-18 feet of water, however, use countdown lures or a jig and minnow. Don't be worried about reaching the shoreline with a cast at this time; the fish aren't there. Position your boat away from shore so you're fishing through the deeper, suspended fish. Quick-breaking points such as G and H are often big fish spots during the last hour of daylight.

Long-lipped, minnow-imitating lures that float at rest and dive on the retrieve rank high on the list of pre-spawn pike producers. The key is their slow, tantalizing wobble. Simply cast them to the shoreline and retrieve them in at a steady pace; be ready for anything!

Switch to a countdown (sinking version) of these same lures for fancasting the centers of deep flats or the junctions of small bays with larger ones. Inactive pike suspend in these areas, and by experimenting with the depth you allow the lure to sink to, you can zero in on and catch these fish at times when the "bank beaters" catch little or nothing.

Most pike fishermen also throw spoons when faced with shallow water fishing conditions, and there's no question that a spoon is a great pike bait. It does not seem, however, to be as productive as the minnow-imitators under these conditions. Also remember this: Choose a very light spoon such as a Blue Fox in this situation. Heavy spoons sink too fast and must be retrieved too quickly to be effective. Be sure to try fluorescent colors when faced with the slightly murky water you should be fishing in.

There are always some fish using the fairly shallow (usually around 8 feet) flats that typically extend up into most bays and feeder cuts. Pike will spread out on these flats, but usually suspend at about mid-depth. The same two bait types used in the shallows work well here, with the spoon now producing more fish than before, probably because you can flutter it and drop it a bit deeper.

Cold fronts are a common springtime Dakota phenomenon, just as they are in all pike fishing country. As in other reservoirs across the country, a cold front pushes Oahe pike from the immediate shallows inside a bay or feeder cut, out into deeper water at the mouths of the bays. Here they usually suspend (in Oahe, typically from 10-18 feet down over 25 feet of water) over deep water. This suspension is often in relation to a quick-breaking point at the bay's mouth, and almost always occurs in relation to the steepest-breaking side of a cut or bay.

In this instance, jig and minnow combos and countdown lures are the way to go. Fish these lures by casting them out, counting them down to various depths (experiment), and then slowly retrieving them. Remember that these deep fish are suspended out away from the shoreline, so don't cast right up to it. Back off a bit and cast to where you think the fish are suspended! You can often detect them with a graph or depth finder!

Spinnerbaits also have their place. We use spinnerbaits most effectively when we've had a pike follow a minnow-imitating plug without striking. Plunk that tandem spinnerbait right back at 'em and you'll usually be rewarded with an arm-jolting strike.

It's important to remember that few pike are caught in gin-clear bays. An ideal situation exists where a tiny feeder creek dumps runoff into a bay. If it colors the water slightly, the bay will warm up a bit faster, since the darker water really soaks up the sun's warmth. Forage fish are attracted to such areas and predators, such as the pike, tag along.

Trolling, especially with an outboard, is generally a waste of time. You're fishing shallow water and if you motor through, even slowly, with a big motor, you'll spook most of the fish. When you enter the mouth of a bay, shut off your outboard and either drift into casting position, or move in with an electric motor. Quiet casting will produce most of your action.

As noted earlier, the pike often group according to size. Large fish—those above 15 pounds—tend to be loners, although there's reason to believe they may form loose aggregates with one or two fish of similar size.

Apparently the really big hawgs go it all alone; perhaps simply because there are few other fish of similar size to associate with. There also seems to be a tendency for the very large fish to relate to points within a bay, while the smaller fish are more "flat" oriented. However, the large fish do tend to move up onto the shallow flats to feed during the low light period that occurs during the last hour or so of daylight. Remember, we're talking here only of *small flats within a bay*, not large flats you'll find out in the main reservoir.

Calm, sunny days produce the best pike fishing. Even on windy days, though, some fish are caught by seeking out wind-protected bays where murky water is present. The more wind-protected an area is, the more the sun penetrates and warms the water.

During Pre-spawn the most intense fish activity occurs during the afternoon. The water in the shallow bays needs a chance to soak up radiant energy and warm up! The fish do the same thing! Most of the really fast fishing for smaller pike comes during mid-afternoon, but the big pike, those over 12 pounds, seem far more active during the last hour of daylight.

What about live bait? Wouldn't it produce some big fish? Certainly, but that's another story. Compared to the mobile and more rapid "casting approach" it's a tedious process. We believe that casting definitely allows you to cover much more productive water and increases your odds for contacting big fish.

The pike population in Oahe is good right now, and within the United States, only the bays of the Great Lakes offer an equal chance at connecting with numbers of real trophies. That's not to say, however, that there aren't many other reservoirs that offer excellent fishing for pre-spawn pike.

A Game Plan For Early Season Pike Fishing

•Pre-spawn pike activity begins just before ice-out as pike move to the vicinity of spawning areas. Ice-out, and a subsequent warming of the water, intensifies pre-spawn activity.

•Spawning usually takes place soon after ice-out in water temperatures ranging from 40°F-52°F. Oahe's best pre-spawn fishing corresponds with water temperatures in the low 40°F's. You can expect the same to be true in other waters.

•Expect the best pre-spawn fishing to occur during the late afternoon on sunny, warm, calm days. Fish basking in the sun soak up radiant energy, warm their bodies beyond surrounding water temperatures and become relatively aggressive. Wind cuts down light penetration, so always seek the calmest available areas.

•In rivers and lakes, spawning habitat normally consists of vegetated backwaters, marshes or bays. Pike often run up feeder creeks to reach such areas. The water may be as shallow as half a foot. In reservoirs such as Oahe, however, the fish search out revegetated flats (vegetated during low water periods)

or sparse vegetation in the very back ends of bays or in the feeder cuts inside of bays. When vegetation is absent, the fish will still frequent these areas although spawning success will generally be poor.

• Slow-swimming, minnow-imitating lures and spoons are the top lure choices.

• Feeding activity slows after a cold front passes. The fish generally drop out a bit deeper but can still be caught with a slow count-down technique.

• After spawning, forage availability and water temperature keys big pike location. In Oahe, the fish usually remain within the bays for the entire year because plentiful forage and cool water temperatures allow them to. In natural lakes, the fish may forage in deeper weedbeds or follow a shallow, open water baitfish (like suspended perch) for a time.

• When water temperatures begin to climb, however, the fish seem to seek the coolest oxygenated water available which also provides an adequate forage source. In some shallow lakes, the fish are confined to thick weedbeds or cool spring areas. In deeper lakes, the fish may use the thermocline region, seek out spring areas, or use thick weeds. In rivers, the largest fish often seek out spring areas.

•Remember, during the Pre-spawn and Spawn Periods the location of spawning habitat, and to a lesser extent forage, keys fish location. After spawning, water temperature and the availability of food are the most important factors.

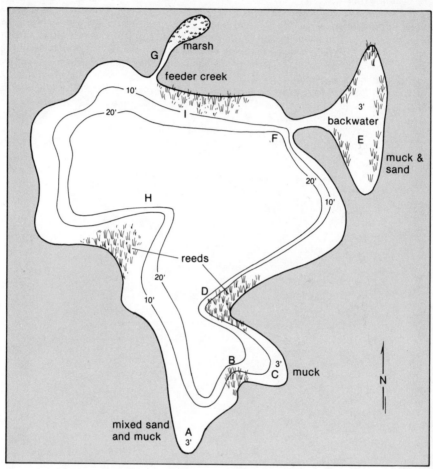

Pre-spawn Pike in Natural Lakes

Even though this chapter keys on reservoirs, pike spawning principles, and thus prespawn pike location, are similar in natural lakes. Let's use these same principles to identify potential pike spawning activity on a typical natural lake.

Bays A and C, backwater E, marsh G, and flat I could all see some early pike activity depending on the circumstances. Pike generally prefer shallow, soft bottom bays with vegetation and slightly colored water. This being the case, on this lake bay C, with its muck bottom, would be better than bay A, with its somewhat harder sand/muck bottom. Bay A would probably attract few pike, but quite a few largemouths, due to its harder bottom content.

Both backwater E and marsh G, however, would be superior to bays A and C because they lie off the deep, cold main lake and thereby warm much faster. Both of these areas have the proper bottom content, although backwater E could also host Prespawn bass activity a month or so later. On this lake, flat I would probably not draw pike. On a lake where backwater E and marsh G were absent, though, it might.

Before ice-out the pike will have already positioned themselves near these spawning areas. Ice-out occurs in marsh G and backwater E first, and the fish will begin running up into these areas while there is still ice on the main lake. Later, under optimum conditions (a warm, sunny, calm day) the fish will also be active and shallow in areas like G, E, C, and perhaps A.

If a severe cold front were to come through, the fish typically vacate the shallows in favor of the quickest-breaking adjacent point. Thus the fish from bay A would suspend over deeper water in the vicinity of point B, and the fish in bay C would either suspend off point B or D. When a sharp-breaking point is absent, the fish suspend out from the steepest-breaking shoreline adjacent to the shallows. Thus, the fish from backwater E would probably suspend in front of and down the shore from the mouth of the backwater. It's hard to say exactly where the fish from the marsh would suspend. Point H would probably not receive any pre-spawn, cold front pike use because there is no spawning area adjacent to it.

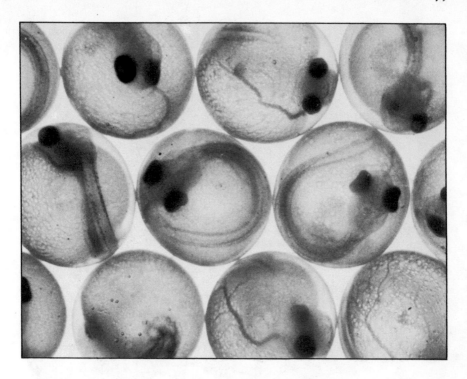

Chapter 11
THE SPAWN PERIOD

"A Time of Tension"

When they're ready to spawn, female pike, often accompanied by two or three males, move into weeds in shallow bays, ditches or bogs. You may be able to see them if the sun is shining. The eggs are a light yellow color, and do not adhere to each other but separate in the water like trout eggs.

Frost and Kipling (1867) noted that Windermere pike spawn along relatively sheltered parts of the shoreline, and in small bays. They usually choose silted and sandy (rather than stony) areas less than 12 feet deep, where there are submerged single or mixed strands of downed or newly-emerging vegetation. Evidence indicates that availablity determines the pike's choice of vegetation. For example, in Minnesota, pike spawn on the dead stems of sedges and rushes.

On Windermere the male pike arrive on the breeding ground first, and sometimes stay for a month. The average length of stay is 14 days, whereas the females usually stay for about 10 days. It appears that Windermere pike repeatedly return to the same spawning grounds; one tagged pike, first caught in 1959, was recaptured on the same grounds in 1960, 1962, 1963 and 1964.

Work done by Munro in Scotland (1957), Healy in Ireland (1956), and Frost and Kipling in Windermere, suggests that most pike spawn for the first time in their second or third year. The evidence obtained so far implies that size, rather than age, determines when pike first spawn.

We had scant knowledge of spawning details until Fabricius and Gustafson (1956) used aquarium tanks (24 ft. X 28 ft. X 14-18 in. deep) to observe pike spawning behavior. They observed that a male pike approached the female by rubbing his nose gently against her head and flanks. If the female was still "un-ripe," she was likely to repulse the male with a convulsive, jerky head movement.

On being accepted by a ripe female, the male took up a position parallel to her, and the two moved forward side-by-side, or more exactly, eye-to-eye. This behavior ensured that the milt emitted by the shorter male was released in front of the eggs, to whirl among them in the jet currents caused by the moving fish. Pike spawning consisted of a series of mating acts every 24 seconds followed by rest periods of a minute or so, extending sometimes to a period of 40 minutes. A portion of milt and a portion of eggs were released when the male flicked its abdomen violently against the side of the female.

The whole operation was completed in one hour and forty minutes by one couple, and in five hours and forty minutes by another. Two or three males usually attended one female, and delivered their mating thrusts in turn from both sides of the female.

Fabricius and Gustafson showed pike spawning was stimulated by a rise in water temperature, and by increased light value. They found no evidence of "territorial" behavior, and all the males in attendance were able to take part in the spawning operation unless the tanks used in the experiment were small. When a small tank was used, one male became dominant and prevented the others from joining in spawning operations.

Pike spawning dates not only vary from year to year depending on the ice breakup, but they also vary according to latitude and climate. In Ireland, northerns spawn as early as February. In Minnesota and Pennsylvania, they are most likely to spawn the first week in April. Saskatchewan pike wait until May to spawn. Spawning reportedly takes place in Alaska, northern Sweden, and Russia as late as July, and never before the end of May. In southern Sweden and Finland, it's about April 30.

The weight of the female ovaries, expressed as a percentage of total body weight, increases from about 2% in August to about 7% in October; 10% in November; 12½% in December; 14% in January; 15% in February; and finally, when fully ripe, up to 18-20%. In male pike, the maximum weight of the testes forms only 2-4% of total body weight.

Water temperature is critical in determining the rate of egg development. Swift (1965) conducted an interesting experiment at the Freshwater Biological Association on the effect of temperature on mortality and rate of development of pike eggs. He found the average number of days required to hatch eggs varied with the temperature, as indicated in the following table:

26 days to hatch in water kept at 6°C (43°F)
17 days to hatch in water kept at 8°C (46°F)
12 days to hatch in water kept at 10°C (50°F)
9 days to hatch in water kept at 12°C (54°F)
6 days to hatch in water kept at 14°C (57°F)
5 days to hatch in water kept at 16°C (61°F)
5 days to hatch in water kept at 18°C (65°F)
5 days to hatch in water kept at 20°C (68°F)

Frost and Kipling reported that the number of eggs laid by a pike of any one size varied widely. For example, a pike of 3 pounds may lay 28,500-41,700 eggs; a pike of 10 pounds, 85,000-122,000; and a pike of 15 pounds, 186,000-226,000 eggs.

Both the age and size of northerns at maturity vary with the latitude the fish are found at. In general, northerns in the southern part of their range are fertile by the second year. In Northern Canada or Russia, it may take pike four years to mature. The size and composition of the spawning run indicate the size of the fish you can expect to catch later in the season. In other words, small spawners mean small-sized pike for anglers.

Egg viability can vary greatly and be as low as 50% or as high as 99%. Loss can be almost total if the water level drops and leaves the eggs high and dry. This is especially true in the reservoirs of the Dakotas. Cold weather is also harmful. Severe weather can slow the development of the tiny organisms that pike depend on to survive in their first few weeks of life. Predators also take heavy tolls.

Newly-hatched fry in no way resemble their parents. The fins are unformed,

and the mouth must migrate to its future position to form the familiar duck-like bill. During this period the fry live attached to the dead grass, sustained by food in the yolk sack. At a length of 1½ inches, scales begin to appear, and at 3 inches the fingerlings are completely scaled. Most young pike move to the lake during the first 25 days of life, before they are an inch long. There they hide in dense vegetation for food and cover.

Increased growth coincides with the increased size of food. As big eaters, pike grow fast. They have been observed to grow at the rate of .7 inches every 10 days.

Pike do not tolerate crowding. When this happens, fry survival nosedives. In fact, a number of studies in the United States and Canada have shown that low populations are preferable to dense ones when it comes to growing large fish.

Before young pike reach maturity, they have to face many enemies. Yellow perch, now instead of being the prey, are the most important predators when they are present. Perch devour little pike, some a third their own size. Back-swimmers can kill small pike by biting them and sucking them dry. Water beetle larvae can kill them until they are up to 3½ inches long. These beetles can kill as many as two or three young pike per day. Other enemies are creek chubs, mimic shiners, pumpkinseeds, mudminnows, crappies and very likely many others.

Northerns start out as fry no more than nine millimeters long, and both males and females grow at the same rate at first. As they get older, the females grow faster. At three years, females are two to three inches longer than males. Females mature at 20 to 22 inches and three years. Females live longer than males (Threinen and others 1968).

Growth varies according to latitude. In Great Bear Lake, on the Arctic Circle in Canada, it take about 7 years for pike to reach 20 inches and 12 years to reach 30 inches. In Pennsylvania, on the extreme southern edge of their range, they reach 20 inches between the second and third year, and 30 inches between the fifth and sixth year of life. In Minnesota's southern, more fertile lakes, growth is 12-18 inches the first year; in the northern part of the state, it is 6-14 inches. Males rarely exceed 24 inches. The largest male reported in Saskatchewan was 30½ inches, weighed 6 pounds, and was 10 years old.

Chapter 12

THE POST-SPAWN PERIOD

"A Time of Recuperation"

This is the recuperation period after the spawn. Big females which have not dropped all their eggs will begin reabsorbing them, and in the process remain quite inactive. The males, although less affected, do not feed that heavily either. Fishing is usually slow for females, and just so-so for the smaller males.

Why is fishing so tough? Well, as with any post-spawn fish, northern pike have just finished taking a physical beating, particularly the females. Perhaps as much as 15% of their body weight was discharged as eggs, and it simply takes time to recuperate.

On the other hand, males don't suffer nearly the abuse the females do, and they'll remain in or near the spawning grounds for days, usually halfway aggressive and catchable. But the larger females are a different story. All they require now is a place to rest and recuperate. They'll eat—but only if it's an easy meal. Anything that requires chasing will be ignored. If you're looking for a big fish, it won't be easy, even if you know where to find them. The dead bait approach is probably the best ticket for lunker pike at this time.

THE POST-SPAWN DISPERSAL— GENERAL RULES OF THUMB

A number of questions arise when it comes to locating post-spawn pike. How long do they remain in the spawning area? When they leave, how far do they go? Where do they go? All these questions, and more, are part of the puzzle. Because fish do different things in diverse kinds of environments, these questions are not easy to answer with a simple formula.

There are a few generalized guidelines, however, to get you started on the right track. For one, the males tend to hang in the general vicinity of the spawning grounds for awhile. They're the first ones into the spawning area and the last ones to leave. The females, however, usually don't waste any time getting in and out. How fast and how far they move after spawning depends on the conditions they encounter. Weather has quite an influence. Stable, warm weather warms the water and speeds the dispersal. A barrage of cold fronts, however, prolongs both the spawn and the recovery period.

Beyond these basic guidelines, the crucial missing link is where they go. And that's no easy question, because the kinds of areas that post-spawn pike use can be radically different from one lake or reservoir type to another. The only way you'll figure out the answer is by taking a good hard look at what a specific lake offers in terms of environmental options, and proceed from there.

Once again, we're back to the case of understanding what the environment offers the fish. Where's the food? Where can the fish rest when they're not feeding? In short, where's the most likely place to find the biggest concentration of the most active fish? Well, the most logical answer is, "Look in the closest place adjacent to the spawning grounds where the pike can stop to rest, grab an easy meal, and recover from their spawning ordeal."

THE POST-SPAWN ENVIRONMENT

Understanding what the environment offers northern pike during Post-spawn is the key to making fish contact. There are logical reasons why pike will be where they are.

First off, lakes generally exhibit a mild temperature difference from top to bottom during Post-spawn. It's not like a thermocline that develops later in summer, but the principle is basically the same. The sun warms the upper layers of water. This warmth slowly transfers downward, but it takes a long time to do so. At this stage of the season, the lake hasn't had enough sun exposure to warm the lower layer yet. So, in most cases, the fish are faced with two temperature layers—one warm, one cold.

The upper layer is where the bulk of the food is. Most minnow and small fish species are preparing to spawn around this time, so they'll be shallow. Suckers and perch, usually key forage fish, are also shallow. In deeper lakes, cold-water species like ciscoes and whitefish, which are fall spawners, suspend (often shallow) and feed on whatever small items they can find.

So, the shallow, warm water environment contains the bulk of the food at this time. Even though there's a cold water environment beneath it in some lakes, that zone is usually pretty slim pickin's.

It has been our experience, at this time of year, that *some* very big fish (if conditions allow) will nevertheless move out and set up a deep, cold, or suspended water existence almost immediately. Meanwhile, the smaller and intermediate-sized pike tend to stay shallow, along with a percentage of the big ones.

One ironic observation has been that some huge pike, which remain shallow, can be visibly spotted at this time, but are almost impossible to catch with artificial lures. However, dead or live bait, artfully presented, can many times turn the trick.

The essential locational item at this time appears to be the presence of forage food, regardless if the pike are remaining shallow, moving deeper or starting to suspend. If an area is devoid of food, it will simply be devoid of active pike (or any other fish, for that matter).

FLATS ADJACENT TO SPAWNING GROUNDS ON OLI, MESO AND EUTROPHIC LAKES

One key post-spawn pike pattern is fish using medium-depth flats (8-12 feet deep) which bound, or are in direct proximity to, spawning bays. This situation commonly occurs on many different lake types. It is particularly evident on oligotrophic lake trout lakes, where the shallow, rocky, infertile bays lack any significant cover and/or forage at this time of year. Faced with this condition, the larger pike simply drop back toward the main lake, and hold in the first available area with adequate depth and cover—generally weeds. However, even in lakes with more shallow weedgrowth and baitfish, pike use these flats when they eventually leave the shallows. Once post-spawn pike retreat to these nearby (but accessible) flats, they often spend at least part of their recuperative stage in the general area.

Pike are usually inactive in these locales—particularly right after they spawn. In fact, they are downright reluctant to chase quick-moving artificial lures. However, they can be induced to strike a very slow-moving live bait, or

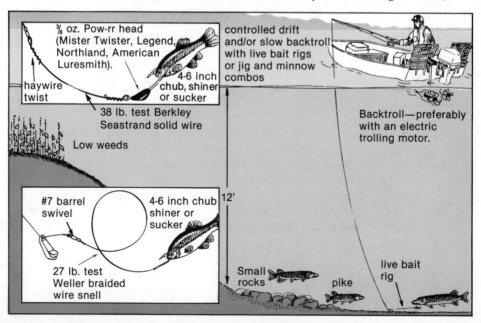

lure/live bait combination. Little by little, as they grow stronger, they become steadily more aggressive, and much more active.

Since pike are generally in a neutral/negative feeding attitude during the early Post-spawn Period, slow presentations are your best bet. Very slowly drag a chub, shiner or sucker right in front of their noses. They may simply mouth the bait, and if you put any undue tension on the line, a pike might drop the bait and not pick it up again. As they begin recovering from the spawn, however, their attitude often switches to neutral or even positive. Under these conditions, they'll strike bait with a little more authority.

Remember that pike laying on these flats *are not* actively feeding. Therefore, they will not necessarily be in classic feeding or ambush stations. Pike can be scattered anywhere on the flat, although most of the fish will usually be on or along the first breakline where the bottom either levels out (*AREA A*) or drops off (*AREA B* on the accompanying illustration).

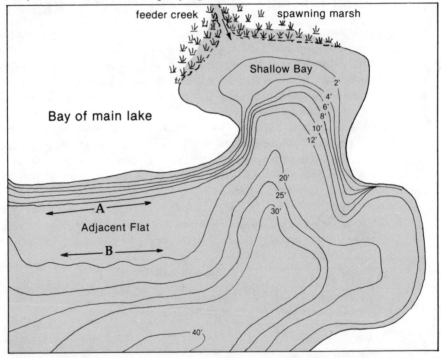

Recuperating pike usually relate to some sort of cover. In rock-bound "oligotrophic" lakes, a boulder patch, clam bed or scattered rock may provide that "something different" to attract and hold resting pike. On meso lakes, which tend to have sandy bottoms on the flats, a patch of gravel or a string of low sandgrass may be the attractor. On eutrophic lakes, last year's surviving vegetation, or whatever new (but sparse and low) vegetation is coming up, might be the "point of relation." A line of hard bottom meeting soft bottom might also serve as a "holding" point.

One of the most effective ways to tackle this situation is very slowly back-trolling and redrifting across the flat. We prefer using an electric trolling motor, rather than a noisy outboard, to cut down the spooking factor. Use a long-line, live bait rig with a chub or shiner, or drag a jig and minnow combination.

Remember, strikes will probably *not* be savage, nor will pike likely run off with the bait once they grab it. Post-spawn "pick ups" are usually light. You just sort of feel some spongy weight.

The trick to fishing a flat, particularly a large one, is establishing where most of the fish are concentrated. You simply work that area thoroughly "eking" out a fish here and there. It may not sound very sophisticated, but it's effective. On some Canadian lakes, pike may hold in flats like this up to 30 days or more, so it generally pays to check this pattern.

HOLES IN EUTROPHIC BAYS
ON ANY BODY OF WATER

Another clear-cut and simple-to-find post-spawn pike pattern occurs in holes in shallow spawning bays. This is particularly common in fertile meso and eutrophic waters, where the bays attract many baitfish in spring. If pike encounter a hole big and deep enough to accommodate them, they may remain there for some time. The bigger the bay, and the bigger the hole, the more fish it will hold.

Sparse, emerging weedgrowth sometimes rims the edges of these holes, and the pike generally use the weeds as a form of cover—if they exist. If rocks, brush or any other form of cover is present, the pike will relate to it.

These cover spots are usually inhabited by intermediate-sized pike as op-

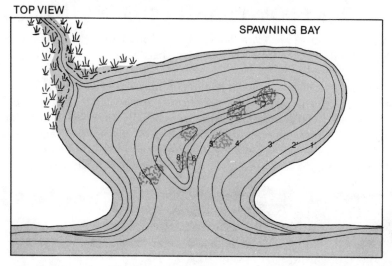

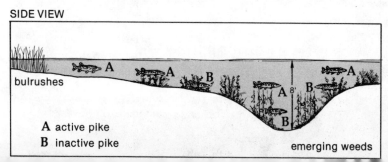

A active pike
B inactive pike

posed to the small, big or lunker class fish. Most times, you can expect to catch fish in the 4 to 9 pound range. However, big pike are occasionally taken from these types of pockets.

The most active fish, and thus the best potential "biters," tend to ride high and roam a great deal. They often swim around the rim of the hole, and can even roam the entire flat. A chop on the water, low light, or, better yet, a combination of both conditions, seems to activate the most fish. Therefore, expect pike to be most active on overcast days.

During bright, calm periods, pike tend to drop down in the emerging weed clumps or cover. In the absence of cover, they simply lay on or near the bottom. These inactive fish won't chase lures. Under these conditions, the best lures are jigs dressed with plastic tails like Reapers or Sassy Shads, or Pow-rr head jigs dressed with live bait like suckers, waterdogs or chubs. These set-ups are best fished very slowly, and jigged and crawled through any weed clumps or cover, or directly along the bottom. Be sure to use a steel leader to prevent bite-offs.

Since active fish chase and strike lures like spoons or spinners, you can either troll or cast these lures. An electric trolling motor won't spook them as much as an outboard motor.

In summary, troll or drift the entire flat area during overcast or low-light days. On bright or clear conditions, work deeper and drop your baits into the pockets and weed clumps to induce a strike.

CANADIAN LAKES
ROCKY POINTS AND CREEK MOUTHS

From the oligotrophic trout lakes of the Canadian Shield, to the meso-trophic pike lakes of the Canadian prairies, there are several patterns for post-spawn northern pike.

As we said, post-spawn pike in trout lakes may pull out of the infertile bays rather quickly, due to the general lack of cover and available shallow food. On the other hand, the fish in fertile prairie lakes usually linger there much longer, feeding on shallow-water prey like minnows, walleyes and small pike. In either case, you find some big pike lingering near, or cruising past, the rocky points at the mouths of spawning bays. These are key, early season spots.

The best rocky points are adjacent to large, shallow spawning bays. A large area, like a reed point with a saddle, leading to a rock or boulder-covered hump (see the accompanying illustration), would be ideal.

Since large, shallow bays warm early, they often attract baitfish and other warm-water fish. Apparently, the pike station themselves at key locations to prey on bait filtering in and out of the bay. The baitfish tend to follow the shoreline, and the rocky points provide ideal ambush areas, or at least places to contact roving prey. Even if the bay attracts few baitfish, chances are some pike will hang at the mouth of the bay to feed on cold-water, main-lake prey like ciscoes or whitefish.

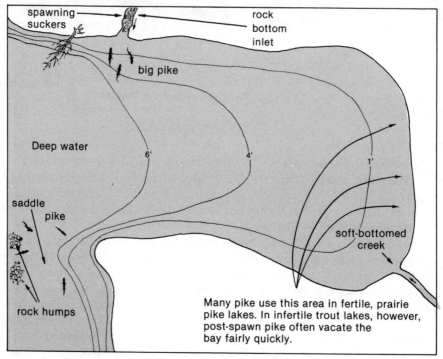

Many pike use this area in fertile, prairie pike lakes. In infertile trout lakes, however, post-spawn pike often vacate the bay fairly quickly.

From this location, pike both have access to deep water and can move into the bay on a feeding binge. In either case, the rocky point, and especially the saddle (if it's available), are key pivot points.

Once you find an area like this, start fishing at the point. Either drift or move slowly along with an electric motor, and start casting crankbaits or spoons toward the point. If there is a reed area near shore, hit that next. Finish up by fancasting the saddle area between the point and rock hump.

Proceed to the shallow bay, and cast spoons or spinnerbaits to any pockets or objects such as fallen trees, beaver dams, reeds, etc. Work around the bay and out the other side.

Before you leave, be sure to check the other rocky point leading into the main lake area. If the bay itself attracts numbers of fish, they'll be in one of two locations. Under sunny, calm, ideal conditions, they'll often cruise the shallows in the back end of the bay, often in as little as 2 feet of water. Under cloudy, windy, unstable conditions, they're more likely to lie inactive toward

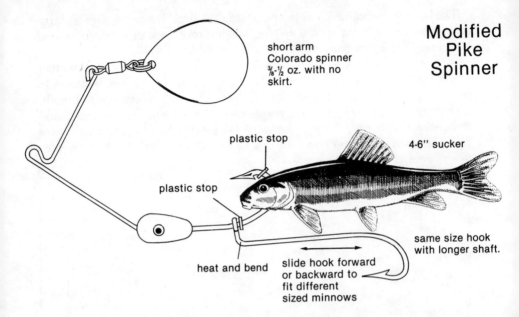

short arm
Colorado spinner
⅜-½ oz. with no
skirt.

Modified
Pike
Spinner

plastic stop

4-6" sucker

plastic stop

same size hook
with longer shaft.

heat and bend

slide hook forward
or backward to
fit different
sized minnows

the center of the bay, relating to a hole or any available weedgrowth.

Remember, you're after active fish located somewhere in the vicinity of key spawning bays. Weather, cover, and available food dictate pike movements. If you spot lunker pike, but they're not hitting artificial lures, use the "dead bait" approach described in Chapter 21.

There is also a distinct sucker/pike pattern associated with the running water from rocky creeks or rivers flowing into these lakes. These areas may be near shallow pike spawning bays, although they're normally located away from the shallowest, marshiest end of the bay. The stream may range from a small brook to a large river, but it must contain a rock or rubble bottom.

Suckers spawn in rocky sections of the flowing water. Huge, hungry northerns will hold below the stream outlet, or move up into the stream itself. In any case, if you see suckers spawning, pike will be somewhere nearby. This is a deadly pattern, and produces many of the largest pike caught in Canada every spring.

Your best presentations are usually suckers or smelt fished on live or dead bait rigs. If the fish appear more active, however, cast a spoon, and slowly retrieve it back with an occasional pause-and-flutter. Be ready!

THE PRE-SUMMER PERIOD

Chapter 13

"A Time of Transition"

The pike's activity during this period moves from neutral to positive. This happens as surface water temperatures rise to the high 50°F's and low 60°F's. At this time small and medium-sized pike are "back on the bite."

The biggest fish will continue (since the post-spawn dispersal) to function in a deeper/open water existence. They will begin feeding regularly and on a more predictable basis.

Apparently, a lull in big pike action takes place after this period. The next period, to take any number of big fish, will be during the Post-summer Calendar Period.

Pre-summer is a time of transition when a lake's or reservoir's surface waters transform from the cooler environment of spring to a warmer environment of summer.

The best example of this is the slower warming waters of the Canadian North. Let's take a closer look at the better locations and presentations.

TROPHY SPRING NORTHERNS

Every year thousands of fishermen head north from the U.S. and cross the border into Canada, with visions of wilderness fishing they can't get back home. Most are after walleyes, hoping to bring back a limit of tasty eaters. Others pursue more exotic species like the lake trout, smallmouth bass or musky. Or, for those with a hefty budget, it might even be a trip to the arctic circle to tackle grayling or arctic char. Whatever the quarry, the picturesque beauty of the Canadian frontier permanently etches itself in the mind. You keep reminding yourself that you've got to go home, although the reasons for doing so seem distant and unimportant when surrounded by this majestic wilderness.

All across the length and breadth of Canada, you'll find another powerful gamefish that usually takes the back seat to the more glamorous species. He's right there in almost every lake, often growing to mammoth proportions. Whether you're fishing for them on purpose or catching them by accident, the sheer power and speed of these long, slim, toothy carnivores will stretch your tackle to the limit. Untold numbers of anglers return with broken lines and tall tales after an encounter with the wild's most fearsome predator, the Great Northern Pike.

Catching a trophy northern within the bounds of the U.S. seems a near impossible task to most fishermen. A few giants are caught each spring and fall, but by and large they're conspicuous by their absence during most of the warm water season. Many frustrated pike hunters consequently make the trek to Canada, where the overall cooler water temperature and plentiful pike population generally provides an active and aggressive trophy pike fishery throughout most of the season.

Yes, Canada's got big northerns and plenty of them. But if you think that all you have to do is toss a lure anywhere north of the border, you're mistaken.

Because with big northerns, just as with any species of fish, there's times when the fishing's unbelievably good, times when it's not half bad, and times when you've really got to scrounge to dig up a few. The trick is reading the conditions and reacting accordingly.

As good as the summer and fall fishing for Canadian pike is, the potential for the trip of a lifetime lies more with the spring season than with any other time of year. The first few weeks after the ice goes out sets the stage for a lunker pike bonanza that's tough to beat. If you want a 20-pounder, this is the time to go. So let's examine some typical pike habitat and see how big Canadian pike behave in early spring.

CANADIAN PIKE LAKES

How do you pin down the characteristics of a good Canadian pike lake when northerns are found just about everywhere from the U.S. border clear up to Hudson Bay? It's not easy. Some lakes are deep and clear, while others are stained and shallow. Some contain chiefly pike, walleyes and whitefish, while others host a complex interrelationship with muskies, lake trout and smallmouth bass. In some the big pike might sit in the shallow weeds and eat walleyes all summer, in others they may run deep with the lakers and feast on ciscoes. It all depends on the available habitat.

Regardless of these vastly differing summer habitats, one clear-cut characteristic *must* be present—good spawning grounds. Without them, northern pike will be rare or absent. And since the pike in all cases must come in shallow to use these spawning grounds in spring, it really doesn't matter if you're in a 200 foot deep Ontario trout lake or a 40 foot deep Manitoba pike factory. The pike in both cases will respond to nature's call in the same fashion. Once you know where the Spawn/Post-spawn areas are and how the pike relate to them, it's a piece of cake. Get ready to set the hook!

SPRING NORTHERN AREAS

Most spring nothern pike activity centers around bays and inlets where a marsh occurs. Pike spawn in the soupy mixture of muck, bulrushes and decayed vegetation, right up in a foot of water. However, since the majority of the spawning activity generally occurs under the ice or right at ice-out, it's pretty tough to get near these big devils until after spawning is complete. Not that they'd bite, anyway. All they're interested in at this time is spawning, and until they're through they'll ignore every trick you throw at them.

It's when the pike finish spawning and drop back out of the marsh that they become vulnerable. They have very few options at this time of year and will concentrate in limited areas. This is chiefly because the food supply in these lakes is very scarce after a cold, harsh winter. The cold water of the main body of the lake hosts little available forage this early in spring. The pike, therefore, are forced to seek out the few scattered areas where food is available.

In most cases, the early spring activity centers around shallow, wind-protected bays. They're the first areas to warm up in spring, thus bringing forth the first new weedgrowth and hatches of both minnow and insect life. In many instances, they're the same bays that the pike spawn in, although they don't necessarily have to be.

After the spawn, some pike merely drop back out of the marsh and take up residence in the adjacent weedgrowth, lounging there until the bay warms. Others, particularly the larger fish, seem to group up in packs and slowly cruise the shoreline of the lake, seeking some source of food. When they encounter a bay that has warmed to the point of producing food, they join with the local fish in a feeding spree that's little short of fantastic.

In order to best understand how northern pike respond to this ever-so-slowly warming environment, let's examine Post-spawn/Pre-summer pike activity in a typical spawning bay. You'll see how the proper set of features combine to make a superb spring fishing spot, while another area lacking even one of the key features might attract few if any fish. It's recognizing such fine points in location that can make all the difference.

CHARACTERISTICS OF A GOOD BAY

The key elements to look for in a prime spring northern pike area are: (1) a shallow, sandy bay bordered with reeds and/or a marsh, (2) protection from harsh winds, and (3) direct exposure to the warming influence of the sun. An area with only 2 of the 3 key features usually turns out to be mediocre—even a waste of time. Yet when you find a bay with the proper combination of elements, you've got a gold mine that you have to see to believe.

SPRING NORTHERN PIKE BEHAVIOR

Northerns typically spend the off-hours (early morning) in an inactive state, either resting in the remnants of last year's cabbage weedgrowth in the center of the bay, or slowly cruising the shoreline. The water is still so cold at this time of year (in the 40°F's), that they show little activity until the sun beats down enough to get them moving. Then they cruise up into the shallows at the back ends of the bays and go on the prowl. On cloudy or windy early spring days, with the resulting lack of sun penetration, they generally remain inactive, and the fishing is slow at best. Thus the importance of good sun exposure.

The very first shallow areas to see heavy pike use are the most sun-baked, wind-protected areas of a bay, as indicated on the accompanying map. When you pull your boat into this prime area and get out of the wind, you can actually feel the heat. You might even have to take your jacket off it's so toasty warm.

Looking in the water reveals that the aquatic environment also responds to this warming effect. The lack of waves allows the sun to really penetrate the water. The first new weedgrowth in the bay consequently begins developing in this same sun-baked area. Minnows are seen cruising through the emerging weeds. The area seems alive, while the rest of the bay seems cold and lifeless. Naturally it's the first shallow spot the big pike begin using.

Don't expect to find the big pike right up shallow in early morning, however. That's because the temperature of the bay drops overnight, chilling the activity. Mornings are usually better spent chasing walleyes. Yet about 10-10:30 AM (on a sunny day) the water begins warming up enough so that a few fish begin penetrating the shallows. At first they simply cruise up and lie right on the sand, sunning themselves in 2 feet of water! You can actually move your boat right up on top of them and poke the fish with your rod tip before they'll move. That's how negative they are. As the sun continues pounding down, though, more and more fish enter the shallows and hit the beach. By noon the shallows are covered with fish—and big ones. And, by now the shallow water has warmed sufficiently to wake them up from their in- active state and they begin looking for food.

Comparing the fishing at 8 AM and noon is like comparing night and day. At 8 AM the shallows are empty. At noon they're alive. Pull into the bay at noon and you'll send swirls and wakes all across the prime area. Spooked pike kick up a cloud of sand/muck that we nicknamed "smoke." It's not unusual to have 4 or 5 "smokers" shoot out away from your boat as you enter the area. Give them a minute or two to settle down and they'll be ready to strike.

In the event the water is clear, you've really got a picnic. Not only could there be pike up to 20 pounds roaming the shoreline, but you can actually see them! Put on your polarized sunglasses and you'll see four 6- to 12-pounders just off the reed bed. To the left there's one about 15 pounds next the to fallen tree. That big shadow above the emerging weeds reveals one of those 18 pound plus monsters lurking within reach. Then you simply pick out a fish, plop your lure down within reach, and wham!—he's on! It's like picking off Pre-spawn bass along a shoreline, except that the average fish is long and green and

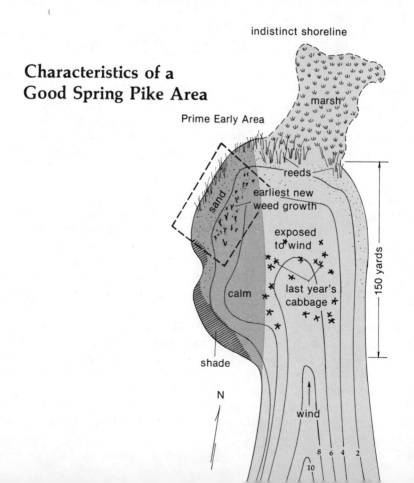

Characteristics of a
Good Spring Pike Area

weighs 4 or 5 times as much! Chances are, under stable weather conditions, you can come back to the exact spot for the next 3 or 4 days, toss out an anchor, and catch big northerns until your arms grow tired.

As the days move on and the bay continues to warm you begin to notice some changes occuring. The original prime area of the bay thickens in with weeds, eventually choking in too thick for the big pike to swim through. What do they do? Well, while the early prime area is thickening, the other formerly dead areas are now beginning to "come alive" too. The overall warming trend starts affecting the rest of the bay. Where there was only plain sand or muck before, now the weeds are starting to grow. The pike begin shifting to these spots. They didn't move far—perhaps 50 yards or so. The new areas now provide the same prime conditions and naturally the pike take advantage of them.

As the warming process continues the northerns continue shifting their preferred areas, little by little, until the entire shallows become so weed-choked that they won't move in. By then, the water temperature in the bay has become a bit more stable, without the drastic overnight fluctuations. Pike activity is now usually concentrated in the center of the bay in the deep cabbage weeds. The fish continue moving out toward the mouth of the bay until the main lake warms sufficiently that most of the big fish leave the bay entirely, taking up residence in main lake weedbeds, suspending in open water, or perhaps even cruising the shoreline until they encounter another bay in the "alive" category.

PREDICTING THE ACTIVE FISH

Picking the bays with the proper combination of sun and wind isn't the only critical locational factor for big spring pike. Some bays tend to warm up earlier than others, proving the peak action at different times. To illustrate the point, let's carefully examine the accompanying lake map. It represents a section of a typical Canadian prairie lake as found in upper Manitoba or Saskatchewan, although the locational factors apply in many kinds of good pike waters.

This section of the lake has 5 distinct bays (A thru E). Most are marshy and prime pike spawning areas. There's also a marsh/beach (Area F) along the shore of the main lake that rates as a "maybe." Which area do you concentrate on?

The trick to really nailing down the productive areas on a day-to-day basis is determining which ones have the proper combinations of sun and wind protection, along with judging how far into the Post-spawn or Pre-summer Period the fish in each area are. Sounds tricky, but it's not as hard as it may at first seem. Let's go through the process step by step, using the accompanying map as an example.

The first bay to shed its ice would most likely be A, since it is adjacent to the flowing water of the river outlet, and has excellent wind protection by the surrounding shoreline. It's the first bay to see use by active pike.

Next up would be bays B or C. Since B is more exposed to west and southwest winds and is partially shaded on its south shore, whereas C is almost totally exposed to the sun and exposed only to a straight south wind, bay C would get the nod as the second choice. Bay B would respond shortly after C, say by 3 or 4 days.

Predicting the Active Fish

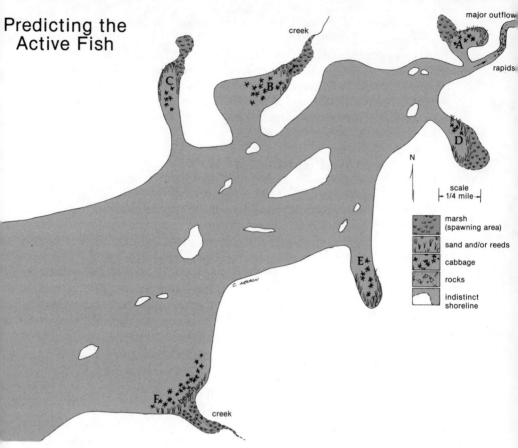

That takes care of the bays exposed to the sun along the north shore. *D* and *E* on the south shore would warm up considerably later—perhaps by a week. They have very little good sun exposure in their back ends since the south shore receives the least sun exposure in early spring. Of the two bays, *D* would probably show some activity first, since it has a marsh to at least attract some pike in the general area for spawning, whereas *E* has only a few reeds and little weed cover. Of all the areas, *E* would be the last of the bays to attract any fish, and even then it might not be many.

That brings us to the fascinating case of *Area F*—the beach. Northerns spawn in the marsh and then drop back into the massive cabbage bed. And in a weedbed that's a mile long and 1/4 mile wide, *Area F* has an astronomical capacity to hold massive numbers of fish.

Here's the catch. Most of the time, in early spring, these fish won't be very active. The area has almost no wind protection, except from southeast winds, and the massive amount of water that needs to be warmed rules this spot out, except under the most ideal weather conditions—a week of warm, calm weather. Get those conditions, and you're liable to go down in history as a local legend. Imagine all those big fish hitting the shallows at once! But for the most part, *Area F* is a hit or miss condition in spring and is only worth an occasional check. But be sure to fish it when the water warms up in summer. It'd be tremendous!

That's the basics of spring pike location. Judge the stage of the Post-spawn/Pre-summer Periods, pick out the most likely bays, and get in there and find the most productive section. If you're on the lake right after ice-out, A and C are the prime spots. If you're there 3 weeks later, you may find the shallows choked with weeds and the peak activity to be over. It rarely lasts longer than 3-5 days. In this case, try a bay that responds later, like *Area D*. Just pick out the most probable area, with good sun exposure and protection from the wind and you've got it made.

PRESENTATION

So you're flying in for the big trip and you don't know which one of your umpteen tackle boxes to bring. Don't panic! You can fit everything you need in *one* small box. Don't believe it? Neither did we until we tried it!

In the Canadian North, "the *spoon* is your life." A spoon is so effective in this condition that you hate to take it off to try something else. If you're brain-washed into thinking that the old Daredevle-type spoon is strictly a no-talent, old-time lure, get ready to be stunned. It'll be hard *not* to fish a spoon after you return.

The slow, lazy wobble of a spoon works magic on these early spring pike. You don't need the rapid, strong action of a crankbait, or the fast, thumping vibration of a spinnerbait either. Try them, but the odds are with the spoon.

Pitch a 3 or 4 inch spoon 8 to 10 feet past a pike and start to work it toward him. The fish will turn and watch it as it comes near, then he'll flick his tail and scoot 2 or 3 feet to smack it. Then you've got all you can handle, as a 15 pound fish in 2 feet of water has nowhere to go except in a long, straight, fast run for deep water. Standard bass tackle is fine for most conditions, but when you're really into the big ones, you might want to beef up and go to a musky rod with 20 pound test line. Sure, the lighter stuff will handle them, but with the heavy-duty tackle you can horse 'em in and then quick catch another one! Pike fever brings out the greed in even the most cool, calm and collected angler.

If the water's clear enough and you can spot the fish, have a field day. Pick out your targets. If it is muddied by rain, systematically work along the shoreline, cast within inches of the shore and slowly work it back. If the fish aren't right up on the bank, make another pass a little farther out, progressive-ly covering the entire back end of the bay. It doesn't take long, perhaps 15-20 minutes, to tell if the big guys are in.

A steady retrieve produces some fish, but is nothing compared to a stop-and-go motion. Reel a few turns, give the rod tip a twitch, and let the spoon flutter back in the fish's face. A curious following pike sees the bait falling right into its mouth and think's it's too easy of a meal to pass by! Gulp—it's gone.

In clear water, just about any color pattern works. The old standby red and white, or a plain silver spoon is great. When the water muddies up, switch to a very visible color like a bright yellow or a fluorescent orange. Give 'em something they can see. If you're caught short, then beg, borrow or steal a can of fluorescent spray paint and give the spoons a once-over. You'll be amazed at the results.

Use an electric trolling motor if you're close enough to civilization to bring your own boat in. On a fly-in, use a slow backtroll through the area with the

Working A Bay

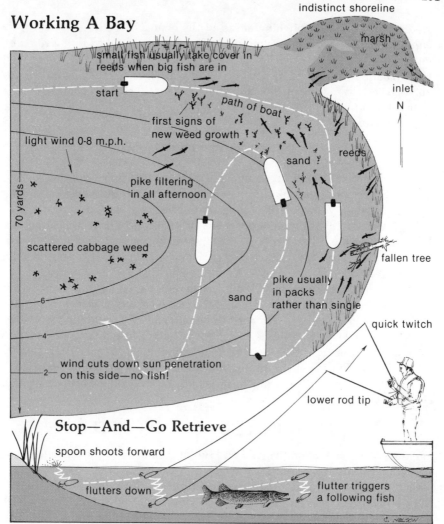

indistinct shoreline

marsh

small fish usually take cover in
reeds when big fish are in

inlet

N

start

path of boat

first signs of
new weed growth

light wind 0-8 m.p.h.

sand

reeds

70 yards

pike filtering
in all afternoon

fallen tree

scattered cabbage weed

6

pike usually
in packs
rather than single

sand

quick twitch

4

lower rod tip

2 — wind cuts down sun penetration
on this side—no fish!

Stop—And—Go Retrieve

spoon shoots forward

flutters down

flutter triggers
a following fish

Quietly pull into the calmest back corner of a bay and take a look. See all those dark shadows silhouetted against the light sand? Boy, are you gonna' see some action!

If the fish are in this heavy, don't be afraid to anchor in the upper right corner, in 1-1/2 feet of water. Let them come to you. If they're not as concentrated, slowly cruise the shore, casting up to the reeds. Cast well ahead of the boat so as not to spook the pike.

If they're just starting to come in, slowly zig-zag back and forth across the back end and pick up the new arrivals as they cruise in. Make parallel drift passes if there's a light wind, or else use the motor to creep along.

Before you leave, go back and check that corner again! You'd be surprised how a pack of big pike can sneak by you. You might slide in 20 minutes later to find another 10 or 15 big fish have arrived.

If your partner could talk you into anchoring off the marsh, chances are together you could catch between 50 and 100 good fish for the afternoon, with some in the 15-20 pound range. Once you find that magic spot, stick with it.

Interestingly enough, if the wind switched from a light north to a 15 mph west wind, it'd be lights out for this area. The waves would hit the back corner, diffuse the sunlight, and attract no fish. Zero. You'd have to find another bay that's wind protected. Yet you can come back tomorrow if the wind is right and make up for lost time.

big engine, constantly pitching ahead of the boat. Or, better yet, drift if the wind is right. Even the most uninitiated fish will get spooked if you run a big motor in shallow water, particularly after you've "introduced" a few of them to the sharp business end of a spoon. And when you're really into them hot and heavy, toss out the anchor and enjoy, partner. Let them come to you. A sunny afternoon will bring waves of big fish within reach and you can wear yourself out without moving an inch.

ALTERNATE TACTICS

Let's pretend we're not up in the wilderness, or that we're working a group of fish that are pretty spooky. The spoon catches some, but you can see some "no-takers" with your polarized sunglasses. Modify a bit.

Pitch a jig and plastic combo out there, like a jig and 6 inch twister tail, and let it sit. Move it a little. A spooky pike just might cruise up and inhale it. You can work this type of lure much slower than a spoon, which is very effective on spooked fish.

Are the fish really spooked? Well, if you're not on a fly-in trip, hopefully you've brought some live bait along. Soak a big shiner, sucker or chub on a plain old ordinary bobber. No need to be fancy. There's nothing more effective on spooked fish than an easy piece of live bait just begging to be eaten. It's the most effective technique for cloudy, windy days. If the pike don't seem to be "in," try anchoring at the mouth of a likely bay and soaking a sucker for a couple of "cruisers." It's not much for action, but will take a few under poor conditions.

BACK IN THE REAL WORLD

Now you're back from the wild and full of memories of the big catch. Too bad you can't do it on your local waters. Or can you?

Don't get the impression that you can automatically catch *tons* of big pike back home, like you can up in the wild. However, you can definitely catch some, on a scaled-down version. It depends on what's available. Find a similar bay off a major river, like the Mississippi, and the same thing happens. A shallow bay off your favorite northern pike lake will probably exhibit similar results. Or if you're adventurous, try a bay, river, canal, inlet or harbor off one of the Great Lakes. There are so many big pike in these waters that don't get fished for, it's unthinkable.

When you do get on the fish in these patterns, it unfortunately doesn't last very long. These environments have more food opportunities, and the fish are prone to scatter sooner. Then, too, these waters warm up more quickly and the fish move off for greener pastures. But in the Canadian North, it could take weeks to achieve the same thing. So keep the pattern in mind and take advantage of it wherever it occurs.

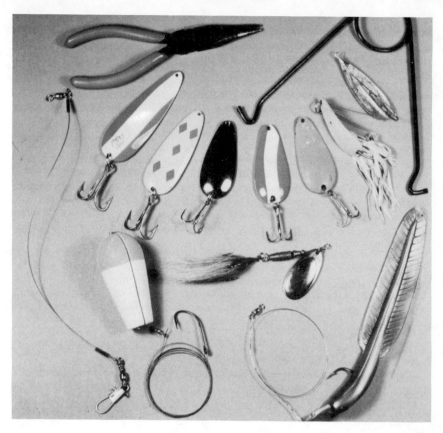

Before you even think of lures, get a long-nosed pliers and a jaw spreader. It'll make life easier, and safer. Squeeze the jaw spreader until it fits in a fish's mouth, then release. It'll hold his mouth while you take the hook out with the pliers.

The wobbling spoons shown here depict some typical pike goodies. Left to right there's a Dardevle in standard red and white, a Fidler #1 Old Killer in the Five-O-Diamonds patterns, and three Evan's spoons, in nickel, red and white, and a homemade fluorescent orange, painted for visibility in dingy water.

For tough, clingy conditions, like rice or heavy reeds, the Timber King and Johnson Silver Minnow are more snag resistant. Their single hooks are far easier to disengage than a standard treble. In fact, consider cutting one or even two of the hooks off of the wobbling spoons. They'll hook just about as good, and are much easier to work with.

Always use a tough wire leader with spoons or a French spinner, like the homemade spinner shown here. Similar spinners like a Mepps, Panther Martin or Vibrax are also excellent spring pike producers.

Your alternate, slower presentations for tough conditions include the slip bobber with homemade wire snell, 27 lb. test braided Sevenstrand, and a jig lure like a large Reaper (leader is 38 lb. test Berkley Seastrand). Hopefully the pike will be active, and you won't need them. But it's always good to have a back-up system when times are tough.

Where are the big pike?

Many Canadian lakes support good northern pike populations. Yet when you plan a trophy hunt, you want to concentrate on a body of water with numbers of trophy-sized fish. Here are a few tips for choosing the right lakes.

You'll find the best populations of big fish in lakes where the pike have a minimum of competition from other predators. We refer to them as transition waters. Let's discuss a few classic cases.

As an example, you seldom see numbers of huge pike in excellent lake trout (oligotrophic) lakes. A few, but not many. Yet as these lakes silt in and age, as the lakers begin to get scarce and you see the beginnings of a walleye population, presto—big pike. The other fish are low in numbers and the pike take the top slot. Late oli/early meso lakes such as this often have numbers of big pike, those in the 15-25 pound class.

When you get into the more meso (slightly more fertile) Canadian lakes, the walleye population blooms into the dominant species. You'll see big walleyes along with medium-sized, but few huge, northern pike. You'll see 10-12 pounders, but not many 18-20 pounders.

As you get out to the western provinces of Manitoba and Saskatchewan, the lakes change from deep gorges to shallow, weedy lakes. There's plenty of broken rocks for walleye spawning, but little food for the walleyes. Walleyes don't grow too big, there's few if any lakers, but there's those big pike again. They dine on whitefish and walleyes and grow to large proportions. The best ones have a walleye/whitefish food source, although you'll see some big pike in far northern "cannibal" lakes where the pike have little to eat except each other. However, growth here is due mainly to a long life span and little fishing pressure. Once these lakes are heavily fished, the average size of the population takes a nose-dive.

Looking for a big Canadian pike? Fish a transition lake in Ontario or Quebec, or better yet, a prairie lake in Manitoba, Saskatchewan or the Northwest Territories. Play the odds and catch the big ones.

Chapter 14 REVISITED
THE SUMMER PEAK PERIOD

"A Time of Separation"

Under our calendar definition, the Summer Peak is a short period of fast-action fishing. This is true for small-to-medium-sized fish. However, the larger pike's real peak may occur during the Pre-summer Period.

In many cases, this is the first really hot, summer weather of the season—and more importantly, the first hot nights of early summer. It's also a time when the larger and trophy-sized pike seem to disappear.

The Summer Peak, although not one of the best times of the year for lunker pike fishing, is nonetheless a period when you can take numbers of small and moderate-sized fish.

This is the time when the different summer niches develop for different-sized pike. Large pike move to avoid or minimize warm water stress, while the smaller and intermediate-sized pike cope with their increased metabolic rate by feeding (and burning it off) and feeding some more. While bass and walleyes enjoy a time of fulfillment, it's a "time of separation" for various-sized pike.

The following two sets of conditions show how the available habitat determines pike location and behavior. In each case, we've matched a very effective presentation technique to the conditions.

A SURE-FIRE TECHNIQUE ON EARLY MESO LAKES

There are many ways to fish. Some require artful manipulations, and others complicated displays of casting prowess; yet some can be very simple. For example, just about anyone can quickly learn to "drag a jig." This simple approach is a boon when you're not acquainted with the "tempo" of a lake, or if you're fishing with inexperienced anglers.

THE SUMMER PERIOD ON EARLY MESO LAKES

Most meso lakes stratify into distinct temperature levels in summer. Since oxygen is present in all but the deepest areas, the various fish species (and corresponding prey) react by settling in their own preferred temperature ranges.

Many of these lakes support alewives, smelt, ciscoes, whitefish and perhaps even stocked or natural trout in the cold water sections of the lake. Generally, walleyes, smallmouths and northern pike live in the cool water areas, and largemouth bass use the warmer water zones. Thus largemouth bass are usually shallowest, walleyes deepest and northern pike somewhere in between. Lakes of this nature are found primarily in northern Michigan and Wisconsin, portions of Minnesota, upstate New York, and north of Toronto, Canada.

The accompanying map is a typical example. In summer, the majority of catchable gamefish are concentrated in a very narrow depth band. Let's look at each section individually.

Area A: Area A would be our number one choice. This spot has enough shallow water cover to support adequate minnow and small fish life, a slow to moderate taper, and a wide band of deep weeds. Along this section, walleyes ply the deeper, hard-bottom zones, northern pike the intermediate levels, and largemouth (as well as some northerns) use the deep weed zones. Because there is a gradual decline in water temperature from the surface to the top of the thermocline, the different species tend to be located at specific temperature levels.

Area A is best because it combines the largest section of slow-to-moderate taper with good weedgrowth. In short, it offers the maximum amount of desirable fish habitat. On early meso lakes this is extremely important.

Areas C, D and E: Areas C, D and E might first appear to be much the same as Area A. But they are not! These spots are primarily hard-bottom sections (sand, gravel, and small rock) and support little weedgrowth. Notice, too, that the drop-offs are very quick, providing limited living space and attracting few fish.

The shallows in Areas C, D and E, although quite extensive, are mostly hard bottom and have very little cover. Primarily, Areas C, D and E would support scattered smallmouths that hang on the drop-off during the day, and run the flats in early morning and late afternoon in search of crayfish, minnows and insects.

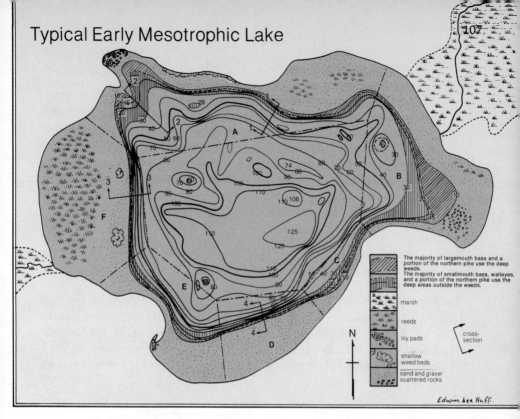

The majority of largemouth bass and a portion of the northern pike use the deep weeds.

The majority of smallmouth bass, walleyes, and a portion of the northern pike use the deep areas outside the weeds.

marsh

reeds

lily pads

shallow weed beds

sand and gravel scattered rocks

cross-section

N

Edwin Lee Huff.

Area F: This section, although it has a quick drop-off, is a good second choice. The extensive reed flat adjacent to the drop-off is home to small pan-fish and minnow life. The bottom makeup allows a narrow rim of weeds; sparse, yes, but important cover in these kinds of lakes.

The drop-off along Area F would hold largemouth bass and some northern pike. Of course, the shallow reeds would attract largemouth bass. But in summer, under a bright midday sun, it would be better to concentrate on the deeper water fish — those that have at least a neutral attitide. Besides, on the drop-off, you have an opportunity to take mixed fish species of fish, including northern pike.

Area B: This spot is our third choice. It has a slow taper, but is primarily hard sand and has little weedgrowth, so prey species would not be as numerous as in Area A. A few northern pike could be found here. But they would not be as concentrated as in Area A. Besides, the adjoining shallow flats do not hold much prey — certainly not as much as in Areas A or F. Therefore, for the most part, Area B would produce fish, but not as many as the other more productive areas.

PRESENTATION

We've observed that presentation (once location is solved) is the number one problem of most anglers. Presentation raises all the subtleties and nuances of fishing to an art. Location is a mechanical process that can be learned by reading. But when it comes to swimming a jig, dropping a spinnerbait or crawling a plastic worm, 95% of all anglers have difficulty. Moreover, some choose line too heavy for a small spinner, or a jig with the wrong head shape for the given situation. Very simply, presentation takes practice and experience.

For these reasons, avoid complex systems when you fish with inexperienced anglers. Instead, simply backtroll (drag) jigs tipped with minnows. Not only is the bait constantly in the fish zone, but the fish strike the jig/minnow hard, so hard that hooking them is relatively easy. And, most importantly, this method produces fish — and a mixed bag stringer as a bonus.

"Dragging" jigs usually works best in deeper water (15 feet or more). You might have a lot of line out (in 25 feet of water, it could be as much as 40 feet). However, with jigs, you don't let a fish run as you might with a live bait rig. A slight pause, and a quick, hard set, are usually the ticket. Many times fish hook themselves on the strike. However, if you don't get a good set or you give too much slack line, they often throw the lure with a simple shake of the head. So, to assure a good solid set and good feel, a relatively stiff rod and low-stretch line are absolutely necessary.

Flexible, "buggy whip" rods don't work for this type of fishing, either. A 6 foot spinning rod (medium-heavy action) with an open face spinning reel is the way to go. Line weight can vary, but 10 pound test is usually the best all-around choice. It's light enough to allow the jig to swim naturally, but not heavy enough to spook fish in clear water. At the same time it's strong enough to allow a quick, hard set.

THE LURES

There are many kinds of jigs, with a wide array of colors and dressing. We prefer nothing fancy—just a plain jighead (no hair or dressing) with a short-shanked hook, dressed with a minnow.

Over the years, we found that northern pike tend to strike a jig/minnow with sparse hair better than those with a lot of dressing. Gradually, we began plucking the hair (or feathers) from jigs, until we were using plain jigheads with great success.

In any case, simple, short-shank jigheads are great. The colors? It doesn't make that much difference, but lighter colors seem to produce better than darker colors.

Generally, chubs are the best bait. Shiners are a close second, and suckers a poor third. Chubs are not only very attractive to pike, but they stay on the hook well. Shiners, although a great bait, tend to fall off the hook and are not durable. Suckers stay on a hook, but they are not as effective as the other two baits. Large fatheads can also be used, and, everything else considered, might be a reasonable second choice.

Balance is the most important factor for jig/minnow fishing. A large chub on the back of a lightweight jighead will "roll." The best way to handle this is to use a minnow with a jighead that keeps the combination "upright." Then you impart action to the lure in a series of lifts, drops, drags and twitches.

THE TRIP

To visualize how to backtroll and cast a jig, we'll take an imaginary fishing trip on the lake depicted in Map #1.

This method is ideal for good fishermen who would like to take the wife and kids out and get them some fish. In fact, it isn't bad for good fishermen who want to turn some fish for themselves!

Area A, with its slow-to-moderate taper, has the best weeds. After a glance at the map, this is the natural starting point.

Noting the direction of the wind, begin working at Point A and make one sweep down the weed edge. This accomplishes two things. First, your partners get used to dragging a jig. Second, you'll spot any fish or baitfish on your

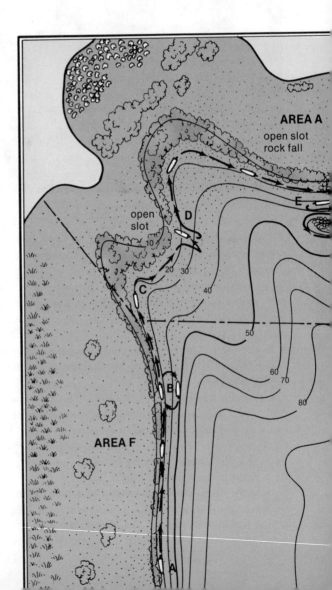

depth finder, or maybe even get a strike to indicate a productive depth.

Let's say you hold the 20 foot contour and cover a depth range from 10 to 30 feet on a backtrolling pass. At Point B, you miss a strike casting up to the weeds, and your partner takes a northern pike. The 'rake' marks on your minnow indicated that fish was a pike also. Immediately swing the boat around after your partners reel in their baits to avoid tangling lines.

The wind is too light to permit drifting over the same area. So you have to backtrack and run the spot again. If you had experienced anglers in the boat you could hover in the area and cast it out.

On the return swing you caught another northern. Two more passes produce nothing, so you continue down the drop-off.

At Point C the taper flattens out considerably. Position the boat to cast the front face of the weedbed, instead of working your jig all the way through it.

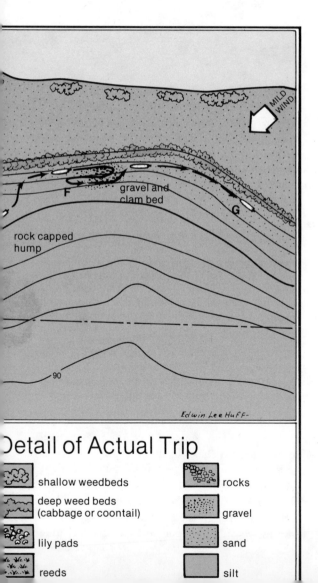

Edwin Lee Huff-

Detail of Actual Trip

shallow weedbeds		rocks	
deep weed beds (cabbage or coontail)		gravel	
lily pads		sand	
reeds		silt	

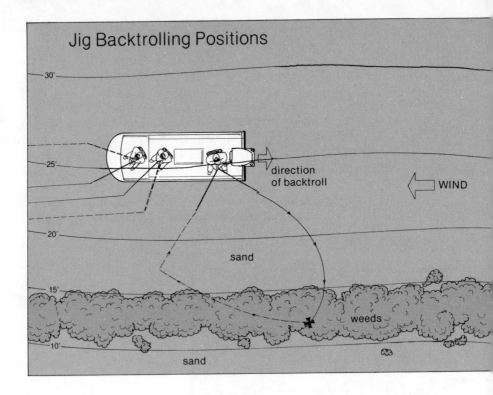

Jig Backtrolling Positions

By correctly positioning three anglers in a boat you can backtroll and cover several zones with one pass and every depth level from 10 to 25 feet can be cleared. The angler in front of the boat slowly moves his rod to the left and the right as he is jigging up and down and covers depths from 22 to 25 feet. The middle person covers the area slightly shallower, say 18 to 22 feet. The passengers simply drag the jig with alternating lifts, drops and twitches. They do not cast or retrieve, unless it is to check the bait or clear off some pieces of sandgrass.

The boat driver, who should be a skilled angler, does cast and retrieve. His job is to keep the passengers in the deeper zones while he checks the areas from the back of the weeds (in this case 10 feet) to just outside the weedline at about 17 feet.

It takes practice to effectively backtroll, keep the boat moving and still use both hands to work the rod. The driver's major job is to keep the boat on course and moving. His casts and retrieves are secondary to this purpose. Sometimes he will use a knee on the tiller handle to turn the boat. At other times he stops in mid retrieve and drags the bait while changing gears. And, occasionally he doesn't cast at all—all for the purpose of keeping his passengers "on" fish.

This illustration shows an ideal drop-off. On faster or slower tapers, the width of the zones will be different. Just remember that it is important to cover all levels—even if it means more than one pass.

Your partners will be working the 18 to 22 foot range. Continue to backtroll until you arrive at Point D. You didn't get a "lick" in the interim!

Suddenly, at a slot in the weeds, you catch a largemouth bass—and then another! You suspect a school, so you swing the boat out and tell your partners to cast into the slot, too. You catch more bass. The fish weren't active, but you trigger them by "snapping" the jigs through the base of the weeds.

You don't get any more fish, so move on. Your partners catch a few pike

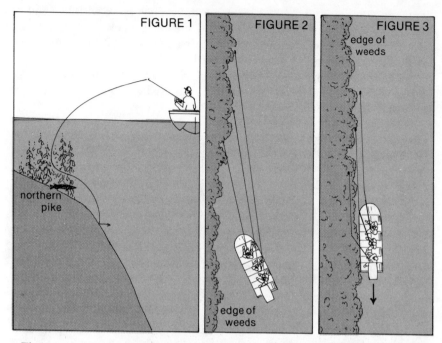

There are times when northern pike will position themselves exactly at the deep front edge of a weedline. In this situation they won't chase a bait, come up or move very far to the side to strike. But they will often take a bait that is dragged in front of their nose. Figure #1 shows how casting fails to get close enough to the fish. What happens is that the jig tends to skirt the top of the weeds and usually doesn't hit bottom until it is out of the weeds. Even parallel casting (as in Fig. #2) misses areas at that all important edge of the weeds. And, once away from the weededge, under these conditions, the jig is out of the pike zone.

The best way to approach a situation like this is to backtroll, keeping your jigs right at the edge of the weeds all the time as in Figure #3. The driver watches his depth finder and holds the boat tight on the edge of the weeds as the other anglers almost vertically fish their jigs. Everybody fishes off one side and simply bobs the jigs up and down. Simple, but extremely productive.

and one walleye from Point D to E.

At Point E, the slow taper changes to a faster drop. There is a break in the weeds where the bottom turns to rock. The map indicates a rock-capped sunken island slightly offshore, with a saddle-like dip in between—obviously a spot to be worked hard. Normally, you'd be better off switching to live bait rings, but this approach requires feel. Working sinkers over rocks without getting hung up takes quite a bit of expertise. Instead, you tell your partners to shorten up their lines and fish almost vertically, lifting the jig each time it strikes bottom. You move the boat very slowly as your partners bounce the lure along. In the area around Point E, you catch 5 small walleyes and 3 nice smallmouths—all in the 20-26 foot depth range. You know there are many more fish in this section, but considering that you're fishing jigs and it's midday, you did very well. After you work the area sufficiently, move back to the 20 foot level and resume a multi-level backtrolling sweep.

At Point F you encounter a gravel and clam bed. You pick up one decent-sized walleye, but can't get any more to pop. There are probably more fish here, and you know you might be able to take a few more with live bait rigs; but you've established your method and intend to stick with it. So again, return to the 20 foot level and start moving toward Point G. You pick up another pike, and hang a largemouth off the weedline.

Using this simple approach, you and your partners take a nice midday catch of bass, walleyes and pike. The method required a minimum of skill, and everyone's happy. What could be better?

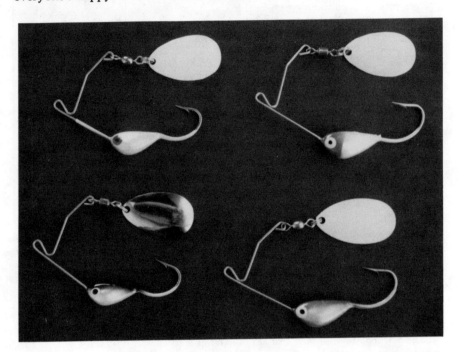

THE SPIN RIG IN ACTION

The Lindy Spin Rig is something of a forgotten lure. Basically, it's a well-balanced spinnerbait without a skirt designed to be fished with live bait. The bait works equally well for casting or trolling.

While the Spin Rig was originally manufactured in 6 different sizes and 11 different colors, experience has shown that 2 sizes and 3 colors are the best for northern pike in natural lakes. Trial and error has also shown that the Spin Rig produces best for old razor jaw just at or inside the edge of a weedline, or along the rim of the first drop-off. This means that the lure will be primarily backtrolled in depths of 12 to 20 feet. Thus the smaller 1/32, 1/16, 1/8 and 1/4 oz. sizes have only limited effect. After all is said and done, if you're looking for pike at the edge of a weedline or along the first drop-off, the 3/8 oz. size is the best.

Most of the time the type of minnow selected as an attractor tends to make more difference than the color of the lure. Nevertheless, during tests of color against color with the same kind of minnow, preferences have surfaced. The lighter colors are many, many times more productive than the dark ones. It appears that "flash" is a very important element in this method of presentation. Through the years, the guide's favorites have been a red/white body with a red/white blade, a silver body with a silver blade, and a yellow body with a yellow blade. On the other hand, solid blacks, purples and browns have been poor producers.

Among Spin Rig fanciers there is some controversy whether to tie mono line directly to the lure, or to use short wire "strikers." Purists claim wire "strikers" produce less hits. Maybe they are right. But if the fish are very active, as they sometimes are, northern pike "bite-offs" occur. Generally, strikers are unnecessary in the Pre-summer Period since fish like pike seldom clamp their jaws over the wire bend. But in the Summer Peak, Summer and Post-summer Calendar Periods, a short, 3 inch wire striker with a swivel is recommended.

While there is a lot of latitude in the choice of rods and reels, the right line is a different matter. In spin rigging, too much line stretch is counterproductive. Six pound test mono is usually too light, and 12 pount test is too heavy. Your best choices are 8 or 10 pound test, low-stretch mono.

Always remember that the heavier the line, the bigger the diameter, and the more it will inhibit lure depth and rate of fall. Don't use anything over 10 pound test—and 8 pound is even better.

TYPES OF BAIT

Again, trial and error has shown that the Spin Rig is best rigged with minnows. Over the years we have hung just about every kind of live and manufactured critter on the back of them. Nightcrawlers have not proven to be any great shakes, and neither have leeches. Frogs, crayfish, hellgramites and water dogs also do not lend themselves to the lure; even dead, they tend to knock the lure too far off its critical balance.

We have also dressed the lures with all manner of plastic creatures—ones that are minnow-shaped, twister worms, lizards, etc. While some, like the twisters, are quite productive, none seem to work as well as a dead (but fresh) minnow. The closest competitor we have found that even comes close to triggering as many strikes as a minnow is the Uncle Josh U-2 split-tail pork rind in white or yellow. In some Canadian waters where minnows were not available or could not be portaged in, we use "pork" extensively. While not as effective as minnows, under these circumstances, the rind is your second best choice.

As far as type of minnow is concerned, we have found definite preferences. In order of descending preference, our list of minnows include:

1) medium-sized shiners
2) medium-sized creek (redtail) chubs
3) large dace
4) very small suckers
5) very large fatheads

We've tried small perch in places where it is legal. Surprisingly, this staple of many a predator fish's diet just doesn't seem to work that well. Why? Well, we don't know. Perhaps the perch lacks the flash the more silvery-colored baitfish do.

Armed with the basics of equipment, we are now ready to look at 3 Spin Rig methods. They are:

1) casting and retrieving
2) straight backtrolling
3) combinations

Remember, these are not the only ways the lure can be used. Vertical jigging next to trees or over deep, suspended fish might be very effective under some circumstances.

THE CASTING AND RETRIEVING SYSTEM

The Spin Rig has a very definite balance and consequent "feel." You can feel the bait vibrate on the "lift." On the "drop,' the pronounced "helicopter" action of the blade creates a slight buzzing. Continuous "lifting" and "dropping" motions create a distinct rhythm.

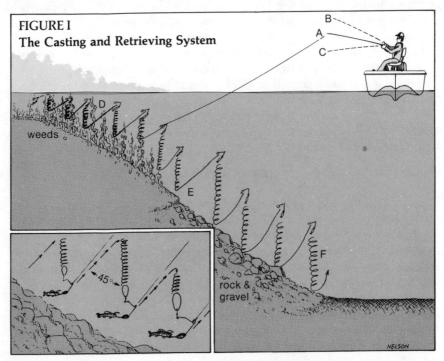

FIGURE I
The Casting and Retrieving System

weeds

rock & gravel

NELSON

The casting method (Figure I) is somewhat similar to jigging. When the bait hits the water, it immediately rights itself and slowly, in an almost perpendicular direction, begins to "helicopter" towards the bottom. Bring the rod up to the 10 o'clock position, and take in all the slack line (rod position A). As soon as the line is taut, start "pumping" by arching the rod upward to set up the "rhythm." This lifting motion advances the bait upward about 2 feet on a 45° angle (as shown in the inset).

At the apex of the lift, which occurs at about the 11 o'clock rod position (rod position B), allow the bait to "flutter" downward again. In order to retain "feel," keep a tight line at all times. Slowly lower the rod tip while simultaneously reeling up the excess line as you follow the bait down with the rod tip, at the same rate that the lure is dropping (rod position C). Continue this motion until you feel either bottom or an obstruction (weeds or brush). Then begin the upward "pumping" motion again. This takes a little practice, but is not difficult to learn.

When working weeds, brush or timber, the bait should just touch the obstruction and then be lifted again (lure position D). On hard, clean bottom, you can sometimes let the lure "crawl" on the bottom a bit before the lift (lure position E). Over soft bottom, "pump" continuously without touching anything on the downdrop. Gauge the length of the drop by the position of your line and the rhythm of your arcs.

It might at first appear that strikes will occur on the "lift," rather than on the "drop." In fact, the reverse is probably true in most cases. The vast majority of strikes occur just as the lure "flutters down." If there is slack in the line, you won't feel a strike immediately. A lot of times, you'll have a fish on the upward pump with no previous indication of a strike. What happens is the fish hit the bait on the "down flutter" and hooked himself. Because of the slack, you didn't feel the fish until you lifted the rod.

Let's face it—good angling demands you set the hook. You can't expect the fish to do it for you all the time. Be alert for any and all strange or unusual line movements, bumps, ticks or even a lack of "feel." These can all be indications of strikes. Anytime the rhythmic feel of the bait is interrupted, set the hook immediately.

With this type of fishing, you often get strikes when you're in an odd position. In this situation, do what we call "crack the whip." Regardless of what "pumping" position you are in, you can set the hook with this method.

Quickly grip the rod with two hands and make a swift, sharp, down-and-upward "whip-like" motion with the rod tip. Keep the rod stoutly arched, and swiftly retrieve any slack while lowering your rod tip slowly, making sure there is pressure on the fish. Then, position yourself to solidly "re-stick" him once again. This takes a little practice, but will save a lot of fish.

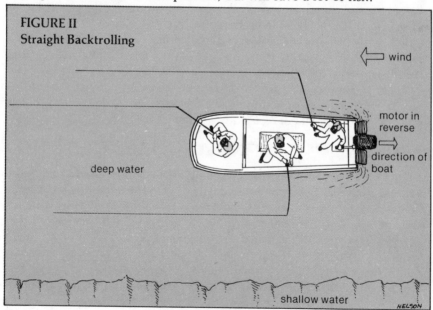

FIGURE II
Straight Backtrolling

wind

motor in reverse

direction of boat

deep water

shallow water

NELSON

BACKTROLLING

Backtrolling (Figure II) is another way to work a Spin Rig. With casting and retrieving you can work down a drop-off and cover a number of depth levels.

But experience has shown that after you make fish contact, it's often best to stay at one level. If you want to work a consistent depth level from the edge of the weedline (or deeper) along a drop-off, the backtrolling system works much better.

To avoid line tangles if two or more persons are fishing, fish as follows: The man in the front of the boat fishes over the tip. The man in the middle works the left side. The man in the rear fishes to the right, using one hand to work his rod and the other to control the motor. This position should be a rigid rule at all times.

Ideally, select a bar or drop-off where the wind is blowing parallel to, or at an angle to, the drop-off. (It's always wise to choose a favorable wind.) These areas, of course, should contain the correct structural elements and conditions for whatever time of the year you are fishing.

Then, place the motor in reverse and back into (or tack against) the wind, holding a consistent depth level. (Obviously, a depth finder can be extremely useful.) On calm days, you may have to place the motor in neutral to slow the boat down. Regardless, a nice even pace is best.

Next, drop the lines into the water, making sure they hit bottom. Now, rather than letting the bait just drag along by itself, "pump" the bait by slowly raising the rod tip. This lifts the bait off the bottom. Then, allow the bait to "flutter" towards the bottom and lower the rod tip at the same rate the bait drops. Simply keep repeating the process—raising and lowering the bait in the controlled manner described. It's really a very easy way to fish.

Try variations of this technique. Allow the bait to crawl along the bottom a bit before lifting, or "hop" it with a high sweep of the rod. Always keep the bail of the reel closed, and secure the line with your index finger. Set the hook, of course, at the slightest indication of a "rap."

This basic backtrolling system is the backbone of the Spin Rig system. This technique covers a lot of water fast, taking the more active and "catchable" fish. It is perfect for relatively inexperienced anglers.

There is another way to use this method—as a "finding" lure. In other words, locate a tight concentration of fish with it, and then, once they are pinpointed, work the school over with another lure.

"COMBO" CASTING AND BACKTROLLING

This system (Figure III) was originally devised to be used in conjunction with the Spin Rig. But it can be used with a whole host of other bait combinations—a single spin spinnerbait and a jig, a wobbling plug, or a plastic worm and Spin Rig. For that matter, any mix of "dragging" and "pitching" lures can be used. This approach allows a great degree of versatility. A wide variety of depth levels can be covered during a single pass. It's possible, under some situations, to "clean" water from 3 to 18 feet, very quickly, in one sweep.

The method is simple. All it takes is coordination of effort and attention so that you avoid tangles. The person running the motor simply backtrolls and flutters a Spin Rig up and down, as during a straight backtrolling run. The man in the middle, however, casts ahead in the direction of movement, into the shallows, with lures like a shallow-running crankbait. As the boat advances, he retrieves enough line so his lure will approach the boat perpen-

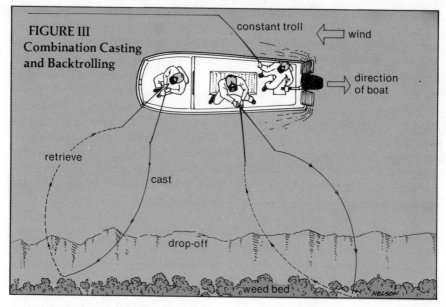

FIGURE III
Combination Casting
and Backtrolling

constant troll   wind

direction
of boat

retrieve

cast

drop-off

weed bed

dicular to the side. The man in the front of the boat could, let's say, use a jig worm. By casting perpendicular to the boat, he retrieves his bait with the usual "pumping" motions until the bait comes to the edge of the weedline. At this point, he allows the bait to stay that distance away from the boat, and uses a dragging or trolling method in a somewhat angular fashion. Then he "pump" trolls the bait for a short distance, retrieves it a bit, and "pump" trolls it once again. When the bait no longer falls back to the bottom, he quickly retrieves and casts out again.

A variation of this movement is continually "beating" the edge of the weedline for a short distance, and then retrieving the lure. The versatility of this system should be obvious, and its applications manyfold.

SOME LAST MINUTE TIPS

Post-spawn, Pre-summer, and especially the Summer Peak are the most productive Calendar Periods for spin rigging northern pike. During summer, the lure's productivity is still good, but it slows up a bit compared to the earlier periods.

The backtrolling/spin rigging method also appears to work best in meso lakes with deeper weedlines—over 12 feet. The 3/8 oz. size works well to 15 feet.

When you're backtrolling, keep the boat moving, but don't go too fast or the lures will lift too high. Also, don't poke along either—it's not necessary. The Spin Rig is a triggering lure, and not a tantalizer like a standard live bait rig.

Chapter 15

THE SUMMER PERIOD

"A Time of Stress" (Larger Fish)
"A Time of Plenty" (Smaller Fish)

Summer fishing can be perplexing. This is the time when the different niches for different-sized pike are set for the summer. Smaller fish are usually in a positive to neutral mood, and fishing for them can be excellent. However, the largest pike (in some lakes) are generally in a neutral, or even "unknown" mood. They're conspicuous by their absence—as most pike anglers can attest. This is also the main fishing season for most anglers taking their summer vacations.

While the Summer Period is a time of plenty for small and intermediate-sized fish—plenty of food, plenty of cover and plenty of distraction in terms of increased traffic, sun penetration, cold fronts and the like—it's a time of stress for big pike. This period is the warmest cycle of an environment for the year. Let's take a close look at some productive Pre-summer/Summer Peak/early Summer patterns.

FIND THESE MAGIC NORTHERN PIKE SPOTS AND UNLOCK THE PUZZLE

This will explore a completely new concept in fishing for trophy northern pike. The supporting evidence has been gathered over a 10 year period on the Minnesota/Wisconsin boundary portion of the Mississippi River, and is known only to a small group of biologists and a few of their fishing companions. There are some indications, however, that the concept also applies to other big rivers and possibly some lakes with the proper environmental conditions.

Fishermen who spend a lot of time on the river occasionally stumble upon a spot that consistently produces big northerns during the hottest part of the summer. Over the years, word spread among local fishermen and a few of these spots have become widely known. Yet the reason for pike concentrating in these spots has remained a mystery.

Our first discovery of one of the spots came strictly by accident. It was late July and walleye fishing on Lake Pepin on the Minnesota/Wisconsin border had been slow, so we were trolling Heddon Sonics along shore trying to locate a productive area. To make a long story short we hooked and played out the biggest northern of our life only to lose it at the boat. Estimated weight of the fish was 25-30 pounds! During the next few weeks, we worked the spot over tirelessly, hoping the big one would strike again. It didn't, but 46 other pike averaging over 10 pounds each did. And they all were taken from an area no more than 20 feet square!

The obvious question was, "Why were these big pike holding in this tiny area when vast reaches of seemingly similar shoreline were available?" At first, the answer seemed evident—there was a sharp drop-off perpendicular to the shoreline in the exact spot where the northerns were taken. Each fish struck at the lip of the drop-off on the deep side. It was the same old story . . . where you find structure you'll often find fish.

But later experiences shed doubt on the structure theory. As we discovered more and more of these magic spots, the patterns simply did not fit. Some had structure, some didn't. Some were shallow, some deep. Some had current, some had slack water. Some had mud bottoms, some had sand and some had rock.

There was definitely something causing these big pike to congregate in tiny areas, but what was it? As with many other fishing discoveries we stumbled upon this one by accident. Following is Dick Sternberg's explanation.

"It was New Year's Day and I'd had it with watching football, so I decided to try some northern fishing. I bought some big sucker minnows and headed for my pike hotspot to try some ice fishing. When I reached the foot of the hill to step out on the ice, I was surprised to see a small strip of open water along the shore in the exact spot where all the pike were taken in the past summer. Tiny springs flowing into the lake were keeping the water open."

Suddenly, it all made sense. The big pike were seeking out cold water when summer temperatures climbed out of their preferred temperature range. After all, the northern is a cool water fish, whose preferred temperature range is substantially below warm water species like bass, crappies and sunfish.

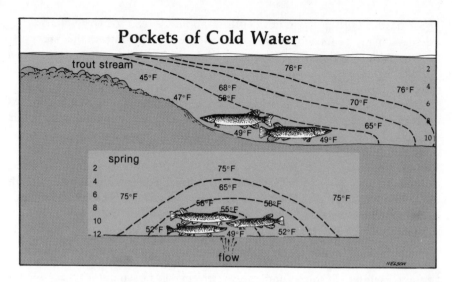

A temperature check of the same area the following summer revealed a tremendous temperature stratification. From the surface down to 12 feet the temperature held steady at 74°F, but dropped to 63°F at 13 feet and way down to 48°F (the temperature of springwater) at 14 feet, which was bottom. Bottom temperature in the rest of the bay was around 68°F.

During the next few summers, Sternberg explored many spots known to be northern pike producers. Without exception, the one thing they all had in common was cold water!

HOW TO LOCATE COLD WATER ZONES

A great number of cold water sources enter most major rivers. And surprisingly, the volume of water need not be large to attract pike. There are no hard and fast rules on locating cold water zones. You simply must explore and know the types of areas to check. Needless to say, an electric thermometer is a must in this search.

As an indication of the types of places to check, let us describe the areas where we've found big pike on the Mississippi. One is a heavily-used small

boat harbor with a maximum depth of about 12 feet. When the harbor was dredged many years ago, springs were exposed on the bottom that still persist today. Although the spring flow is small, it is enough to create a narrow layer of 49°F water in a 500 square foot area. In most years this area is completely bypassed.

Another spot is a long, narrow, dead-end slough used as a boat harbor with a maximum depth of 7 feet. The cold water source is a nearby fish holding pond fed by a large artesian well. Overflow from the pond enters the slough and stratifies along the bottom. A temperature check showed 74°F from the surface to 3 feet, 62°F at 4 feet and 49°F on the bottom (7 feet). Although fished fairly heavily by local residents, fish are continually drawn in to this spot from nearby Lake Pepin. Last summer, two fishermen bagged a limit of 10 northerns here weighing a total of 130 pounds.

The next area is a large backwater lake which has been dredged to a depth of 40 feet to provide fill for building an adjacent railroad grade. Dredging exposed huge springs which provide enough flow to maintain an open water zone all winter. Surface temperature here persists to about 12 feet, but then drops rapidly, and by 15 feet reaches 50°F. A few years back, DNR crews were forced to discontinue test-netting in this area because their nets were being shredded by big northern pike! Yet few fishermen are ever seen in this spot.

A shallow sand flat at the mouth of a large trout stream is yet another example. Maximum depth is about 4 feet. Water temperature in the stream was 60°F on a day when the air temperature was 80°F and the surface water away from the influence of the stream was 78°F.

Most fishermen work the flat around the stream mouth, but some run their boats right up in the lower reaches of the stream. This spot is known to a small group of fishermen and each summer several northerns in the 20 pound class are taken here. DNR crews regularly collect big northerns with electrofishing gear in this spot for display at the Minnesota State Fair.

A spot where cold water from a drain tile pours into the main stream of the river has also drawn big northerns. On an electrofishing expedition on this stretch of the Mississippi (which has a very low northern population), the only pike captured was a 15 pounder taken in the exact spot where cold water from the tile entered the river.

Finally, there is the mouth of a tiny coulee stream entering Lake Pepin. The bluffs along the Mississippi are peppered with springs which flow into ravines and eventually find their way to the river. Dozens of coulee streams flow into the river and the larger ones attract big pike.

Usually summer levels are too low for northerns to ascend far up these coulee streams, but at times when the water is high they will enter these streams and swim as far upstream as they can, which is usually no more than several hundred feet.

Many other areas along the Mississippi area known to attract big northerns, but the 6 types mentioned here are representative of most other spots. Note that none of the areas mentioned have any significant current, since this would dissipate the cold water immediately and not attract pike. You probably know of similar areas on big rivers with which you are familiar, and if pike are around, chances are they will be near some type of cold water zone during mid-summer.

Zones that stay colder in the summer also stay warmer in the winter, since the temperature of ground water varies little throughout the year. Small open water areas often persist around these spots, even on the coldest winter day. Finding these areas is a good winter project! Walk the river banks, locate the potential spots, and be sure to check them out next summer.

The smart fisherman will take careful note of these areas and check them during the summer for thermal stratification. Strong winds destroy temperature stratification by mixing the water from top to bottom and creating currents which carry the cold water away. When this happens the pike leave. It may take as much as 2 or 3 days after a strong wind before temperature stratification is restored. Stratification is more likely to be affected in open areas exposed to the wind than in sheltered coves or harbors.

It's wise to check for cold water before fishing, even in areas that have produced well in the past. After giving up on a favorite spot the past summer, Sternberg checked the temperature only to find it was the same from top to bottom where a few days earlier there was a 26°F difference. There should be at least a 10°F differential to attract pike from the surrounding waters.

HOW TO FISH FOR PIKE IN COLD WATER ZONES

Most cold water zones are relatively small, usually no more than a few hundred square feet in area. So the pike are extremely concentrated and are not actively swimming about in search of food. Instead, they lie relatively motionless and wait for prey to come to them. Like any cold-blooded animal, the northern's metabolism drops in cold water and its activity decreases.

Although we've taken dozens of big pike in these areas by trolling or casting with artificial lures, bait fishing with big minnows is by far the best method in most instances. Here are some details on fishing techniques.

SLIP-BOBBER FISHING

For some reason, big pike often strike a minnow dangled in front of their nose for a period of time while artificials casted or trolled through the same area produce nothing. Since two-line fishing is legal on the Minnesota-Wisconsin Boundary waters, we often still fish with a slip-bobber rig while casting with some type of artificial lure. We'd estimate that 75% of our fish have been taken on the slip-bobber rig.

The basic slip-bobber rig used in walleye fishing fills the bill nicely, but heavier line (about 12 pound test) should be used. Always use a steel leader, whether bait fishing, casting or trolling. Although northerns are not particularly line-shy, you may want to remove the snap swivel and attach the hook directly to the loop in the leader to reduce visibility. The bobber is set to place the minnow in the zone of coldest water.

Big fish like big minnows. Your chances of taking a trophy northern (15 pounds plus) double or even triple when using a 9-12 inch sucker instead of the standard 5-6 inchers sold by most bait shops. We usually use suckers since they are readily available. But pike are not choosy; they will hit big shiners, chubs, or anything else that looks edible. Hook the minnow through the upper lip only with a #1 or #2 short shank Eagle Claw hook. You may have to wait several minutes before setting the hook when using minnows of this size.

We've found that it's a waste of time to try to "wait them out" when fishing for big pike. If they are around, they will usually strike within a few minutes. If nothing strikes within half an hour, there is a good chance that either someone has beat you to the punch or else the area has been destratified by strong winds.

TROLLING

Since cold water is heavier than warm water, it settles out in a thin layer (sometimes no more than 1-2 feet deep) on the bottom. When trolling, it is vitally important to keep your lure in the cold water zone. This can be difficult without the proper equipment. The best way to keep your lure at the right depth without dragging bottom and picking up debris is to fish with lead-core trolling line. Let the lure bump bottom occasionally, but then reel up enough line to avoid dragging. You will find that northerns can be enticed to strike by varying your trolling speed, sometimes almost stopping the lure. The strike usually comes when the lure slows down.

We've taken pike on a wide variety of lures, but surprisingly, big musky lures have not produced as well as smaller (5-6 inch) joined plugs like Pikie Minnows and L & S Mirrolures. Equally surprising is the fact that dull brown has been the best color, despite the murky quality of the water. Another lure that produced about 50 big pike one summer was a red and white Heddon Super Sonic.

The main problem with trolling is that many of the areas are so small that your lure is in the fish producing zone only a fraction of the time. It's a rare occasion when a pike is taken outside the zone of coldest water.

CASTING

If the pike are really feeding, it's possible to take a few on unbaited bucktail jigs. But your odds will improve dramatically by tipping the jig with a 5-6 inch minnow hooked through the upper lip. The type of jig is not too important; in fact, a plain jighead works as well as anything when tipping with minnows. A stringer hook is unnecessary since pike usually swallow the entire jig and minnow. Don't bounce the jig up and down, but instead drag it slowly along the bottom, stopping it occasionally. Resist the urge to set the hook immediately when a fish strikes and let it mouth the bait for a few seconds. When the pike begins to move off, set the hook hard and hold on.

Other types of lures are difficult to keep in the cold water zone unless they are heavily weighted. But in shallow areas, like sand flats near stream mouths, bucktail spinners like the Mepps Giant Killer can be dynamite.

DO PIKE BEHAVE THE SAME IN OTHER WATERS?

Without a doubt! Although Sternberg rarely fishes for pike anywhere but in the Mississippi River, several experienced fishermen have told us of situations in other areas that could be easily explained by the cold water theory. Here are some of their reports:

CASE I—A medium size, eutrophic bass/panfish/walleye lake in central Minnesota. For many years, local fishermen have taken big pike near the mouth of a tiny inlet stream during mid-summer. We've never checked the temperature of the inflowing stream, but it's a safe bet that it's at least 10 degrees colder than the surface temperature of the lake.

CASE II—A large, mesotrophic northern Minnesota walleye lake. Here again pike are attracted to a stream mouth in mid-summer, but only a few fishermen know about it.

CASE III—A shallow, fertile reservoir in southwestern Minnesota with a varied roughfish/gamefish population. Here a local fisherman has specialized in taking big northerns for many years. His favorite spot? An area where a small spring runs into a bay! His favorite time? July and August!

CASE IV—A dredged boat harbor on another large southern Minnesota River with a varied roughfish/gamefish population. Like several such harbors on the Mississippi, this one also produces big pike each year, but only for a tight-lipped few.

The physical requirements of northern pike are the same, regardless of their place of residence. There is every reason to believe that pike seek out cold water in mid-summer, throughout their range.

In oligotrophic and mesotrophic lakes, they can undoubtedly find water cold enough to suit them simply by descending into the hypolimnion (below the thermocline). But in eutrophic lakes, this option is not open to them since the hypolimnion is likely to be devoid of oxygen. And swimming deeper does no good in rivers or shallow lakes, since they are generally the same temperature from top to bottom.

So, obviously, fishermen would have the best chance of finding pike near cold water sources in eutrophic lakes, in shallow mesotrophic or oligotrophic lakes, or in rivers. His poorest chance for locating pike near cold water sources would be in deep oligotrophic lakes or in deep mesotrophic lakes with sufficient dissolved oxygen in the hypolimnion. The fish are there, but it's most likely a needle-in-the-haystack proposition.

Dick Sternberg, Director of the Hunting and Fishing Library, was instrumental on zeroing in on the pike's cold water nature.

EARLY SUMMER LUNKER PIKE—
SPEED UP THE PACE

When is the best time to catch trophy pike? Not single fish, but numbers of beautiful, thick-bodied lunkers? Anglers fishing the Missouri River reservoirs may catch lots of big pike just after ice-out, while midwestern pike fanatics eagerly await the cooling temperatures of late summer that trigger a big pike "feed" over shallow, weedy flats. Over in England, where moderate temperatures prevail, a "specimen" hunter will tell you winter is a favorite time to battle huge, wide-jawed, bream-munching pike. As you can see, *where* you fish pretty much determines *when* to fish.

One factor does remain constant, though, wherever you wet a line: Lunker fish taken in quantity most always come during seasonal peak periods. Seasonal peaks occur when large numbers of fish concentrate in certain locations and show a high degree of activity or aggressiveness. Find the fish, use the right presentation to match the conditions, and catching them can be fairly easy.

Part of the problem is how people view lunker pike, and the types of waters they fish. Most people see a true lunker northern being at least 17 pounds. But fish this size are rare, and only certain waters produce them with any regularity. Typically these waters are large, deep, cold water environments harboring ciscoes, herring, trout or other types of soft-finned baitfish that nourish pike to such huge proportions. Examples are: oligotrophic Canadian shield lakes with large meso bays, early-to-mid meso (moderately fertile) lakes common to north-central and northeastern states, and some large reservoirs like those found on the Missouri River system.

LAKES IN TRANSITION

Fortunately, there are other lake types where the lunker pike population moves into shallower zones in early summer, congregating in more easily-definable and catchable patterns. The secret is switching locations from traditional lunker lakes to smaller, often bypassed, more eutrophic waters. Not small, stunted "snake" lakes, but waters where trophy, pike-producing meso conditions are rapidly changing to eutrophic.

Eutrophic (very fertile) lakes by themselves normally don't have the conditions necesary to produce many large pike. But take a meso lake, which may support a good lunker population, and change it from a deep water to a shallow water-oriented environment, and you now have large numbers of big pike concentrated in shallower, more reachable zones. These pike won't average as large as those from true lunker lakes, but what's wrong with catching 10 to 14 pound pike with an occasional fish over 15 pounds?

Because they possess both middle-aged and older features, and pinpoint classification is hard to define, we will simply label these *transition* lakes. They usually appear as two lakes in one. One half might have steep-breaking, well-defined, hard bottom structures with clear water and weeds growing to 15 feet. The other half could be shallower, consisting of softer, sloping, less-definable (eutrophic) structural elements with weeds growing to only 7 feet. These lakes offer the best early season trophy pike fishing.

Although transition lakes seem like exceptional situations, they are really quite common and easy to find. Transition lakes can be found throughout Minnesota, Wisconsin, Michigan, northern Indiana, Iowa and parts of New York. Wherever you have meso waters subjected to fertilization from human sources, there is a strong likelihood of finding rapidly-changing conditions. Waters situated on fertile farm belts, or weekend lakes with heavily-populated shorelines, are likely candidates.

Transition lakes generally vary in size from 400 to 1000 acres, though some may be larger. One large, deep-water basin often dominates the lake, but there is usually a good balance between open water and shallow bays. The average deep water should be at least 35 or 40 feet. One major drop-off circles the main lake basin, and structural elements near deep water are well defined. Underwater islands or saddles topping off at drop-off depths may be present, but aren't common. On some larger lakes, deep secondary breaklines and underwater islands may be present, but these generally aren't important locations for early summer pike on these waters.

Did you ever wonder how an angler can tear up a strange water the very first time he fishes it? Well, it's not necessarily luck or magic. In fact, with a little study and application, you can do it yourself. If you want to catch big early-summer pike, here is how it's done.

First, obtain contour maps of all the lakes you wish to fish in a given area. Next, spend a day or weekend just driving and observing which lakes physically look most promising. Walk out on a deep pier and look at the water color. Dark water is a key ingredient prompting shallow pike movement and more consistent fishing. Summer algae blooms can turn clear lakes to pea soup—making fishing easier. Check to see if the necessary pike spawning grounds exist: shallow sloughs, backwater bays, and tributaries.

The first blast of hot summer weather, with 3 to 5 consecutive days of high 80°F or 90°F plus temperatures, signals the beginning of the Summer Peak Period. Smaller lakes warm first, followed by progressively deeper waters shortly thereafter. Whereas pre-summer pike were scattered all over the lake, summer peak northerns show remarkably consistent, easily-identifiable patterns. They are very active and aggressive at this time, and easy to catch.

Summer Peak location is a piece of cake. Work the larger structural elements near the deeper main lake basin, and you'll find lots of pike. These areas don't have to be near the actual *deepest* water, but should be near *deeper* areas. For instance, if main basin depths vary from 30 to 55 to 70 feet, respectively, structural elements located near the 55 or 70 foot basin should draw the larger fish. Spots near the 30 foot basin should hold smaller pike. Bigger pike always take the preferred areas.

In many transition lakes, larger forage species spend the Summer Period schooling and suspending over the deeper, main lake basin. In early summer, forage begins moving out of the shallows and gathering on the deep weed edge, or suspending over the main drop-off before they school in summer locations. At times, baitfish can be found around all major points and bars near the deep basin, or as few as one. Wherever they are, you can bet pike will be near. It is common to catch a white bass, snag a crappie or spot sunfish dimpling the surface in areas where pike are located.

Weedbeds are fully developed by now, but by themselves are not all-

LATE SPRING/EARLY SUMMER PIKE LOCATION

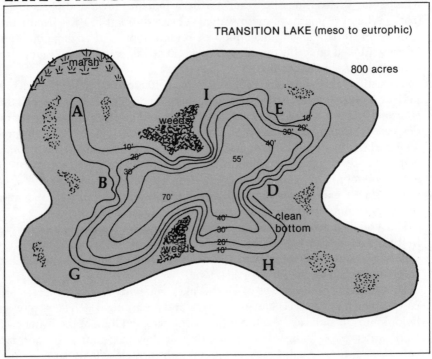

TRANSITION LAKE (meso to eutrophic)

800 acres

Early Pre-summer: *The pike are somewhat mobile. They begin showing up in the first deep water edges (AREA A) outside their spawning marshes. As the water warms, they progressively work their way along the deeper slot toward the main lake to areas like B. Being fairly shallow, AREAS A and B will probably have soft, mucky bottoms, but will hold fish at this time.*

Late Pre-summer: *The northerns are active and mobile. The warming water causes them to scatter and roam all around the lake's basin. Structural elements like B, C, D, E and F could draw fish, although even poor-looking spots like G, H and I might attract pike as well. Weedbeds are still poorly developed this early in the season, so many pike will probably relate to the drop-off.*

Summer Peak: *Big pike now group up on structural elements near deep water. B and E, by comparison, are near shallow basin areas (30 feet), and would probably attract only small fish.*

AREAS C, D and F are prime locations. Although lacking good weedgrowth, AREA D could attract many big pike due to its large size and many points and pockets. Areas like D and F will probably attract more big pike than C, even though C is near very deep water, simply because C lacks numerous points and turns to hold the fish. In addition, D and F are adjacent to large, food-producing shallow flats, whereas C is off by itself with little area to attract shallow baitfish from.

important in determining the better big pike areas; forage determines that. But weed *location* on individual structural elements is important because it dictates how fish relate to the areas.

Points or bars located in the clear water, more meso parts of the lake might have deep weeds growing right to the edge of the drop-off. Pike using these locations usually hold tight to the weedline, suspend off the edge or even move up into the weeds under ideal conditions. But, at the same time, northerns us-

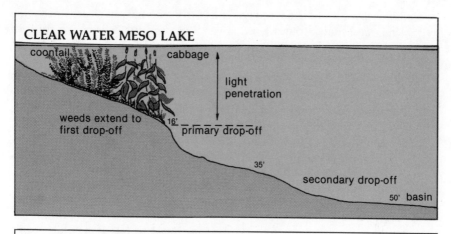

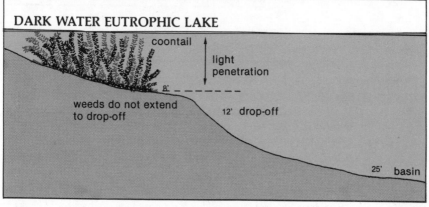

Water color significantly affects fish location and behavior. For instance, most meso (fertile) lakes are fairly clear. Light penetration often extends to the first drop-off, and deep weeds grow out to the edge. The key early summer pike spots are usually right along the deep weed edge.

Contrast this with the darker water condition common to eutrophic (very fertile) lakes in farm country. High nutrient levels frequently cause algae blooms, cutting light penetration and preventing weeds from growing all the way to the drop-off. Large, early summer pike might not move all the way across the clean lip up to the weed edge. Instead, they're liable to lie along hard-bottomed points and turns along the drop-off, in easy range of a trolling approach.

"Transition lakes" often exhibit some sections with meso features, and others that are more eutrophic in nature. This condition combines the tendency to grow large pike (meso lakes) with a darker water color (eutrophic lakes) that tends to keep pike shallower. Fishing-wise, it's like having the best of both extremes.

Transition lakes (late meso and early eutrophic) are common in areas of heavy agricultural run-off or metropolitan activity. Man's introduction of nutrients into the water causes these lakes to age rapidly. They're more fertile than they might at first appear, and if adequate pike habitat is available, they can grow some surprisingly large fish.

ing bars in more eutrophic areas of the lake might ignore weeds. Darker water, eutrophic conditions may limit the depth weeds grow, and they may end some distance from the drop-off. Big pike hardly ever move far up on a flat a long way from deep water to use weed cover in early summer. In clear water, pike love to hide and hunt around weed cover; but dark water is also a form of cover, and in eutrophic conditions, big pike will freely use areas without any form of cover.

Whether using cover-free structural elements or weedlines, pike relate to points, turns and pockets. They use these ambush spots in two ways: (1) single fish, or small groups, hold tight to the side of a point or back of a pocket, waiting for unsuspecting forage to come by; and (2) large groups of fish hunt in packs, running schools of forage up the side of a point, or into a back pocket. Points, turns and pockets always hold the larger pike. If forage is present and equally distributed on all likely areas, more big northerns will tend to use the larger bars with more point and turn areas.

LAKE TYPE

	June 1 →	June 15 →	July 1 →	July 15 →
EUTROPHIC	Pre-summer	Summer Peak		
LATE MESO/ EARLY EUTROPHIC		Pre-summer	Summer Peak	
MID-TO-LATE MESO			Pre-summer	Summer Peak

Pre-summer and Summer Peak are outstanding times to troll for pike along deep weed edges or the first drop-off. However, all lakes do not reach their seasonal peaks at the same time. Moving from lake to lake as each reaches its "peak" potential is a big key to staying on active, catchable fish.

The accompanying chart demonstrates a typical time sequence in the Midwest. Shallow eutrophic lakes don't grow the largest pike, but they do warm up the earliest. Begin your fishing here. Then, as the weeks pass, shift your attention to deeper "transition" lakes as they begin to warm. You'll probably catch larger pike, too. Finally, as the peak pike fishing on transition lakes begins to wind down, switch to deeper meso lakes and try for some real trophies. By following the warming environment and fishing each at its best potential, you can take advantage of as much as 6 to 8 weeks of superb fishing.

EUTROPHIC LAKES

Since shallow lakes warm faster than deeper ones, they are the first to "turn on." Small eutrophic lakes (under 400 acres) usually don't support many huge pike, but can have abundant populations of 7 to 8 pound fish. This is especially true if white bass are the main forage. Lunker hunters should not ignore eutrophic lakes. Many lake records or large fish can be taken during early summer. There won't be many, but occasionally a pike from 12 to 16 pounds may startle you.

Main lake basins are rather small in these lakes, and rarely average over 40 feet deep. The main lake drop-off is usually shallow (6-12 feet) and located a long way from shore. Water color may be a very dark green or milky-white color, and weeds may stop growing at 4 to 6 feet, some distance from the drop-off. Points and bars around the main basin are small, sloping and muck-covered. With the scarcity of weeds extending out to the deep water, hard bottom areas along the drop-off are key Summer Peak locations. These occur as slightly higher spots, or as points and turns. Hard bottom areas may be small and hard to find, but are very important in eutrophic lakes.

LATE MESO/EARLY EUTROPHIC TRANSITION LAKES

A few weeks after small eutrophic lakes reach their Summer Peak, slightly deeper lakes with more meso features come into play. These lakes have a good mixture of both eutrophic and meso features. Water color can fluctuate from one end of the lake to the other, or from season to season. The spring and late fall water color may be very clear, but may have a darker, eutrophic-looking color in summer. Depending upon the water color, weeds may grow right to the drop-off edge in 10 or 12 feet of water, or stop growing a long way from the drop-off. These lakes have larger areas of open water that can average 50 or even 70 feet deep.

These rapidly-changing transition lakes can have surprisingly large populations of good-sized pike. During the Summer Peak, big pike may average 8 to 12 pounds with an occasional fish over 14 pounds. This lake type can produce pike over 15 pounds, although usually later in the season. Hard bottom areas with points and turns are key areas.

MID-TO-LATE MESO LAKES

These are the real "horse" lakes. During a typical summer in the central Midwest, the middle part of July is the time to fish deeper, mid-meso lakes with dark water color. These lakes are usually 1000 acres or more with large areas of deep, cold water. It takes time for these waters to warm up and turn on, but they're worth the wait. Big pike can average 10 to 14 pounds, with some reaching 18 or 20 pounds.

Dark water color is the key to easy fishing. These lakes have large, well-defined, steeper structural elements surrounding the basin, with weeds growing to 15 feet or more. But through over-fertilization, summer algae blooms may prevent a lure from being seen only a foot or two under the surface. This unnatural, dark water condition moves the pike shallower, for a longer duration, than if it were clear.

WEATHER, ACTIVITY AND POSITION

Northern pike are often touted as a good species to fish after a cold front, because some small fish are usually in a neutral mood, or a catchable position, under most weather conditions. But *lunker* pike are very sensitive to weather changes, and may be one of the hardest species to catch during post-frontal conditions—especially in early summer.

Summer weather is dominated by huge, slow-moving, high pressure systems that pump in warm, southerly air. Weather change occurs as a systematic series of high and low pressure, and can be quite predictable. Since weather systems generally move west to east, watching national weather maps for future trends and keeping an eye on local sky conditions will let you predict fishing success.

During the first day or two following a cold front (high pressure), skies are usually very clear, with the exception of some puffy, snowball type clouds, with winds coming from the north or northeast. Lunker pike will suspend out over open water during these conditions and be in a negative mood. Some smaller pike may become active on main lake points and bars, usually later in the afternoon.

By the second or third day, high, whispy cirrus clouds appear and mark the beginning of weather change. Heavier, low pressure systems scrape the ground as they move along, pushing water vapor, pollutants, and various other particles up and in front of them for many hundreds of miles. Cirrus clouds are the frontrunners of heavier "hazy" conditions. By the time hazy skies move into an area, the approaching low pressure has pushed the clockwise rotating high pressure far enough away that hot air from the southwest dominates the scene.

This combination of hot, muggy, hazy conditions really gets lunker pike active and moving. If a low pressure system is slow-moving, causing these conditions to linger in an area, lunker fishing will stay good until conditions drastically change. Generally, these aren't cloudy days, but enough haze is present to block out bright, direct sunlight.

As the actual storm approaches, skies become dark and threatening, and the barometer begins to fall. These pre-frontal conditions account for some of the biggest pike taken, but by and large the hot, partly sunny days before the front passes provide the most consistent action for numbers of large fish.

If low pressure holds, creating a cold, light rain with some lightning high in the clouds, a few big fish might be taken, but fishing is much more difficult. When the front passes and the sky becomes bright and clear, it's all over until the next warm, hazy days.

Even with perfect weather conditions, lunker pike rarely stay active all day long. Small pike can be taken throughout the day, but it is more common for lunker pike to be active for only an hour or two. Very early and very late in the day are the best times to fish—especially on "weekend" lakes with heavy daytime traffic. If pike aren't active early or late, midday from 9 AM to 2 PM is a top time to fish. A good plan for weekend anglers is to fish from 8 AM 'til dark. That way you'll have enough sleep to fish hard all day, and be on the water for all the prime times.

Pike often appear to feed in 24 hour cycles, give or take an hour. If you caught fish around 4 PM, fishing should be good around 3 PM or 5 PM the following day. If the weather remains stable, fish will hold these cycles.

Be alert for nature's signals. Little changes in conditions, which we humans hardly recognize, prompt lunkers to become active. Examples are: a dark day turns darker; an already hot day suddenly becomes muggy and sticky, forcing you to take your shirt off; a slight shift in the wind, or an increase in wind, puts a nice little chop on the water; or a very sunny day is suddenly broken by a thin band of thick clouds. Take note of conditions the next time you land a lunker. You'll be surprised how often they happen again.

The position of various-sized fish also helps you determine what's happening on the water. As we said before, big pike like large structural elements with numerous points, turns, and pockets. When large fish aren't active, small pike will be using these choice locations. But when the lunkers move in, small pike are forced off to the sides, up into the weeds or onto the flat. A typical active period has large fish holding on points and turns, with smaller pike positioned along straight drop-offs, or on short points and turns on shoreline breaklines.

Small pike aren't the only ones pushed around by big northerns. Although most bass stay shallow when pike roam the deep water zones, lunker largemouths (4 to 6 pounds) like to group up on the same points and turns pike prefer. If a lake has few good drop-off areas, it's not uncommon to find big largemouths positioned only a few yards from large northerns. But even lunker bass give way when numbers of lunker pike take control of a spot. Bass are pushed off to the sides of or up shallow onto a bar, perhaps holding over soft, mucky, less desirable bottom. Finding largemouths on the outside edge of a good spot is a good indication that big northerns are using other locations.

Now that you know where and when to fish summer peak northerns, let's go catch them.

TROLLING

During the late Pre-summer, Summer Peak and early Summer Periods on mid-meso to early eutrophic transition lakes, active pike take up positions along the deep edge of the weedline, near the drop-off or somewhere in between. This depth may be anywhere from 6 to 16 feet, depending on water clarity and the physical makeup of the lake. Because of the warmer water temperatures and heavy feeding requirements at this time, pike are often in a very aggressive, active mood. This is a perfect situation to use a fast-moving lure and cover lots of water. Crankbaits really come into their own in these conditions. But instead of casting a crankbait, try trolling one.

Modern crankbaits are excellent trolling lures and come in all shapes and sizes. Some folks may prefer wooden or plastic models, but a favorite for trolling transition lakes is a sinking model called a Spoonplug. Spoonplugs are particularly effective trolling lures. Made of solid brass, they can take a beating, bang off rocks and other objects, and still run remarkably true. Once adjusted, you don't have to keep retuning them like other crankbaits, and the lip won't break off.

Spoonplugs come in various sizes that run at precise depths—the key to their success. Even though pike are active, different speeds or actions may be needed to prompt a strike. Once you determine how much line is needed to make it run at a certain depth, a Spoonplug will stay there. By simply varying boat speed and position, you can run the lure very fast or very slow at the same depth, or make it bounce bottom or ricochet off a weedline.

If you use floating-diving crankbaits, numerous adjustments with added weights and length of line may be needed to achieve the same control. These floater-divers are most effective when you need a large bait in shallow water, or for trolling weed clumps. If you're fishing a situation where weeds grow erratically at various depths, you can slow down a floating lure, make it float over higher weeds, and then speed up to dig down again. In most late-meso to eutrophic transition lakes, however, darker water color stops weedgrowth at a specific depth, forming a very definite edge. When working a precise weed edge or drop-off depth, you need a lure that will hold that depth. Spoonplugs were made for this situation.

Spoonplugging is a great way to map an unfamiliar lake. Instead of motoring around looking at the locator, trolling a Spoonplug as you check a lake will tell you the bottom content, type and depth of weeds or wood cover, and even tell you if the pike are active. If you have done your homework and fish the right lake at the right time, the first loose trolling pass around the main lake basin might produce some beautiful fish.

Let's take an imaginary fishing trip and see how Spoonplugging works for early summer northern pike.

It's the third week in July. The weather has been hot, hazy and very humid for several days. Weather maps indicate an approaching frontal system perhaps two days away. We select a late-meso lake of approximately 1000 acres with a large basin of deep water up to 90 feet deep. We have never fished the lake, but by advance scouting we know it produces some good pike and the water color is on the dark side.

We launch in one of the creeks feeding the lake, and notice numerous bulrushes and lily pad fields as we motor torward the main lake. A check with a contour map indicates three large bars near the deepest water, and one good-looking area halfway up between the shallow eutrophic end where we launched and the deeper meso basin. Since we don't know much about conditions, we'll start with the "in between" area and troll the drop-off around the entire lake basin.

We're using a 16 foot, V-hull, flat bottom aluminum boat with a 25 h.p. engine. A 14 foot boat with a smaller engine might be easier to control, because larger boats tend to slide on the turns, making presentation sloppy. Our tackle consists of 4½ foot, stiff-action, solid fiberglass rods with some flex in the tip. The reels are light saltwater trolling models like the Penn 109 or the old Pflueger Rocket. "Rocket" trolling types have an advantage, because you can use the star drag for trolling, and when a fish is hooked, flicking a lever puts it in direct drive, so you can play the fish with your thumb. If you can convert your reel to direct drive, you'll never have a big pike snap your line when he takes a power dive near the boat. Bandage or tape your thumb so you don't get burned.

We use two rods: One rigged with No-Bo trolling line, and the other with mono wire. Lures are attached with a small snap—not a snap swivel. No-Bo line is pre-metered, non-stretch monofilament designed for easy trolling and greater feel. It comes in 12, 17 and 20 pound test. Twenty pound has a thicker diameter and a lure will run shallower on equal amounts of line. A lure will run deeper on 12 pound test, but tends to keep going deeper once the lure digs into the bottom. Seventeen pound holds the most consistent depth.

If you're working a lure just off the bottom and want it to bump, simply slow down and the lure will walk nicely. Each lure runs a little different on various lines. It is important to become familiar with a certain lure and know how it will run with different types and lengths of line.

When we arrive at the first area, we notice the drop-off is 15 feet deep and the water is very dark green. We select a chartreuse 700 series Spoonplug and

No-Bo line. Lure color is rarely very important as long as you stay with certain lure color/water color trends. Bright yellows are very productive colors for dark water. Chartreuse, hot yellow, brass or any variation of yellow will work. In clearer water situations, white lures work great: white, red and white, green and white, etc. Either white or yellow should produce in most situations. Color is really up to the individual. Whatever you have faith in generally works best. It's much more important to have a well-tuned lure.

Before we begin fishing, we check to see if our lures run properly. Let out about 6 or 8 feet of line and increase boat speed until the lure is pulling hard. Now point your rod directly at the lure and see if it runs to the right or left. If it is not running perfectly straight, use a small screwdriver to bend the small metal hook in the lip in the opposite direction. If the lure is thumping and jumping up and down, bend the entire brass lip slightly up or down until it runs straight. If you can't make a lure run straight with a good, even rhythm at very fast speeds, replace it.

With about 25 yards of line, a 700 spoonplug should run about 14-15 feet. We loosely troll the drop-off on our first pass, slowly moving shallower and deeper. Try not to do anything fancy on the first pass—just get a general lay of the area. Once you get an idea where the points and turns are, the second pass can be a little sharper, running the lure just off the bottom or edge of the breakline, occasionally bumping the bottom.

Run the first few passes rather slow and smooth. Use just enough speed to produce a good, even, humming vibration. In order of how different species react to speed, bass strike the fastest speeds, walleyes medium speeds and pike consistently hit slower speeds during warm water periods. When fishing for pike, it's a good idea to use slower speeds unless you have to go faster. This is especially true if you're fishing unfamiliar water.

Once you know the general shape of the area, work the drop-off with four different speeds to check it thoroughly. Make one pass at the breakline edge with the lure just off the bottom at very fast speed, and another pass with a very slow speed. These lures should only touch bottom once in awhile to let you know your lures are on the money.

A third pass should be made skipping the bottom. Slow down or let out some line until the lure hits bottom. The ideal action is a lure digging bottom, then swimming, digging, swimming. If the lure begins to plow hard, slow the speed, take in some line or move the boat slightly out. On the fourth pass, you want the lure coming up onto or moving off the point. Make straight line passes over deep projections, or zig-zag shallow and deep (*Area A in Figure 1*). Fish sometimes prefer this motion.

After working the breakline without results, we move shallower and notice a weedline begins at 12 feet. Since this is a more eutrophic structure with gradual contours, we'll stay with the No-Bo. Pike rarely bite off a fast-trolled lure, but for fishing weedlines, you may want to add a wire leader. Leaders help slice through the weeds and keep your line from fraying above the lure.

Twenty to 25 yards of No-Bo should get a 100 series Spoonplug down to 12 feet, or you can stay with a 700 and shorten your line length to 10 or 15 yards. Running larger lures on short lines is great for working tight weed contours.

Your trolling passes are basically the same. Try very fast and very slow speeds, just off the bottom at the weed edge. We try to bump the bottom, but

Figure 1

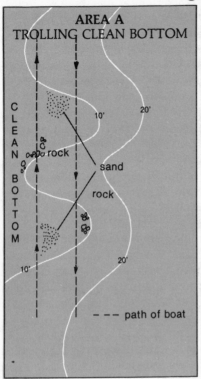

AREA A
TROLLING CLEAN BOTTOM

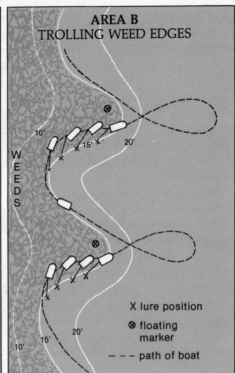

AREA B
TROLLING WEED EDGES

AREA A *has two "finger" points and a pocket. The bar is clean without any form of cover. The top is soft, mucky bottom but the edges are hard.*

The most effective way to cover this situation is to make straight trolling passes using shoreline sightings. Fish find a lure coming up onto, or moving off of, a bar very appealing. The lure will run free, but when it starts bumping bottom, reel in line until it is lightly skipping, not plowing. If the bottom is soft and trashy, just let the lure touch once in awhile, letting you know it's near the bottom. Hold the lure at the same depth, and let it swim off free into deeper water. Repeat the process in the other direction, letting out a little more line as you work progressively deeper.

AREA B *is a similar bar with weeds growing right to the drop-off, forming a weed wall. Place floating markers up into the weed points as reference points. Use larger lures with No-Bo or wire line, and keep your line short. Follow the weed edge, trolling as tight as possible, occasionally bumping the weeds. As you approach a turn, let the boat move up shallow over the weeds for a short distance, and slowly move back to deeper water. This keeps the lure in position as you make the turn. Make a turn outside the marker and repeat in both directions.*

Successful speedtrolling is an art, not just dragging a lure around. As you become more familiar with an area, you'll be able to "tickle" the weed edge or zero in right on the breakline. That's when you really catch fish!

soft, mucky conditions prevent this. Our next pass bumps the weeds themselves.

Most transition lakes have thick coontail weeds which are fairly easy to troll. Coontail grows thick at the top, but the base is sparse. A lure run parallel to the thin, lower stalks bounces off without too much snagging. When your lure starts hitting weeds, move slowly toward deep water until it swims free. Then move back shallow until it starts bumping again. If the lure collects weeds, pull back on the rod, then, throw the rod back to the lure creating slack, and heave it back again. This motion, plus the boat speed, will snap the lure free (*Figure 2*).

Only two small pike are taken, so we troll along the shoreline drop-off, heading toward other potential areas at the lake's deeper end. On the way, we catch some more small pike from short points and turns along shoreline breaks. The pike appear active, and weather conditions remain favorable.

These next areas present an entirely different condition. The water is a little clearer near the deeper basin, and weeds grow right to the edge of steep-

As you troll, keep the rod braced against your knee. This takes the pressure off your wrist and arm, making speedtrolling less tiring.

Make sure your transducer is on the same side as the driver. This aids in positioning your lure exactly with the depth indicated on the locator. By knowing exactly where your lure is, you can place your partner's lure in better position, too!

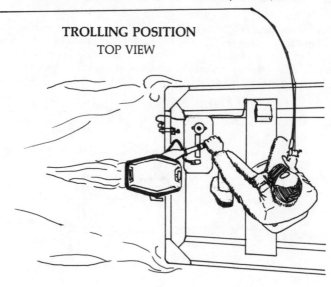

TROLLING POSITION
TOP VIEW

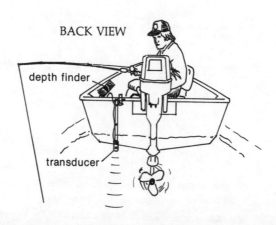

BACK VIEW

depth finder

transducer

breaking points in 15 feet of water. Our first pass with 700's on 25 yards of No-Bo is very ineffective. The breakline is so steep that if we move slightly out, the lure is over very deep water, and if we try to move in, we become hopelessly snagged in the weeds. A change in tactics is needed.

Now we go to the monel wire line. With thin-diameter wire, our lures run deeper, so we can shorten up our line length and troll the erratic weedline more precisely. After several passes, we know the general shape and throw markers up into the shallow weeds on tricky points and turns. Then we try to run our lures as tight as possible without continually hanging up. When we hit a pocket, we turn our boat slowly and smoothly out. For a brief time our boat is over very shallow water, but our lures remain in contact with the deep edge (*Area B* in *Figure 1*). We hang a lot of weeds, but they can usually be shaken free without stopping the boat.

After several hours, our trolling passes become more accurate. Now we experiment with different speeds and actions. We run lures fast and slow just off the weed edge, and even bounce off the weeds. We also start catching some

Most weeds can be easily shaken free from a Spoonplug. Using two hands (left hand on the rod just above the reel), lean back, pulling the lure hard (A). Then snap the rod straight at the lure, creating slack line (B). Then lean back and repeat step A (C). With slack line, the boat's movement creates extra torque, ripping weeds free. Simply pulling and jiggling usually isn't as effective.

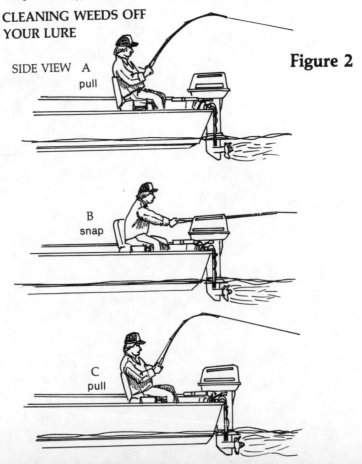

CLEANING WEEDS OFF YOUR LURE

Figure 2

nice pike, noticeably in the sharp bends and points. It's debatable whether the pike suddenly became active and moved in. More likely, they were there all the time. Our presentation simply wasn't tight enough to catch them.

When you hook a big northern trolling, keep the motor running. If the wind is blowing into the weeds, put the motor in reverse and pull the fish into open water. This will save a trophy.

Pike usually slam a lure and hook themselves, but there are times when they follow a lure and just nip at it. You might feel a tick, tick, and then he's on. But other times they nip at it and let it go. When pike are hitting this way, "throw" the rod back at the lure with your wrist, much the way you shake a weed off. Non-chasing pike often take a lure that stops and falls after they nip it. Pike don't often strike like this, but when they do, it's a good method to use.

With fish coming from pockets and the sides of points, we begin casting out some small pockets that were bypassed by trolling. We work the lure from shallow to deep water, hoping to horse the fish out to open water. Spoonplugs are good lures to cast in this situation. Let the lure sink to the bottom, reel fast or pull hard on the rod, and then let it sink again. Smaller plugs like a 250 or 200 series have better vibration for this method. Unlike many lures, fish hit a Spoonplug as it rips off the bottom—not when it sinks.

A jig and twister tail lure, like a creature, is also a good choice when casting for active pike. Pike hit these on the fall. I like to start with a bright yellow creature and go from there.

Precise trolling takes time and experience. If you stick with it, and fish the right lakes at the right time, you'll eagerly await the early summer season. It's one of the best times to catch big northerns, and when you're on 'em, you can catch a bunch.

Although you normally troll on opposite sides of the boat, two trollers can work the same side. Use wire line and keep it short. The front man should run a little less wire to avoid tangling. This works great when pike hold tight to a weed wall, and the outside troller might never see a fish!

TROLLING A WEED WALL

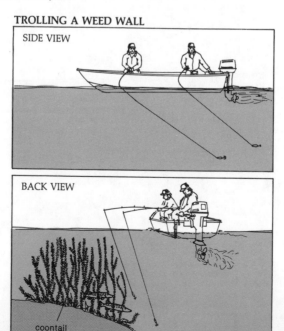

coontail

Chapter 16

THE POST-SUMMER PERIOD

"A Time of Impending Change" (Smaller Fish)
"A Time of Refreshing" (Larger Fish)

Post-summer, in effect, is the reversal of the Pre-summer process. It is a time when a body of water starts changing back from a warmer to a cooler water environment. This period takes place during the tail end of summer. Hot days with dead-calm periods, followed by cool nights, are typical. The days grow shorter, and this becomes the cosmic signal to the ecosystem that things are slowing down.

Pike can respond to these environmental changes in a variety of ways, and a variety of patterns can emerge. Interestingly, even the most marginal anglers manage to start catching a few fish—just as they did during the Pre-summer Period—and for much the same reasons.

Just prior to this (in the Summer Period), the various-sized pike groups might have been doing a lot of different things. Thus, the angler had to be very specific in his presentation, and many times your approach had to be quite refined. But now, in Post-summer, these very defined patterns break down, and fish of various niches start moving about more. In many cases, fish from one area mingle with other groups, forming loose, short-lived concentrations. Pike also now tend to hold in feeding periods longer. When you add all these factors up, pike fishing is easier; in fact, it can be fantastic.

The following are two very effective ways of capitalizing on Post-summer pike.

BIG JERKS—BIG PIKE

Jerkbaits get their name from the fact that you must repeatedly give them the old heave-ho to impart action to the lure. If you simply reeled them in, they'd do nothing at all! But with a variety of jerks, they'll dance like living things.

The majority of jerkbaits fall into two categories: tail baits and stick baits. Each works a bit differently.

Tail baits like the Suick and Bobby Bait have more-or-less rectanglular bodies and a metal tail fin at the rear. You adjust the depth the lure dives on the jerk by *slightly* bending the fin up or down. A little extra twist of the fin to the left or right side will cause the bait to wobble a bit more than usual.

Stick baits like the Lindy Teddy Bait Big Jerk, Fudally Reef Hawg and Eddie Bait are cylindrical in shape and don't have a tail fin. This design causes the lure to dance more in a side-to-side fashion, as opposed to a tail bait's tendency to dive up and down. In short, each style has a bit different action. Standard tail baits will dive to perhaps 3-3½ feet at the maximum, whereas standard stick baits only dive to about 1-1½ feet on a good jerk.

The desire to make "jerks" dance like living creatures, and the constant effort to make some tail baits dive deeper, causes the vast majority of fishermen to jerk these baits like mad. Yes, this will get the little something extra out of 'em. But it's brutal on the back, arms and shoulders! Yet that's the accepted technique for keeping wooded jerks down. As soon as *you* slow down, they start popping back up to the surface!

Jerkbaiters usually spell relief "W-E-I-G-H-T." That's right! Instead of flailing away like a madman, it's infinitely easier to add weight to jerkbaits to *keep* them down. That takes pressure off you, and enables you to concentrate on working the lure, instead of *first* maintaining the depth and *then* working the lure.

As we said, most standard jerkbaits are made out of wood, and their natural buoyancy causes them to rapidly pop back up to the surface when you stop moving them. Some are weighted somewhat to keep 'em down a bit. The key to relief is to add more weight.

THE SECRET

Plop a standard jerkbait in the kitchen sink and see how it floats. It sits pretty level with its entire back slightly out of the water, doesn't it? The trick is: adding (1) the proper amount of weight in (2) the proper location to make the lure sit *slightly nose down* at rest. This will both decrease the lure's buoyancy and make it dive deeper to boot!

Grab a handful of bullet sinkers in the 1/8 to 3/8 ounce range. Use a pair of side cutters or pliers to trim the tips off the sinkers to make them roughly flat on both ends. These are your counterweights.

Pick a mid-size sinker and rest it on top of the jerkbait near the head. What did the lure do? It sat a bit more nose down, didn't it? Now slide the sinker back a half inch or so, and compare it to the previous position. Now move it forward an inch and eyeball the results.

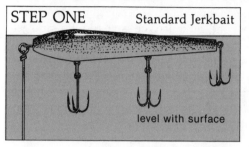

STEP ONE   Standard Jerkbait

level with surface

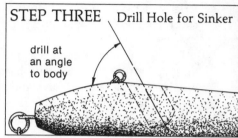

STEP THREE   Drill Hole for Sinker

drill at an angle to body

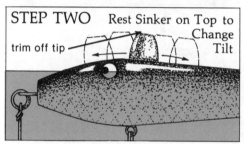

STEP TWO   Rest Sinker on Top to Change Tilt

trim off tip

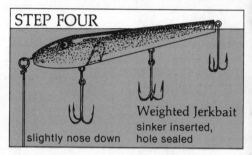

STEP FOUR

slightly nose down

Weighted Jerkbait
sinker inserted, hole sealed

Very simply, moving the sinker back and forth will change the angle of tilt. Remember, you want to make the lure tilt slightly nose down. If you can't get the results you want, switch to a lighter or heavier sinker, and repeat the process. Sooner or later, it'll look right. That's the combination of weight and position you need.

Next pull the jerkbait out of the sink and mark a spot on the underbelly of the lure directly below the sinker position. Then drill an angled hole into the lure body just large enough to insert the sinker. If all looks well, coat the inside of the hole with a little nail polish to waterproof it and hold the sinker in place, and slide the sinker into the hole. Then seal the outside of the hole with some extra nail polish or silicone cement, or, as we prefer, with an electric glue gun.

Congratulations! You've just gone a step further than the majority of jerkbait anglers. Once you've tried the lure and see how much you like it, you'll probably want to weight some more. Now you can get fancy!

Try weighting some lures a little more than others to achieve a little different action. Perhaps you'd like a lure that's almost neutrally buoyant. Well, put a large sinker in near the head, and a smaller one about halfway back to sort of level it out again. Sure, it's almost level, but the extra *total* weight will keep the lure down and cause it to run deeper than your other models. There's no end to what you can do! Just be sure not to overweight lures to the point where they are thrown out of balance.

Customizing jerkbaits is easy and kind of fun. But don't get lazy. Each bait comes slightly different from the manufacturer and must be individually tuned. Dont' think you can weight six baits with the same amount of weight in the same spot; they might all turn out different! So take time to do it right and you'll be in good shape.

WORKING THE LURES

Yes, you still have to "work" them, but it'll be much easier. Instead of heavy jerks that twist your back from side to side, now you can glide them with short, choppy jerks of about 1½-2 feet and get much the same results—and get deeper!

Fire a weighted jerkbait out, point your tip down at the surface in front of you, and give it a moderately sharp twitch of about two feet directly back toward you. The bait will dive and glide a few feet. As it begins to slow down, reel up the slack with a short flip of the reel handle and give it another jerk. Down she goes again. Keep it up all the way to the boat.

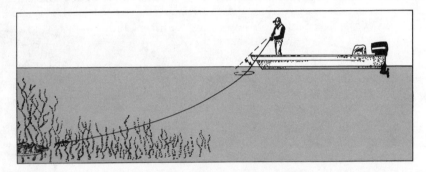

This retrieve works very well with both stick baits and tail baits. Besides, the straight-in-front-of-you, drop-the-rod-tip retrieve eliminates the common sideways/heavy-jerk retrieve that's so punishing on your back. Tail baits will pop up and down with ease, and stick baits will shoot back and forth in the familiar "walk the dog" fashion they are noted for.

Once you get good at it, you can get stick baits down 2½-3½ feet, and tail baits down 4-6 feet! The only jerks pike have ever seen have been up above them, and now you're putting it right down in their face. Boy, does it get results!

EQUIPMENT

Proper equipment always makes the job easier, but is particularly critical in this case because of the large lure size. We prefer a fairly stiff, heavy-duty 5'9" graphite rod because it's easier to work jerkbaits with than a soft rod. A good alternate would be a fiberglass musky rod. Casting tackle is by far your best bet.

Use a heavy dacron line like 30 pound test Berkley Alert, Gudebrod or Cortland, and always use a "Uni-Knot" to tie the lure on. The key to landing a big fish is to stick him good on the hook set and then loosen the drag a bit. Trying to muscle the fish with such heavy tackle will tear the hooks free, and is probably the main reason people lose fish on musky tackle! But by backing off a bit and fighting the fish with the drag instead of toe-to-toe, you put the odds in your favor.

147

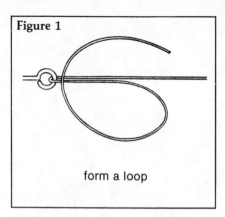

Figure 1

form a loop

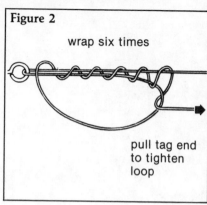

Figure 2

wrap six times

pull tag end
to tighten
loop

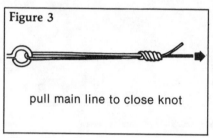

Figure 3

pull main line to close knot

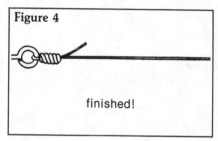

Figure 4

finished!

The Uni-Knot *works much better for braided dacron line than an improved clinch or similar knot, which are better on monofilament line. Try it!*

Ron Kobes, a member of the Lindy/Little Joe fishing team, has fine-tuned the art of balancing jerkbaits and their specialized presentation.

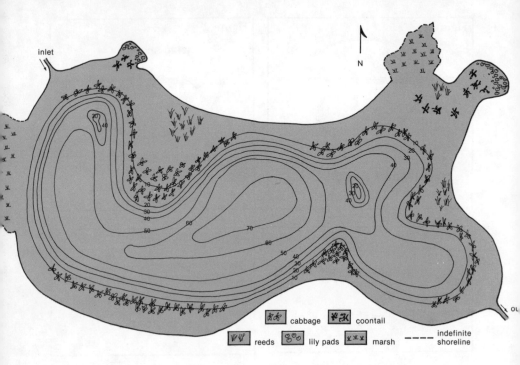

inlet

N

🐟 cabbage	⚘ coontail		
〰 reeds	🌿 lily pads	✕✕ marsh	- - - - indefinite shoreline

THE CONDITIONS

It's mid-September. Summer is drawing to a close. The daytime temperature is still warm, but once the sun goes down the air becomes noticeably chilly—no more of those hot, muggy nights. Fall is definitely drawing near.

The word is that over the past few days several big northern pike have been caught on Tooth Lake, that nearby "tough" son-of-a-gun. It's got the reputation of being tough because it's so deep and clear, but it sure puts up some giants. In fact, it's the best lake in the area for both *big* northerns and walleyes.

You also know the methods the majority of the "locals" use to fish Tooth Lake for northerns. Most of the time they troll spoons or "soak" a big sucker beneath a bobber. Normally, they're not very successful, especially for big fish. But now that these folks are starting to catch a couple of trophies, you know that the big snakes are entering the shallows in range of even the casual fisherman. You're excited, because you know where and how to get in on the action.

Those are the conditions. If you think there's not much information to go on, *you're wrong*! That's the kind of information you normally get. After all, it's very seldom that someone runs up to you, gives you a marked lake map, hands you the "magic" lure and says, "Go get 'em!" Life should always be so easy!

Take the subtle information that's been listed here, give the accompanying lake map a good looking over, and plan your strategy for taking a 15 pound plus northern pike. If you play your cards right, there's no reason why you shouldn't nail a couple of giants. Then compare your answer and ours.

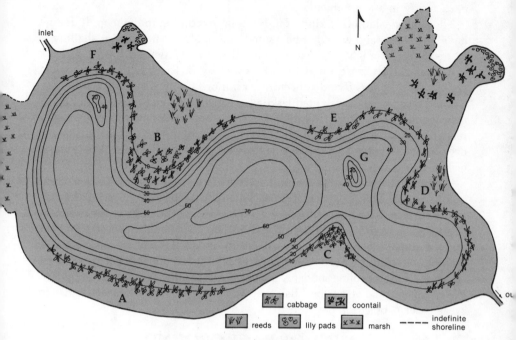

cabbage   coontail

reeds   lily pads   marsh   indefinite shoreline

SOLUTION

The first thing we do is look at the lake map and pick out the points and flats that will hold weeds and large fish. Flats, in particular, have abundant cover and will draw and hold fish all day long at this time of year. Narrow weedbeds on sharp-breaking shorelines, by comparison, will usually only hold big pike morning and evening, with the fish suspending outside the weeds during the day.

There's an area on the south side of the lake we'll call *Area A*. It's a sharp-breaking shoreline weedbed that we'd probably hit first thing in the morning. After that, we'd go to the all-around best-looking spot on the lake, which we'll call *Area B*. It's a giant weedy flat that's ideal for trolling bucktails or working jerkbaits. Under normal fishing conditions, we'd spend a lot of time there.

We like the little point which we'll call *Area C*—especially the sharp-breaking west side. There's enough of a flat to hold fish and a good break to deep water. We like the sharp-breaking side better than the actual tip of the point because of its short, easy access to deep water. The big fish can move directly up onto the flat from deep water.

The point on the east side—*Area D*—looks real good, even though it doesn't have quite the fast drop-off of *Area C*. According to the map, *Area D*'s best weedgrowth is on the tip of the point, although we'd have to check it out to make sure.

Area E isn't much by comparison, although it could draw a couple of good fish and would probably be bypassed by most tournament anglers. We'd probably just troll a Hellbender or other crankbait along the edge to quickly check it out, but then concentrate on other areas.

Finally, *Area F* has some potential, although it's so close to fantastic *Area B* that *B* would probably draw most of the fish. Still, it's worth a quick look—

particularly in a tournament.

The sunken island G is kind of interesting. According to the map, it doesn't have any weeds and wouldn't be a good pike spot. But if it gets as shallow as 12 or 15 feet, it might have weeds—and fish. We'd have to look for sure.

Basically, then, we'd hit A first, followed by B. Faced with a tournament crowd, we'd bypass B and concentrate on more subtle areas like C and D.

We'd mostly fish a weighted jerkbait, particularly since most of the fishermen would probably be trolling bucktails or bobber fishing. That gives us a real edge—that something different. We'd begin by hovering just outside the deep weedline, pitch a jerk up inside the weeds and work it back. We get a lot of fish that way.

We don't strictly fish the break, however. In a good area, we'll move right up on the flat. This is particularly true when the weeds don't come all the way to the surface. Say the weed tops are 2-3 feet below the surface, for example. Most anglers would skip the area and fish where they could *see* weed tops poking out above the surface. But we'll get up on the flat and zig-zag across it, looking for weeds on our locator. Or let's say the weedline and drop-off don't coincide. If the weedline suddenly swings up on the flat, we'll follow it by *feel*. We've taken some of our best fish that way. We get a lot of our better fish in areas other people don't even fish!

A BIT OF BACKGROUND
ON POST-SUMMER TROLLING

The beauty of a trolling system is its stark simplicity. Anyone can do it. You don't need sophisticated equipment. A plain old boat, motor, rod and reel fills out the entire equipment list. If you are familiar with a body of water, you can even leave your depth finder at home. What's more, you don't even have to know how to cast or even be able to detect a strike or set a hook. What can be simpler than that?

This system is actually a throwback to the old days, or prescientific era, if you will—the days of big lures, black braided line, backlash-prone reels, square-shaped steel rods, one-lung clunker motors and wooden boats.

The reason the system survived the switch from the heavy and grueling to the light and delicate is obvious. It worked! In fact, it still works better with some of the old tools, like big clanging metallic bucktail lures, short stiff rods, no-stretch braided line and small short-shaft motors. No, you don't have to trade in your super sleek fiberglass rig for a wooden scow, and you can even keep your favorite boron bass or musky stick. About the only thing you might have to pick up is some black braided line.

The major problem of trolling the shallows for pike is not so much how, but when and where. Once you know when, which we previously explained, plus have the understanding of where—which we will now explain—then the matter of how is relatively simple.

One fact of life with this pattern is that you need large areas to effectively use the system. Short runs and stop-start tactics are counter-productive. If a weed patch is small and isolated, the chances that a lot of big pike are relating to it are remote. Besides, these spots are better fished by methods other than trolling. To potently troll the shallows for these brutes you need room to roam, so the more extensive the structural piece the better.

WHAT TO LOOK FOR IN VARIOUS LAKE TYPES

Although the shallow trolling system works on most of the different lake types that we've tried, the classic pike movements occur on big sprawling meso lakes. Specifically, the ones which have extensive weed-studded shallow water flats. Throughout the summer on these kinds of waters anglers catch small skinny "snake" northerns in the weeds and even a few medium-sized fish along the drop-offs, but the big pike remain strangely aloof. But come the first blasts of cold polar air from Canada, and the vegetation on the flats comes alive with bruisers.

An ideal flat would be one with a slow taper and a lot of 5 to 8 foot deep water peppered with patches of weeds. While a weed-choked flat can draw

This map shows a typical mid-mesotrophic lake with sections of big flats in the 5 to 8 foot range. Two different types of flats are illustrated here. Flat A, an extended flat, is the most common. This one happens to project off a point. However, other flats could exist off a stretch of shoreline as well. The important thing is that there is a wide band of slowly tapering water in the 5 to 12 foot depth range. Cabbage weeds generally grow in clumps along a flat in this depth range.

Flat B shows a typical formation found in a bay. These usually occur at the mouth of a big weedy, shallow bay. The bigger and flatter the bay the better. On the outside rim where it starts to taper out into the main lake basin, you will many times find cabbage beds in the 5 to 15 foot levels. Where the contours flatten up along the rim is where you should concentrate your trolling efforts.

Two Kinds of Flats

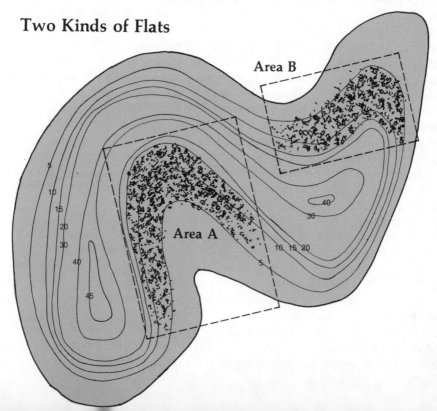

fish, those with sporadic growth concentrate the fish more and are much easier to fish. So again, those flats which are sandy and have clumps of cabbage or coontail (or combinations of both), as opposed to heavy continuous growth, will be best.

Will big pike only relate to cabbage or coontail? Although these weeds are best, how about other weeds? Well, it's primarily cover which draws and holds the fish, so any kind of weed that is dense enough to provide the needed cover for hunting and off-hours rest will do. In the thick matted weeds, however, a pike has a hard time creeping up on its prey. The fish also have a tougher time zeroing in on a fast-moving lure and pouncing on it. Although pike will relate to many types of weeds, trolling the shallows works best in cabbage and coontail that is not thick and choked, but has the necessary holes, pockets, clean open areas and umbrella-like fronds that allow the pike concealment and an open field of fire to lunge at prey.

In Canadian shield lakes, big pike mill in bays in early spring, move out to the points or areas in the main lake during the summer, and return to shallow weedy bays for a short spell in late summer. An ideal bay in a Canadian lake that would attract a lot of big pike in late summer is one that is large and relatively shallow. A 20 or 30 acre section with perhaps a 10 or 12 foot deep hole somewhere, and with extensive parcels of 5-8 foot water with small patches of scattered weeds would be close to ideal. This growth does not have to be expansive, or thick. In these barren waters small stringy tufts will often provide enough cover. The bottom in these bays could be sandy, silty or mucky. The big pike don't seem to be troubled by the soft bottom.

The presence of stained or darker off-colored water would be a definite asset in such a bay. This could be the result of an inflowing stream or draining marsh. The bays in these waters might also contain reeds. The front face of a reedbed which is along a slight break in depth will attract big pike late in summer. Lunker fish sometimes position themselves nose out in the reeds and feel quite secure here, even with the approach of a boat. Most of the time they will only back up a bit. Trolling passes can be made right along the reed banks along the front face, as long as the depth is at least 5 feet. Although sporadic, these spots produce, and are always worth a quick pass through. However, these spots are sometimes better to cast to.

While this trolling system is easy to employ in the aforementioned kinds of lakes, eutrophic bodies of water present a different set of circumstances. Most flats or bays in these lake types are not extensive, and many are weedchoked and quite shallow.

The amount of big fish available is also usually much less on these waters. So you are faced with limited amounts of fish, plus difficult conditions to troll and maneuver in.

Even so, big pike which lay all summer long in a spring hole or stay buried in the weeds become active in late summer. While they spread out through the weed beds, it's been our experience that weeds in the 5-8 foot range, or along the front face of weedlines are best.

Fishing the front face of the weedline poses a bit of a problem, however. Most of these weedlines end at 8, 10 or 12 feet, and with one side completely open, the fish are very apprehensive to come up and hit shallow riding lures.

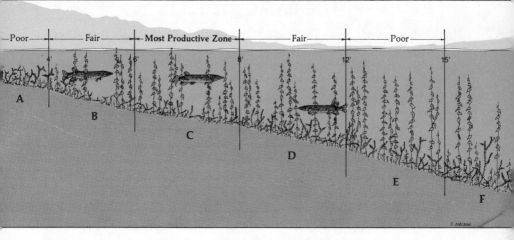

All Weeds Levels Are Not Created Equal

Shown here is a side section of a flat. For purposes of illustration it appears that the weeds continue uninterrupted from the shallows to the drop-off. In actual practice, however, they would most likely be found in scattered clumps in these depth ranges. Area A, the depths shallower than 4 feet, are generally unproductive with our trolling technique. From this point shoreward you'll start spooking the fish by trolling over them. You're better off casting to the fish in these levels.

Area B, in the 4 to 6 foot depth range, usually has weeds growing all the way to the surface. These are tough waters to troll in. In fact, you need a totally weedless lure in order to work through these areas and the prop will cut up weeds and leave a trail which we've found to be counterproductive. So these kinds of sections are only fair producers.

Area C, in the 6 to 8 foot range, is usually the ideal depth range. Here the weeds often grow only to within 2 or 3 feet of the surface, which leaves an open water section above them and is perfect for trolling. The fish will lay suspended high in the weeds and will come up to hit the baits as they pass.

Area D, the 8 to 12 foot range, is only fair. The pike will be present here but they are not as likely to rise up and strike a shallow buzzing spinner as they are in the 6 to 8 foot range. At this depth you may want to run the lures a little deeper. You can do this by moving slower. In the deeper sections, like 12 to 15 foot ranges shown in sections E and F, you are better off using other methods.

Under these conditions you must modify your approach a bit.

In some eutrophic lakes that have a big bay or flat where you can maneuver, you would fish just as you would on a Canadian shield or mesotrophic lake. But, on these waters the bays are very shallow and have dense weeds close to the surface. The flats are also narrow, so you are better off concentrating your efforts along the edge of the weeds or in the rim of weeds bounding the front face.

To summarize then, we are looking for a big weed-studded flat on a meso lake, a big weedy bay on an oligotrophic Canadian shield body of water, or a full cabbage or coontail edge on a eutrophic lake. Location is basically that simple. Now that we know the when's and the where's, let's look at the how.

THE BASIC SYSTEM

In the days before depth finders, trolling was a less precise art than it is today. Although floating markers were sometimes used to establish a course, holding an exact depth level was well nigh impossible. Still, the old-timers caught fish.

Sometime in the mid 50's our trolling system using big bucktail lures and spoons began. As we understand it, it started in Canada and filtered down into the U.S. Whatever the case, the method worked then and does today. Its strength is in its shotgun approach—you cover a lot of water fast. You're fishing eager feeding pike, so there is no need for finesse.

The primary equipment is simple. A stiff rod, black braided trolling line, a big, shallow-running lure, a boat and motor and you're ready to go.

The stiff rod is necessary to hook and control the fish. You're fishing in weeds for big, strong northern pike—an open invitation for hang ups and lost fish. Most folks don't realize it, but with a stiff rod and no-stretch line, you not only have increased control, but you can actually feel the fish fight better. Every shake of the head, twist of the body or powerful surge is instantly telegraphed back to your head.

Braided line allows you to detect and even shake off the weeds by snapping the line in a whip-like manner. With stretchy mono you could pick up a piece of weed and not know it and drag a lure for long distances. Berkley's 20 lb. Medallion black braided nylon, Gudebrod's 20 lb. black braided dacron or Cortland's 18 lb. black Musky Master braided dacron are all top choices for this system. Twenty pound is heavy enough to set a hook well and fight and control even a big pike, but is not so thick as to keep the lure from riding a few feet beneath the surface at a brisk speed.

Why black line? We really don't know, but for us it seems to work better than the white, banded or camouflage lines. Al once kiddingly said that the black line helps lunker pike better zero in on the lure! Who knows? It's hard to argue with success!

We usually attach a 6 inch, 20 lb. test steel leader to the braided line. Yes, just like in the days of old. Any free spool trolling or casting reel that'll hold the thick line will do. You won't be doing any casting, so all you need to do is be able to let out, reel in or store line.

LURES

Of all the various lures that can be used, the two types which are by far the most productive are spinners (both the straight-shaft and the safety pin types), and big, lightweight spoons. We experimented with plugs, such as Rapalas, Pikie Minnows and the like, and have caught fish. But these lures dive considerably deeper than the spinners and spoons and tend to pick up too much vegetation. What you want is a bait that has lift to it—like a spoon or spinner.

There are a number of big, straight-shaft spinners on the market, all of which can be productive. The big bucktails that are designed primarily for muskies are perfect for big northerns as well. Straight-shaft spinners have less water resistance than safety pin tandem models, and you can get a little deeper with them on a fast troll. Some prime examples are the Mepps Giant Killer, the Marathon Big Slim and Musky Hound, Grassl's Rampage (with reversed bucktail) and Mark Windel's Harasser. These baits are of heavy-duty construction with good solid shafts and quality hardware.

One important feature to look for when selecting a spinner is a weighted treble on the back hook. These were originally added to make casting easier and stop the lures from tangling end-over-end in the wind. Yet the 3/4 oz. weight on the back hooks also makes a big difference in the depth you can achieve when trolling fast. An unweighted spinner will often break the surface or turn on its side when moving at high speeds, whereas the weighted models generally run true.

We have been the most successful with the safety pin tandem spinners. These lures tend to ride a little bit higher than the straight-shaft versions because of the increased water resistance created by the two big blades. That extra vibration created by those blades also has a good deal of calling power that raises a fish. Besides being more noisy underwater, they are also less prone to foul in weeds because of the way the overhead shaft protects the upturned hooks. Again, a heavy weighted treble on the back is essential to get that depth at higher trolling speeds.

Some good trolling baits are the Lindy Musky Tandem or Mr. Twister's Musky Tandem. These baits are well designed and come with good hooks, hair and hardware. The addition of 3 or 4 inch Twister tails on the rear hooks often helps to stimulate strikes.

The color of the baits can sometimes make a difference. One of the most consistent color patterns we have used is the black body with hot orange fluorescent blades. Fluorescent blades seem particularly attractive to northern pike. Hot yellow is another good producer, as is the standard red and white bucktail with silver blades. Experiment with various colors until a productive one is found.

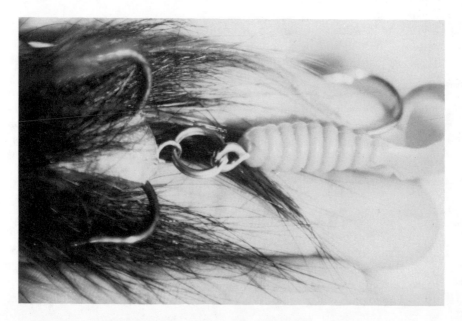

TROLLING

Once rigged with the proper equipment and choice of baits you are ready to begin trolling. This trolling method is most effective with two people. Although it is possible to troll with 3 lines out, this will increase the odds of tangled lines, especially when a big fish is hooked. One man should fish on the left and the other on the right, to keep the lines as far apart as possible and cover as much water as you can.

Once the boat is positioned for the start of a forward trolling run, shift into forward gear and let out between 20 and 30 feet of line behind the boat. It is usually best to begin with 2 different types of spinners and have one man let out 5 or 10 more feet of line than the other until you can establish a pattern. You don't need to trail the lures way back either—30 feet is plenty of line. Big pike often come right up and hit the spinners in the wake of the boat. In fact, it is advantageous to keep your lures close to the boat so that you have better control of them and also more hooking power when the fish hits. Make your trolling passes in forward gear at approximately 3 to 4 miles an hour. This is fast enough to keep your baits running about 2 feet below the surface.

The type of trolling pass you use largely depends on the individual lake you are fishing, and the way the weeds have grown. In most meso lakes the bulk of your fishing should be concentrated up on the flats in the 6 to 12 foot depth range. Since these flats will usually taper gently in this range, there are no real distinct breaklines or bottom contours to follow. You will usually be fishing right over and through patches of cabbage weeds which grow on the flat. So it helps to have a pair of polaroid sunglasses to see the weedgrowth.

Get out on those weedbeds and just start trolling through them. At first you may want to weave a trolling pattern that snakes up and down in depth as you move across the flats. When a fish hits, hold that depth range and try to concentrate your trolling efforts at that level. On huge flats you may want to throw a marker to better help you correlate where you are in relation to the weedbeds.

We should warn you, though, in many cases there is no distinctive depth pattern. The fish will be found in certain weed patches regardless of depth. They are just in there, and there is no sense in questioning it. You just fish them.

As you troll your way along pay attention to the weedgrowth and even minor variations in depths along the flat. There may be a little bend, point, dip or greener clump in the cabbage that will be holding fish. Don't hesitate to troll over the same beds more than once. Use a systematic pattern so that you thoroughly cover the beds. When coming through a very thick patch you will want to speed up and raise your rod tip. When you come to a gap or pocket in the weeds you should slow up a little and drop your rod tip so it sinks down a little deeper.

One interesting thing to note is that big pike often strike on the turns. There are two schools of thought as to why this occurs. First, the bait on the outside of the turn speeds up while the one on the inside tends to drop a little. Secondly, an S-shaped trolling pass pulls the lure through areas that the boat hasn't passed directly over. In case a fish moves to the side when you pass overhead, the S-shaped path will get him. Whatever the case, it pays off to use a few ran-

TROLLING A FLAT

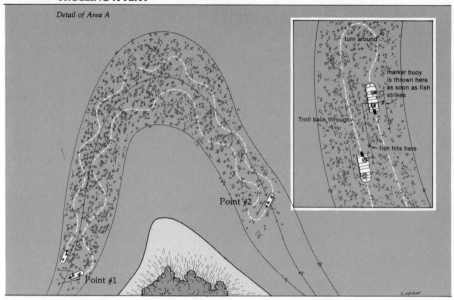

This drawing shows one good way to fish a weedy flat. Illustrated is a typical trolling pattern. Begin the trolling pass at point #1 (roughly 7 feet of water). Cover the entire flat by zig-zagging back and forth between 5 and 10 feet until the weeds thin out at point #2. If you catch a fish or get a strike somewhere in between, throw a marker, switch directions and run right back through the same weedbed. Many times there will be more active fish within one weedbed or in a given section, so it pays to go right back through it immediately.

If you make the initial pass without any action by the time you reach point #2, turn around and begin zig-zagging back through the deeper 10 to 15 foot range. However, slow up a little at these depths so you can get the baits down a little deeper. This way, you can cover the whole flat thoroughly.

dom turns when your baits are coming through key areas. You need not turn much, only a mere 10 or 15 degrees, to achieve this affect. By keeping an eye on your line you can follow the path of your baits and direct them more efficiently.

The length of the trolling sweeps you make will, of course, vary from lake to lake and spot to spot. But long runs are generally the most productive. You can cover a lot of water in a relatively short period of time. Remember to troll back and forth a number of times through areas where a fish is taken.

When a fish hits you will know it. Northerns smash into these spinners hard and fast at this time of year. Often they will boil the surface as they attack. You should set the hook with authority, but need not overdo it if you have a stiff rod and heavy braided line. The impact of trolling at that speed will generally set the hook for you. But you should rear back and nail them a couple of times to make sure you get the hooks in the fish. It is important to keep your drag set tight to assure proper hooking and get them coming your way.

Once you've achieved a good set, shift the outboard into neutral and fight the fish. Don't turn the motor off. You may want to slip it in gear to follow a big, fast-running pike. After all, there's no rush. Don't fall to the temptation of leaning on him with all you've got with that heavy equipment. If you do, you'll most likely rip the hooks out. Just take it easy and enjoy the fun. Big northerns in that 15 lb. plus class are extremely powerful and make lightning runs for freedom.

The technique is simple enough so that anyone can do it. Find a lake that grows big pike, head out there with some big spinners and spoons, and do a little late summer trolling over the weedy flats. You'll be surprised just how easy it really is.

Chapter 17

THE TURNOVER PERIOD

"A Time of Turmoil"

First, all bodies of water do not experience the Turnover Period. The most classic (drastic) turnover situation occurs in bodies of water which set up (stratify) in distinct temperature layers during summer. Since cold water is heavier than warm water, the warmer water stays on top and the colder water sinks and builds up on the bottom; in between lies a narrow band of rapid temperature change from warm to cold called the thermocline.

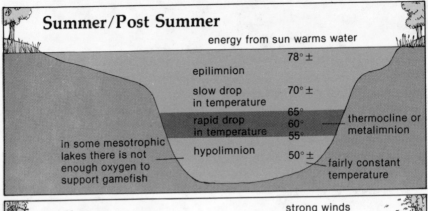

Summer/Post Summer

energy from sun warms water

epilimnion — 78°±

slow drop in temperature — 70°±

65°
rapid drop in temperature — 60° — thermocline or metalimnion
55°

hypolimnion — 50°±

fairly constant temperature

in some mesotrophic lakes there is not enough oxygen to support gamefish

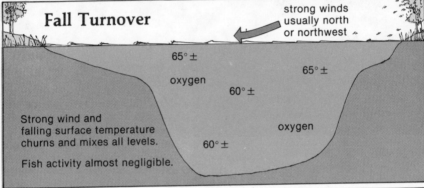

Fall Turnover

strong winds usually north or northwest

65°±

oxygen

65°±

60°±

Strong wind and falling surface temperature churns and mixes all levels.

oxygen

60°±

Fish activity almost negligible.

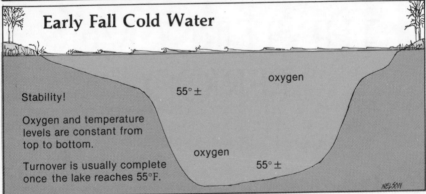

Early Fall Cold Water

oxygen

55°±

Stability!

Oxygen and temperature levels are constant from top to bottom.

oxygen

Turnover is usually complete once the lake reaches 55°F.

55°±

NELSON

In these waters, a thermocline condition usually remains in effect throughout most of the Summer Peak, Summer and Post-summer Periods. But during the tail end of the Post-summer Period, as the sun grows less direct, seasonal hard, driving, cold winds and rain begin chilling the surface temperature of the water very quickly. As the heavier (colder) water begins sinking, it comes in contact with the warmer water below. This action forces the lighter, yet warmer, deeper water back to the surface. Eventually, the narrow thermocline layer ruptures and a mixing or "turning over" process takes place. As the wind beats the water, the mixing action continues until it thoroughly homogenizes the water to a point where the whole body of water is the same temperature. This process also reoxygenates the deep water.

The actual Turnover process itself takes place once the thermocline layer has ruptured. But the turmoil that takes place usually adversely affects the fish for a period of time after this event actually occurs. Fishing doesn't pick up again until these conditions stabilize. In general, once the water temperature drops to about 55°F and the water clears perceptibly, cold water fishing patterns emerge.

Fishing during the Turnover Period on bodies of water that actually thermocline is tough, to say the least. However, since all bodies of water do not turn over at the same time, it is usually best to switch to waters which have already turned over—or bodies of water which have not yet begun to—or to waters which don't thermocline and turn over so drastically.

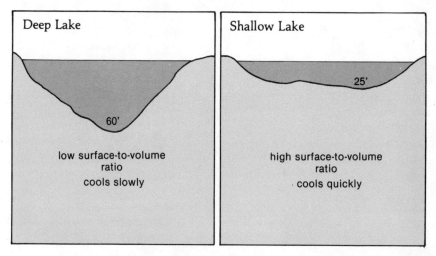

Small, shallow, dark, warm lakes turn over faster than big, deep, clear, cool ones. In a given area, some lakes could have turned over, others could be just turning over, and some might not have begun to. By being able to read the seasonal signs, and by knowing your lakes, it's possible to stay on active, big pike by moving to different waters.

After the Turnover, some big fish (usually in low numbers) can be caught up shallow. Basically, the Turnover Period is a time of turmoil when fish activity grinds to a halt, although action will pick up as conditions gradually stabilize.

Chapter 18
THE COLD-WATER PERIOD

"A Time of Stability"

During the Cold Water Period the water temperature drops to the lowest of the year. And the pike's metabolism follows. However, being the coolest of the cool, pike can be quite active as the cold water unlocks many barriers.

In lakes where small and intermediate-sized pike inhabit weedy flats in summer, the fish may now drop down and concentrate on steep drop-offs or move to deep flats. These areas are usually located near the deepest depths of the lake. In reservoirs, pike can gather around points. Drop-offs with forage hold the key to fish location.

Pike will hit a moving crankbait sharply in the early Cold Water Period, yet slow to prefer a jig-and-minnow or jig-and-waterdog "teasing" presentation by the end of the period. Thus, as the water cools, you should slow down your approach.

The Cold Water Period, however, is a time of stability. The combination of stability and cool water temperature make this the most consistent period of the entire year for catching big pike.

WHEN PIKE FISHING'S TOUGH . . .
THE TOUGH GUYS START JIGGING!

We love a tussle with a pike as much as anyone, and we're not fussy what technique puts 'em on our line. In fact, versatility—being able to employ a number of different techniques depending on the fishing conditions—is important to taking northern pike, or any fish, on a consistent basis.

Jigging techniques do more than "complement" traditional late-season pike fishing methods such as trolling big spinnerbaits or plugs, or casting spoons; jigging techniques "complete" a pike angler's arsenal. This features two commonly ignored techniques that tempt many pike during late summer and early fall. Our first option—"flippin' the dog"—is a new approach that we have used effectively. We call our second option the "do somethin'" approach. These techniques consistently bag big pike, no matter how everyone else is doing.

Jigging for pike isn't just a "fun" technique; it's productive. In fact, it may be the most consistently productive late-summer and fall pike technique, especially on lakes that are fished hard. The right jigging techniques allow you to take active and aggressive fish, as well as cautious individuals that are normally passed over with traditional methods.

It's been said, "that most of the fish (big ones, too) are in a neutral feeding mood, most of the time." Jigging is the best option available to trigger neutral pike.

Where are pike during late summer and early fall? Let's make that, where are a *majority* of pike during the late summer and early fall? All fish of a species seldom react alike at the same time. There may indeed be pike roaming open water at this time, but a good number of pike are usually weed-oriented by late summer. But there are weed areas, and then, there are weed areas!

Key weed types vary from one body of water to the next. But as a general rule, weeds should offer either: (1) overhead cover, heavy cover or both; and (2) distinct edges; or (3) areas with indistinct edges or scattered weeds, adjacent to areas of heavy weedgrowth or good overhead cover. The combination of these three characteristics looks and sounds perplexing, but isn't.

Overhead cover or heavy weedgrowth isn't so much for pike as it is for the baitfish that pike feed on. Heavy cover and/or overhead cover attracts prey species. In most lakes, the best overhead cover is provided by either pondweed species (*Potomageton* species: cabbage, especially broad leaf or tobacco cabbage) or coontail (*Ceratophyllum* species). In lakes which do not offer these weeds, any dense weedgrowth that provides a distinct edge that is located near deeper water may suffice.

Pondweed or coontail growth usually offers distinct inside and outside edges, and pockets usually form on weed flats. The area above thick weeds must also be considered an edge—a top edge.

Distinct edges are important to pike because of their body characteristics. Their long body type, and the fact that most of their fin surface is located at the tail, allows pike to move straight ahead with tremendous speed. But they are not readily able to change directions. Their eyes are also set far enough forward to have binocular vision, allowing them to accurately judge depth and distance. They are not, however, as adept as some fish at scanning 180°

Pike Mood Affects Pike Position and Our Presentation

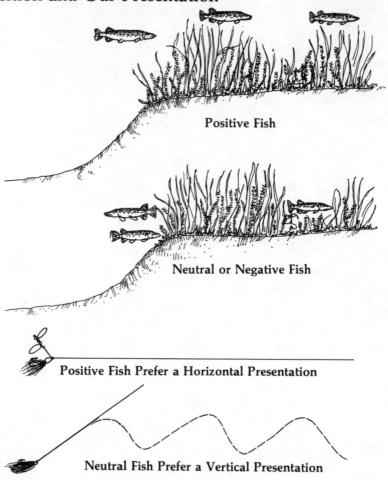

Positive Fish

Neutral or Negative Fish

Positive Fish Prefer a Horizontal Presentation

Neutral Fish Prefer a Vertical Presentation

Although the distinction isn't quite so clear-cut, we usually characterize fish as being in one of three moods: negative, neutral, or positive. All fish are not in the same mood at the same time, although a majority of fish may be in the same mood at the same time. Prime weather conditions, such as overcast or rainy days, offer the best chance for many pike to be active. Wind also helps, and early morning and evening are also prime pike activity periods on some lakes.

Active, aggressive, positive fish usually roam on top of flats or high along the outside edge of a weed breakline. Neutral fish, on the other hand, usually drop into weed pockets on a flat, or position tight to the outside edge of a weed breakline. Neutral or negative fish on the outside edge of weeds may be found anywhere along the weed face, and especially at the base of the weeds. Although nothing may activate negative fish, neutral fish are vulnerable to a properly presented bait.

Pike mood not only affects pike position, but also the way they prefer a bait to be presented. Basically, positive fish prefer lures to be presented horizontally, while neutral fish prefer a vertical or dropping presentation. Active fish love a trolled bait, but when they get the least bit turned off, as they are most of the time, a jigging presentation is far more productive!

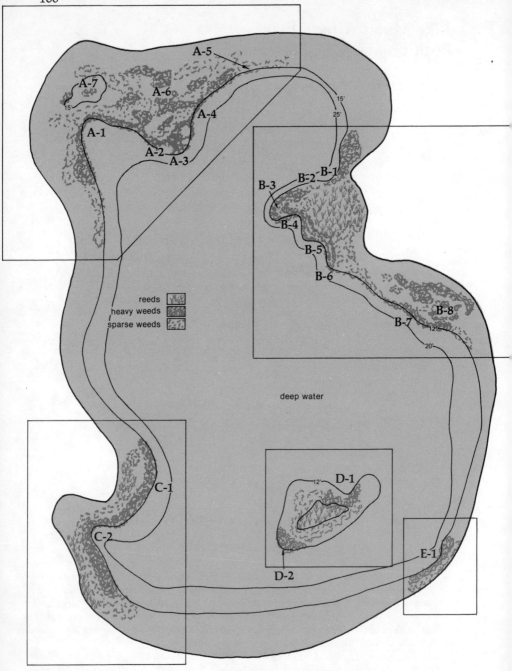

reeds

heavy weeds

sparse weeds

deep water

PIKE LOCATION DURING LATE SUMMER
AND EARLY FALL

Late summer and early fall pike location isn't a mystery. Let's use this lake map to make some key points about pike location. First, let's evaluate how AREAS A-E compare to one another.

The first priority for late summer and early fall pike fishing in natural lakes is weedgrowth. Generally, you can count on large bars with good weed cover to attract more pike than small bars. Using the criteria, "large bars with heavy weedgrowth draw the most fish," AREA A is best, followed by AREAS B, C, D, and E, respectively, in order of importance.

Of course, there's more to pike location than "large weedy bars draw the most fish." The total "edge area" offered by weedgrowth is equally, and perhaps more, important. Pike are ambush predators, and "edges" allow pike to practice ambush tactics effectively.

An edge is an area of change; it's where two different areas meet. Open water meeting the front face of weedgrowth (the outside edge) is an obvious edge. Other edges form on top of bars; for example, patchy weeds provide pockets and create additional edges. This is more attractive to pike than continuous, solid weedgrowth. Areas where heavy growth butts against thin growth also constitutes an edge. Actually, this edge concept isn't just important when you're fishing for pike; walleyes, muskies, crappies, bluegills and other fish are also drawn to edges.

We need to go one step farther, however. Once you identify a distinct edge, such as the outside edge of weeds facing deeper water, it's time to probe for less distinct edges along this larger edge. In essence, you're looking for "edges on edges." Say you were working along the front face of AREA A on the map. A-2 is an abrupt change, and constitutes an "edge on an edge." These areas tend to draw more pike.

Considering the "edge factor," AREA A is again our first choice. Not only are there nooks and crannies in the outside weed edge, but the adjacent flat offers plenty of patchy weedgrowth and many weed pockets. AREA B is our second choice, and then it's a toss-up between AREAS C or D.

Let's evaluate each area on our Pike Lake Map.

AREA A:

A-1—Pike make use of inside turns in bars or weedgrowth because these turns allow pike to use their ambush tactics effectively.

A-2—Distinct pockets that form inside turns draw pike. Just what you're probing for along the continuous face of a weedline.

A-3—Worth fishing, but weed points usually do not attract as many pike as inside turns.

A-4—The more distinct an inside turn, the better the chance that it'll hold fish. Not a great spot, but you'd fish it as you worked your way along the weedline.

A-5—Thin weedgrowth butted against heavy weedgrowth constitutes an edge that may attract pike. Worth spending a little extra time on.

A-6—A weed flat filled with pockets and alternate heavy and thin patches of weedgrowth will definitely attract a lot of pike. The standard approach to fishing A-6 is to troll large spinnerbaits over the top of the growth. That's fine when the fish are going strong! The jigging approaches detailed later will allow you to take fish more consistently, especially when things are tough—as they usually are!

A-7—A depression on a flat is a good area for pike to drop into when they're in a neutral mood. These spots almost always hold some fish.

AREA B:

B-1—An inside turn. Great!

B-2—A distinct edge. Great!

B-3—A weed and bar point. Usually not the best producer; however, the flat on top of the point looks great, and is small enough to be covered from a boat position outside the edge. The area between B-2, B-3 and B-4 has a big fish on it. Bet on it!

B-4—A good looking inside turn.

B-5—Ditto.

B-6—Same as A-5.

B-7—The front face is no great shakes, but should be covered.

B-8—A miniature A-6, and thus a good spot. B-8 isn't near an obvious point, and would probably be overlooked by many anglers. That's fine!

AREA C:

Fish Area C quickly, spending the bulk of your time on C-2.

AREA D:

D-1 should attract fish.

AREA E:

AREA E is a small spot that won't hold many fish. Such spots are likely to be bypassed by most anglers, however, and several such spots can make for an interesting day of fishing. Make a quick stop at E-1.

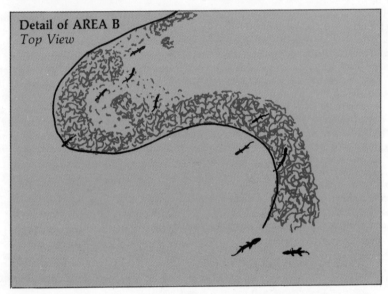

Detail of AREA B
Top View

Expect fish to be up on the flat, as well as along the front face of the weedline. Also, expect more fish to relate to inside turns as opposed to points.

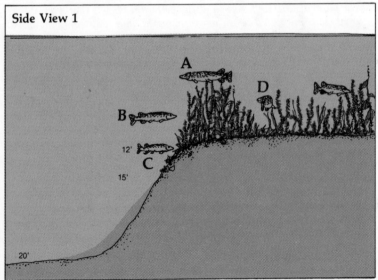

Side View 1

Fish relating to the outside edge of weedgrowth can be expected to ride high (A), be at any level along the front face (B), or lie at the base of the weeds (C). Although inactive pike often settle to the bottom, pike also feed aggressively in this area. High-riding pike up on flats (D) are usually active.

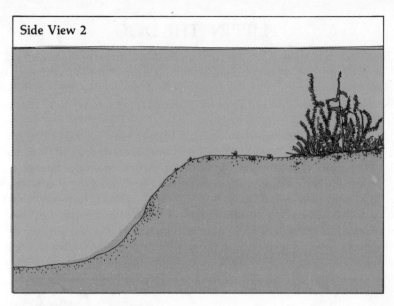

Side View 2

The weed condition found in Side View 1 is the premium condition for attracting pike. If possible, weeds should grow to the very edge of the drop-off. In eutrophic lakes, however, conditions found in Side View 2 may be all that's available. In that case, you can expect this weed edge to draw fish.

around them. These characteristics make the pike an ambush predator; thus they function best in open, unconfined water. Certainly pike roam with open water species such as ciscoes or whitefish. But other prey are usually concentrated near weeds. In order to survive, some pike function along the open-water edges of weedgrowth.

Obviously, then, distinct edges formed by heavy weedgrowth attract pike. But so does light weed cover, as long as it is near heavy cover which offers protection for, and draws, baitfish that occasionally filter into the light growth.

The largest, shallow bars with cover usually attract forage and pike. A look at a lake map will produce a starting point on most lakes. Of course, you want to motor around any point, flat or bar before fishing it to be sure it offers the proper weed cover.

While large bars normally attract many pike, smaller areas may receive less fishing pressure, and thereby hold nice fish. We suggest you start fishing along large bars, but don't pass up smaller areas—areas you're likely to pinpoint only after spending time on a body of water.

Is adjacent deep water important? Yes, there should be comparatively deeper water adjacent to the weed bars. But don't get carried away with this distinction; deeper water is almost always adjacent to fishable areas. It doesn't have to be the deepest water in the area, although such areas are definitely worth fishing because they offer a distinct edge. But distinct weed edges are where the best action is; and better if a weed edge is adjacent to a good drop-off.

Points usually play second-fiddle to *inside turns* on bars or in weedgrowth. Inside turns probably attract pike because they offer a confined area, allowing pike to practice their ambush tactics efficiently. Inside turns also act as funnels to push prey into a defined corner or area.

FLIPPIN' THE DOG

There's much to be said for standard jig fishing approaches for weed pockets and weed edges. But, as usual, a slight modification of a basic approach often produces better results. The most unique and productive jigging technique we've fished is a new, and pretty outstanding, technique we call "flippin' the dog."

"Flippin' the dog" translates to: using a flippin' stick to cast or flip a weedless, rubber-legged jig tipped with either pork, a waterdog, chub or sucker. This option'll do almost everything. You can work down the face of a weed edge, or vertically jig below the boat. Work it fast through or over pockets, or work slow and methodical. Even with all these options, however, this technique works best as a jig'n live bait method when pike are difficult, they way they are most of the time. Even a neutral pike has a hard time turning down a chub or sucker. And a juicy waterdog is the most deadly pike live bait we know of.

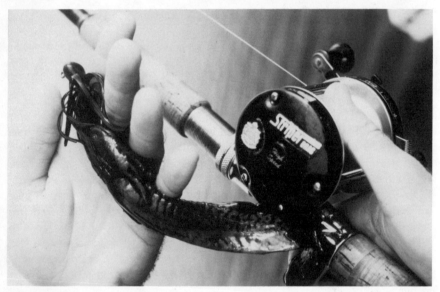

A Flippin' Goodie

A 7-inch dog. A rubber-legged jig. Frankly, waterdogs are great bait for walleyes, bass and pike, but dogs aren't always easy to obtain.

Why almost no one has been using a flippin' stick to present jigs to pike remains a mystery. The long rod (most flippin' sticks are 7½ feet long) allows you to swim jigs above weeds and work them in weed pockets much better than a standard rod. You can really stick it to a pike with the long rod, too; big fish that threaten to dive deep into the weeds are much easier to control with a flippin' stick. Last, but not least, it's great fun to battle a pike on a flippin' stick.

Let's make one thing clear. We're actually flipping baits only about 1/4 of the time. It's easy to make a short cast, say 30-60 feet, with 3/8 to 5/8 ounce jigs on 12 or 14 pound test line.

The reason we prefer using rubber-legged jigs with weed guards is because they work through weedgrowth so easily using the slower, less-aggressive retrieve employed with this approach. By far the best hooking jigs are those with flattened, oval heads. Rubber-legged jigs from the Arkie Bait Company and Blakemore Company are examples of good jigs. Many other companies offer outstanding jigs as well. Subdued colors such as black and brown have worked very well for us. Fluorescent-head rubber-legged jigs are better, if you can find them, or create your own by painting them.

If you can get waterdogs—the larval, gilled (aquatic) stage of the tiger sala-mander—by all means do so. They're tough—we often catch several pike per dog—and for who-knows-whatever-reason, pike can't resist them. Six to 8-inch dogs work well tipped on jigs. Just hook them up through the lips; don't bother to use a stinger hook, as bigger pike usually hit the head of the bait. Dogs larger than 8 inches become difficult to cast, although they flip OK. We admit that waterdogs have not been easy to obtain.

Chubs or suckers of 4-7 inches are a second option following waterdogs. "Meat" helps trigger extra fish, and a 4-7 inch bait adds size—often a "plus" during the late season. Pork that adds motion, such as the "Crawfrog" or "Flippin' Frog," is usually a third choice. However, if the fish are aggressive and you wish to fish fast, pork is a better option. Yet you may be better off fishing our next featured jigging option, the "do somethin'" approach, or tak-ing a standard trolling approach if the pike are really poppin'. The "flippin'" technique does it all, but really comes into its own when pike fishing is tough.

Let's work down a weed edge for pike. There are two of us in the boat; one of us is running it from the bow with a trolling motor and we've positioned the boat about 30 feet from the edge. To start, the bow angler's job is to cast up onto the weed flat and work the jig over the tops of the weeds, and into weed pockets, until it gets to the weed edge. At that point, he allows the jig to drop several feet, and then swims it back to the boat at about mid-depth.

By a swimming retrieve, we mean: Cast the jig out and count it down until it hits weeds. At this point, lift the jig (raise the rod tip to 1 or 2 o'clock), and reel to move the jig along. After you've reeled the rod tip from 3 o'clock to 1 o'clock, and moved the jig towards you about 6 feet, let it settle again, until it almost contacts weeds, before lifting again. Repeat the process. Of course, while you're doing this, there's nothing wrong with twitching (actually "nod-ding" would be more descriptive) the rod tip to give the jig extra action. But don't overdo it.

In the meantime, the stern angler flips or casts just beyond the edge. As soon as the jig hits the water, engage the reel and allow the jig to ride a tight line towards the bottom. Stop and lift the jig only if it contacts weeds or hits the bottom.

After the jig hits the bottom, your retrieve should be of two varieties de-pending on the mood of the fish. If they're fairly active, yet positioned somewhere near bottom, use a 2 or 3-foot lift, followed by a tight-line ride back to the bottom. The other alternative is to lift the jig off the bottom a mere 6 inches to a foot before letting it settle.

You may think both anglers should switch to fishing a particular way, say

172

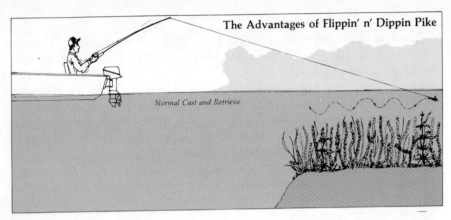

Advantage: *A long rod allows a more appealing swimming movement. It's possible to gently swim a lure into the tops of weeds and back out again, providing a better trigger for reluctant pike.*

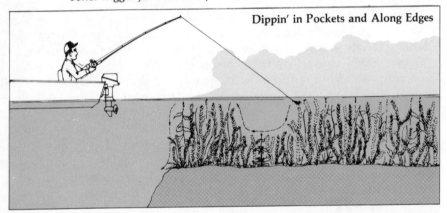

Advantage: *A long rod allows a more vertical fall, if that's what you want, as well as better control of what the jig's doing when it's in the pocket. The same's true of fishing the jig along the front face of weeds.*

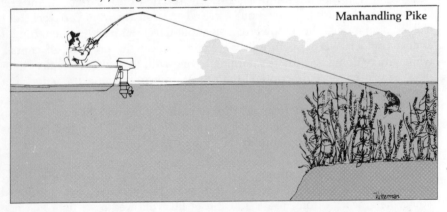

Advantage: *Fish this technique and you're going to tie into a good one. Big fish can bury in heavy cover and tear off. The extra "oomph" provided by the long rod helps keep this from happening.*

Two Basic Retrieves for Tough Pike

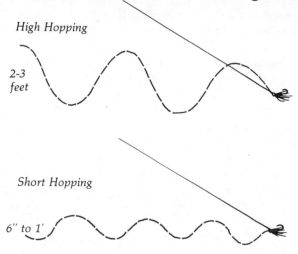

High Hopping

2-3
feet

Short Hopping

6" to 1'

"High hopping" or "short hopping" can be performed either: (1) above weeds, (2) in or through weeds, or (3) on the bottom. High hopping is accomplished by lifting the rod tip from 3 o'clock to about 1 o'clock, and then allowing the jig to settle a count or two as you reel the rod tip back to 3 o'clock. Watch your line for a telltale twitch. High hopping is for fairly active fish.

Short hopping is performed by holding the rod tip at about 2 o'clock, and just "nodding" the rod tip to about 1 o'clock. When a fish hits, drop the rod tip to 3 o'clock, and reel to tighten the line before sticking the pike. Short hopping is great for pike that are really turned off.

up onto the weed flat, if the bow angler catches several fish. Perhaps. Experience indicates, though, that pike aren't so easily patterned that way. Pike may be up on the weed flat, along the face of a weed breakline, or at the base of the weed breakline all at once. This technique is for tough pike fishing situations. If most of the fish are neutral, there are likely to be scattered fish. Active fish are easier to pattern.

What we're getting at is this: Both anglers should continue fishing their particular areas even if the other is presently catching a few more fish. Further down the weedline, things may change and the other angler may be into more fish. Keep fishing systematically, to thoroughly cover an area. If you tire of fishing over the weeds, switch assignments.

Your initial probing should take the form of moving slowly down an edge or over a flat, looking for fish. But if you contact fish on a particular area, don't just continue down the bar; use a controlled drift to go back through the area from another direction. Allow the wind to move the boat. As you drift, make directional changes by using the electric (or gas) motor.

Two anglers should still work as a team with each fishing a particular section of water. A common approach is for one angler to crawl a jig along the bottom, lifting it only six inches or so as you move along. The other angler should swim the jig several feet off the bottom.

THE DO SOMETHIN' RETRIEVE

The flippin' option is a great approach for pike, but there's something to be said for fishing faster at times. Enter the "do somethin'" approach to late-summer pike angling.

The old "weed doctor," Tony Portincaso, first showed us this retrieve more than five years ago; so it's not new. Indeed, the retrieve has enjoyed popularity in parts of Wisconsin and Illinois for many years. But alas, the rest of the country has neglected it. We haven't changed the retrieve; we've only given it a snappy name befitting the technique.

The "do somethin'" approach utilizes blank (no hair or other dressing) wedge-shaped swimming jigheads (3/8 and 1/2 oz.), as well as shad-head jigs (1/2 - 1 oz.) often used for striper fishing. The emphasis is on adding large

Do Somethin' Goodies

Do somethin' goodies for pike are larger and heavier than normal jigging lures. Taking the jigheads from left to right, heads 1 and 3 are Mister Twister shad heads in 1/2 and 1 oz. The second head is a 1 oz. swimming head made by Grassl Tackle Company. Head 4 is a saltwater jig of unknown origin and the last head is a homemade 3/8 ounce Pow-RR Head.

Now for the plastic dressings. Dressings 1, 2, 3, and 6 are creature bodies from the ZETAbait Lure Company. Number 4 is a 7-inch Mar-Lynn Reaper, and number 5 is a 4-inch Mister Twister Sassy Shad.

Thread the plastic baits onto the jighead, and add a touch of Super Glue to hold them securely in place.

plastic dressings such as the ZETAbait Ding-A-Ling, a 7½-inch creature body. These plastic bodies are threaded on to a jig hook and secured with a touch or two of Super Glue. Cementing a plastic body onto a jig lets you work it through weeds without having to rethread the plastic body back onto the jig after each cast.

Charley Brewer, a renowned Ozarks-area angler who developed the "slider jighead," also coined the term "do nothin'" retrieve to describe his approach to fishing his swimming jighead. We can't do justice to Charley's approach here; however, basically, Charley casts the slider jig out, counts it down to a certain depth and then ever-so-gently and easily swims the jig back in. The entire process is ever-so-delicate and tender.

The "do somethin'" retrieve is the opposite of Charley's "do nothin'" approach. Where the "do nothin'" retrieve is refined, the "do somethin'" is a rip-snortin' paradox. The emphasis, as mentioned before, is on fishing faster than usual. Instead of easing a cast out, fire out a line drive, quickly engage the reel, and count the jig down to a desired depth. Point the rod tip towards the lure (3 o'clock rod position) as opposed to holding the rod tip at 1:30 or 2 o'clock as is the practice with normal jigging retrieves. The retrieve is a combination of 4 or 5 rapid turns of the reel handle to make the jig scamper along, followed by a pause (no reeling), during which the jig darts toward the bottom on a tight line, followed by a quick pop of the wrist to free the lure of weeds. Return to step one. This process is repeated until the lure is near the boat.

The "do somethin'" retrieve is great for aggressive fish, but the retrieve's speed also acts as a triggering mechanism on neutral fish. We're frankly not sure whether the increased size of the bait has anything to do with triggering bigger fish. But we do know that a good weedline can be unsuccessfully fished by standard pike techniques, but going back through with the "do somethin'" retrieve will often trigger a fish or two.

Easily the best pike producer is the combination of any of three heads: the Grassl Swim Head, the Pow-RR Head, or the Mister Twister Shad Head, with a brown ZETAbait Ding-A-Ling creature body with a hot-orange tail. When this combo is run along or darts toward the bottom, the hot-orange beaver tail flaps madly from side-to-side. In order to kill the creature, pike almost always hit the head of the jig. A secondary color is a black-bodied creature with a pink tail, and a completely yellow creature is also an excellent producer in some lakes.

To handle jigheads larger than 1/2 ounce, use a stiff spinning rod preferably 5½ to 6 feet long. Heavier jigs call for 12 pound, or at times, 14 pound test line. Any reel that handles such heavy line should suffice. Screw the drag down tight, or you'll have trouble popping free of weeds. You can backreel a caught fish, loosening the drag after the initial hookset and run.

The "do somethin'" retrieve can be used over weed flats, but is typically a weed edge technique. Position the boat about 30 feet out from an edge with an electric motor. Cast about 30 feet up over the edge, and use the aforementioned retrieve procedure.

A STANDARD JIGGING APPROACH

Now that we've highlighted our two overlooked jigging techniques, let's review a standard jigging approach that has accounted for one-heck-of-a-lot of pike. Pitching a leadhead jig, dressed with a piece of pork, small chub or sucker, is still the standard by which other jigging techniques must be judged.

Using this standard approach is simple if you employ the right jig for the right purpose. For casting into weed pockets on weed flats, or up into a weed-line from a position outside the weedline and working the jig back through weeds, your best option is a jig with a swimming or standup head. The Lindy/ Little Joe Dingo Jig is a good example of a jig with a standup head. A good swimming jighead is the American Luresmith Jighead. Mister Twister's line of "Nature Jigs" also offers a Pow-RR head style jig dressed with bucktail. Carry an assortment of 1/4 and 3/8 ounce jigs, in gaudy (orange and chartreuse), subtle (yellow and green) and subdued (black or brown) colors.

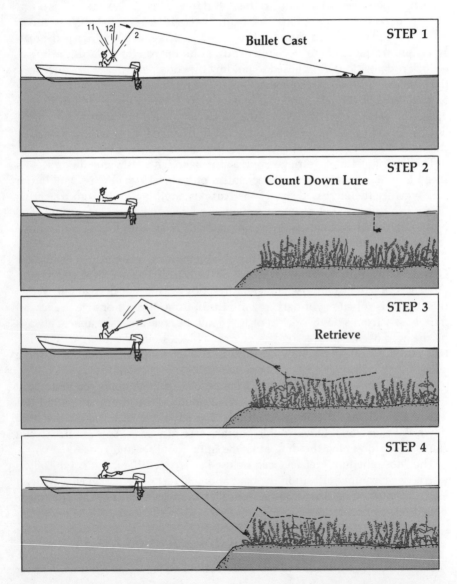

As mentioned, the most common dressings are pork or live bait such as chubs or suckers. Pork will take active, as well as neutral, fish. The best pike-fishing pork strips provide movement. Try Uncle Josh's No. 14 Flippin Frog, a U3 Twin Tail or a No. 25 Crawfrog. They all wiggle and kick attractively on the back of a swimming or falling jig.

When pike are extra tough to come by, switch from a pork attractor to a 3-4 inch chub or sucker. Live bait definitely helps attract hesitant (neutral or non-aggressive) pike.

The basic method of presentation for these baits is to cast them past the weed edge (up onto the flat) while the boat is positioned outside the breakline. Pike may position at the top of weeds, somewhere along the face of the weed edge, or at the base of the weed edge. You need to use retrieves that'll cover these various positions.

A common retrieve is to swim a jig, keeping it just above the weeds until nearing an edge. At that point, allow the jig to fall on a tight line until it contacts weeds. Using pork, you can vigorously snap a jig free of weeds and, in the process, often trigger pike. Don't pop the jig free quite so vigorously when using live bait.

This jigging technique is best executed with a stiff, 5½ or 6 foot spinning rod and reel combo loaded with 10 pound test line. A wire leader is a must for

The Do Somethin' Retrieve

STEP 1 *The "Do Somethin'" retrieve, a rip-snortin' approach to jig fishing weeds, starts with a bullet cast. Bring the rod tip back to the 11 o'clock position, and then quickly snap it forward with your wrist, stopping abruptly at 2 o'clock and snapping the wrist and rod tip back to 12 o'clock. The lure is now traveling close to the speed of light (give or take a little) towards your intended fishing spot. Now stop the lure so that it doesn't roll or create a fish-startling disturbance when it hits the water. You also want to get the rod tip to the 3 o'clock fishing position. That's because you're fishing a fairly heavy lure, and you must be ready immediately to begin the retrieve after the lure hits the water; otherwise it'll settle too far into weeds.*

After snapping your rod tip back to the 12 o'clock position, the line is shooting off the spool. When the lure is almost to the intended entry point, grab the line with your trigger finger, stopping the lure almost in mid-air. Then ease the rod tip from 12 o'clock to 3 o'clock, all-the-while putting tension on the lure and allowing it to drop easily. Done properly, the stop isn't too abrupt, the lure enters the water gently, and your rod tip ends at the 3 o'clock retrieve position. We can guarantee this: It's tougher to explain than it is to do.

STEP 2 *With your rod tip at 3 o'clock, count the lure down to an intended depth: "One thousand, two thousand," etc.*

STEP 3 *Scoot the lure along with 3, 4 or 5 quick turns of the reel handle. Allow the lure to settle (glide) towards the weeds—again, count the lure down—all-the-while watching your line for a telltale twitch (more like a jerk) that indicates a strike. If your lure contacts heavy weeds, you may need to pop it free with a quick and powerful snap of the rod tip (use your wrist and forearm, not your entire arm) back to 1 or 2 o'clock. Quickly reel in any slack and return the rod tip back to the 3 o'clock position. Resume your retrieve.*

STEP 4 *When you reach the edge of weedgrowth (that includes fishing pockets up on the flat), allow the lure to settle all the way to the bottom before alternately swimming it back to the boat.*

toothy pike, and we suggest making your own out of Berkley Sea Strand (38 pound test) and a good swivel. A Berkley Crosslock snap (size 10) can be used to attach the leader to the jig, but we suggest tying direct using a haywire twist to secure the leader to the hook eye. The leader should be about one foot long.

When fishing immediately outside a weed edge, employ any type of jighead, but still tip the bait with pork or a live chub or sucker. If we had to key on just one type of jighead for this fishing, however, we would choose a round jighead, preferably painted with a fluorescent color. A heavy-hooked Jack's Jig, tipped with a chub or sucker, fits the bill.

Standard jigging lures include (from left to right): Two American Luresmith Spin Rigs; a Mister Twister Nature Jig complete with a Pow-RR Head; a Lindy-Little Joe Dingo Jig; and two Jack's jigs, including a heavy-hook version on the right. Tip these standard baits with pork that provides movement: an Uncle Josh #14 Flippin Frog, a U3 Twin Tail, or a #25 Crawfrog. Switch to tipping with meat—3/4 inch chubs or suckers—when the fishing's tough.

We might as well focus on two colors—fluorescent orange and chartreuse—for a moment. Why pike in many (probably most) bodies of water are particularly attracted to these colors is not clear. Perhaps they see these colors best? For years, anglers observed that hot orange was particularly attractive to walleyes. Then came scientific confirmation of the walleye's ability to distinguish this part of the spectrum better than others. The colors often help attract pike and focuses their attention on the real object of their desire, the pork or meat on the back of the jig.

Round, fluorescent-headed jigs can be cast parallel to weed edges or into pockets, backtrolled along an edge, or fished with a controlled drift. One standard approach is to combine backtrolling with casting. The person running the boat in reverse, 30-50 feet off a weedline but parallel to it, casts to the weed edge, while the angler in the bow of the boat vertically jigs the drop-off.

Being armed with pike fishing techniques allowing you to trigger fish when others are having a hard time should motivate you. That's what these two overlooked jigging techniques are supposed to do, motivate you, and a whole lotta pike, too!

Chapter 19

WORLD CLASS PIKE

Plus

U.S. and CANADIAN RECORDS

Pike of 40, 50, 60—even 90 pounds! No need to pinch yourself! You're not dreaming! Without bass and muskies to divert them, European anglers are pike crazy—big pike crazy to be exact!

From the lochs of Scotland, the loughs of Ireland, the broads of Britain; from the shallow, poulder waters and canals of Holland; from the huge lakes and reservoirs and the gigantic, brackish Baltic Sea of the Scandinavian countries; from the pits, seas, and mountain lakes of Switzerland, Austria and Germany; from the marshes of Spain; from the Rivers Danube, Drau, and Rhine in Central Europe and Shannon, Avon and Stour in Great Britain; from a multitude of waters in Poland, Czechoslovakia, Bulgaria and even Russia; come legendary, monster pike!

Well, not really "legendary." Monstrous European pike are a fact! But there are plenty of authenticated records showing pike approaching 100 pounds taken on hook and line. Verifiable fish larger than the present 57 pound world record—bonafide 60 pound class fish—have been taken within the past few years! The European "Big Pike List" first compiled by Englishman Fred Buller didn't even include pike that weighed less than 25 pounds, and an updated list may exclude pike below 39 or 40 pounds!

Europe sports a wonderful diversity of lakes, rivers, reservoirs and streams. Admittedly, many European waters do receive heavy fishing pressure, but many of the waters are also huge and can take it! The brackish Baltic Sea between Finland and Sweden is gigantic! Sweden also has two lakes, Vänern and Vättern (reported 60 pound fish), approaching 100 miles long and 20-50 miles wide. And each European country except the smallest has waters of 5-15-25,000 or more acres, ranging from very shallow to 400 feet deep. Loch Lomond in Scotland (fish approaching 50 pounds) is 27 miles long and up to 5 or 6 miles wide.

While the Loch Ness monster is not a pike, Loch Ness is huge and does contain pike. For that matter, the Rivers Danube, Rhine or Shannon are no mere trickling brooks either. The River Shannon is almost 1/2 mile wide at Meelick, where pike approaching 50 pounds have been caught and a 90 pound fish was found dead.

Not that water size has much to do with huge European pike, mind you. Fifty pound fish have been caught from small sand pits. Anglers on Scottish swamps typically drag huge pike from drainage ditches only 50 feet wide!

So, the following is a listing of some of the world's largest pike. Notice that U.S. and Canadian pike do not enter the ranks until the fish drop below the 50 pound mark. The top of the list is dominated by Ireland. Perhaps this is a little bit of "Leprechaun" magic? Or could it be that Ireland hosts the finest trophy pike conditions in the world?

The Big Pike List of Europe and North America

WEIGHT lbs.	oz.	LOCATION	COUNTRY	DATE	METHOD
96		Broadwood Lake, Killaloe	Ireland	Unknown	Unknown
92		River Shannon	Ireland	1822	Lifted out
92		River Shannon	Ireland	1839	Unknown
90	8	Lough Derg	Ireland	1862	Trolling
90	plus	River Shannon	Ireland	1926	Found dead
78		Lake in County Clare	Ireland	1830	Rod and reel

75		Ilman Lake	USSR	1930	Live bait
72		Loch Ken	Scotland	1774	Live bait
70		Endrick River	Scotland	1934	Found dead
69	8	River Rhine	Germany	1850	Unknown
68		Llangorse Lake	Wales	1846	Spinning
65		Lough Derb	Ireland	1849	Unknown
65		Lower Lough Erne	Ireland	1880	Trolling
64		Lough Derb	Ireland	1856	Pitchforked
63		Lough Conn	Ireland	1875	Live bait
61	15	Vahojärvi	Finland	1944	Unknown
61	11½	Lynbi Lake	Denmark	1857	Unknown
61	11½	Vänern Lake	Sweden	1915	Unknown
61		River Bann	Ireland	1894	Clubbed
61		Derries Lough	Ireland	1948	Shot
60	10	Omutinsk Reservoir	USSR	1972	Spinning
60		Dowdeswell Reservoir	England	1896	Found dead
59	½	Lake nr Hamburg	Germany	1978	Spinning
58	6	Grarup Lake	Denmark	1929	Jug fishing
56	3½	Sâkyhan Pyhajarvi	Finland	1905	Unknown
56		Lough Erne	Ireland	1885	Jug fishing
56		Drum Lough	Ireland	1894	Lifted out
55	15¾	Lipno Reservoir	Czechoslovakia	1979	Live bait
55	4	Günzstaus Lake	Germany	1975	Found dead
55		Lough Gur	Ireland	1909	Otter board
53	11	Lough Sheelin	Ireland	1901	Shot
53	9¼	Lake nr Darmstadt	Germany	1981	Unknown
53	5½	Feld near lake	Austria	Unknown	Unknown
53	4	River Nida	Poland	1976	Live bait
53		Tomgraney Lake	Ireland	1881	Rod and reel
53		Lough Mask	Ireland	1898	Trolling
53		Lough Key	Ireland	1900	Trolling
53		Lough Conn	Ireland	1920	Trolling
52	14½	Keurafjarden Lake	Finland	1912	Spinning
52	4	Sieversschen pit	Germany	1971	Live bait
52		Whittlesea Mere	England	1851	Beached
52		Lough Macnean	Ireland	1898	Spinning
51	12¾	River Drau	Austria	1974	Live bait
51	7¼	Kuivajärvi Lake	Finland	1953	Unknown
51	2¼	Klopeiner Lake	Austria	1976	Live bait
51	2¼	Bundia Marshes	Spain	Unknown	Unknown
50	12	Irr Lake	Austria	1978	Live bait
50	8	Lough Mask	Ireland	1966	Netted
50	2½	Tyrifjorden Lake	Norway	1976	Trolling
50		Duke of Newcastle's Lake	England	1823	Choked
49	14	Loch Alva	Scotland	1784	Live bait
49	10	Mälaren Lake	Sweden	1973	Spinning
49	9½	Baltic Sea	Lapland	1954	Netted
49	9½	Unterbacher Lake	Germany	1972	Live bait
49	6	Hörhäuser gravel pit	Germany	1977	Spinning

49		Lake Tschotagama	Canada	1890	Unknown
49		Lough Derg	Ireland	1838	Unknown
48	13½	Old River Rhine	Germany	1973	Rod and line
48	11½	Vihti Lake Region	Finland	1894	Unknown
48	8	Maaninka Lake Region	Finland	1942	Netted
48	8	Gravel pit	Denmark	1952	Spinning
48	8	Moat of Wickrather	Germany	1968	Rod and line
48	8	River Juutuanjoki	Lapland	1969	Plug fishing
48	8	Vesjoloskoje Reservoir	USSR	1977	Unknown
48	8	Weikerl Lake	Austria	1977	Live bait
48	8	Baltic near Tammisaari	Finland	1979	Plug fishing
48	5	Unknown	Denmark	1970	Plug fishing
48		Morira River	Canada	Unknown	Unknown
48		Furnace Pond	England	1830	Beached
48		Lough Corrib	Ireland	1905	Gaffed
48		River Camlin	Ireland	1910	Unknown
48		Lough Corrib	Ireland	1961	Nightlining
48		Lough Mask	Ireland	1958	Netted
47	11	Loch Lomond	Scotland	1945	Live bait
47	6¼	Unknown	Denmark	Unknown	Unknown
47	6	Öyeren Lake	Norway	1976	Plug fishing
47	4	Unknown	Sweden	Unknown	Unknown
47	4	Greyerzer Lake	Switzerland	1978	Live bait
47		River Peene	E. Germany	1969	Rod and line
47		Near Duisburg	Germany	1911	Netted
47		Summer Castlelake	England	1799	Beached
47		Lough Sheeling	Ireland	1896	Unknown
46	13	Vannsjø Lake	Norway	1975	Spinning
46	4¾	Murten Lake	Switzerland	1965	Spinning
46	2	Sacandaga Reservoir	USA	1940	Plug fishing
46		River Inn	Austria	1909	Speared
46		Rozstepniewo Lake	Poland	1970	Live bait
46		Chillington Pool	England	1822	Unknown
46		Lough Mask	Ireland	1957	Netted
45	12	Basswood Lake	USA	1929	Rod and line
45	8	Hohenwarte Reservoir	E. Germany	1971	Rod and line
45	8	Kriebstein Reservoir	E. Germany	1971	Rod and line
45	8	Lough Conn	Ireland	1917	Trolling
45	7	Unknown	Norway	1977	Plug fishing
45	4	Schlier Lake	Germany	1979	Netted
45	3¼	Pit at Höxter-Fodelheim	Germany	1961	Found dead
45	3¼	Platten Lake	Hungary	1968	Rod and line
45	3¼	Kärtner Lake	Austria	1971	Rod and line
45	3	Öyeren Lake	Norway	1976	Plug fishing
45		Windermere	England	1813	Dragged out

45	Loch Leven	Scotland	1880	Unknown
45	Lough Lene (Westmeath)	Ireland	1956	Unknown
45	Lough Conn	Ireland	1957	Netted
45	Lough Corrib	Ireland	1965	Long lining

U.S. and Canadian Northern Pike Records

STATE	WEIGHT lbs.	oz.	DATE
Alaska	38		1978
Alabama	No record		
Arizona	24	3	1981
Arkansas	16	1	1973
California	No record		
Colorado	30	1	1971
Connecticut	29	0	1980
Delaware	No record		
Florida	No record		
Georgia	18	2	1982
Hawaii	No record		
Idaho	27	5.28	1982
Illinois	22	12	1976
Indiana	26	8	1972
Iowa	25	5	1977
Kansas	24	12	1971
Kentucky	9	8	1981
Louisiana	No record		
Maine	10	8	1982
Maryland	19	8	1979
Massachusetts	29	3	1979
Michigan	39		1961
Minnesota	45	12	1929
Mississippi	No record		
Missouri	18	9	1975
Montana	37	8	1972
Nebraska	29	3	1976
Nevada	27		1978
New Hampsh.	20	9	1978
New Jersey	30	2	1977
New Mexico	36		1974 & '78

STATE	WEIGHT lbs.	oz.	DATE
New York	46	2	1940
No. Carolina	No record		
North Dakota	37	8	1968
Ohio	22	2	
Oklahoma	36	8	1976
Oregon	No record		
Pennsylvania	33	8	1980
Rhode Island	24	12	1980
So. Carolina	No record		
South Dakota	35		1972
Tennessee	10	13.6	1982
Texas	18	4.5	1981
Utah	19	2	1982
Vermont	30	8	1977
Virginia	22	9	1976
Washington	18	6	1980
West Virginia	16	.77	1982
Wisconsin	38		1952
Wyoming	22	8	1982

PROVINCE	WEIGHT lbs.	oz.	DATE
Brit. Columbia	No record		
Alberta	37	8	1974
Saskatchewan*	42	12	1954
Manitoba	42	7½	1977
Ontario	42	2	1946
Quebec	49		1890

*No official listing of fish caught since 1975

Chapter 20

GREAT LAKES PIKE

The Great Lakes provide a unique environment for trophy northern pike. With the possible exception of the Missouri River reservoir system, no place in the United States even comes close to growing big pike like the Great Lakes. The bountiful food supply, cool water and wide-open spaces add up to lunker northerns. If you're looking for a trophy pike within the U.S., *this* is the place to go.

Northern pike are actually quite common throughout much of the Great Lakes. They spawn in shallow sloughs and inhabit rivers, canals, bays and small lakes connected to the big water. A few people make the effort and take some giants by casting spoons in marsh areas in April and May. But when the water warms and the northerns disappear from the shallows, so do the pike anglers. A surprised salmon fisherman may tie into a 15- or 20-pounder once in a great while, but that's about it until next spring.

Well, not quite. There's a very rare breed of cat that fishes the bays in September, October and November. His buddies are all out chasing muskies or sitting in duck blinds. He weaves his small boat through the marina, dodging the big salmon rigs as they head out into the fog. Instead of following them, though, he suddenly veers 90° and begins to parallel the shore, looking for, of all things, *weeds!*

THE FALL MOVEMENT

Weeds? In the Great Lakes? You're kidding!

Nope! Take the time to cruise the water 15 feet and shallower in the adjacent bays, canals or rivers sometime. You'll be surprised. What you thought was strictly rock may turn out to be thick, healthy stands of green cabbage weeds. It almost looks like the shoreline of an inland lake. And, since it looks like one, it stands to reason that these areas might function like an inland lake. As a matter of fact, they do to a large extent. Many bays serve as small, cool water environments attached to the huge, cold main lake.

These weedy areas hold some northern pike all summer long, although generally not the gigantic ones. Once the water warms above the high 50°F's in the spring, the big pike—the 12 pound plus bruisers—seem to disappear. Exactly where they go is open to contention. Some are caught suspended *slightly* out into the bays—not way out with the salmon, but still somewhat out into

the cooler water just outside the warmer shorelines. You'll also catch an occasional good summer pike *in* the weeds, but they're generally skinny, with a sunken stomach that suggests inactivity. Sure, you occasionally get a wind switch that blows unusually cold water into the bays, and all of a sudden you may catch a couple of big pike until conditions return to normal. But all in all, it's usually tough to tie into a large concentration of good pike in summer.

As the summer wanes and turns into fall, a mysterious change occurs. The big pike suddenly appear from out of nowhere. It's like somebody threw a switch. All of a sudden, they're there to stay. You can catch them all the way until freeze-up.

We've discussed this situation with a number of authorities and feel that the best explanation lies in a combination of *temperature* and *food*. For one, this in-shore movement doesn't hit high gear until the water drops to about the 50°F mark—well within the comfort range of big northern pike.

Secondly, the appearance of the big pike generally coincides with a definite in-shore movement of several varieties of suspended baitfish. Scout outside the edge of the weeds with your depth finder and you'll spot large concentrations of small suspended fish. Once the food comes in, the big guys aren't far behind. When they move in and join the resident pike, you have a cold water aggregation that you have to see to believe.

The difference between the two types of fish is like night and day. A resident weed fish is usually long and thin. An open-water fish—outside of obviously being downright huge—is built thick and deep. There's no comparison. It's been eating high-fat herring, smelt, alewives or maybe even a small trout or two, and it shows. It's not unusual for an open-water fish to weigh 15 or even 20% more than a resident weed fish of the same length!

SPECIFIC LOCATION

Almost without fail, one particular type of structural element is *the* classic fall northern pike spot: a sharp inside turn in the deep weedline where an area of healthy green weeds borders a fast drop to deep water. The combination of

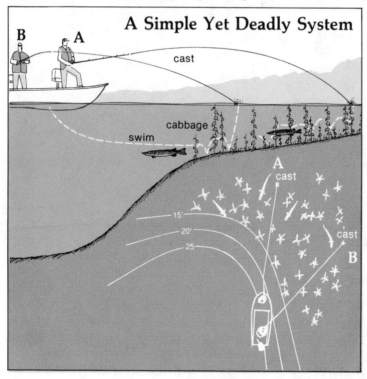

A Simple Yet Deadly System

Position the boat just outside of the deep weedline and pitch the jig up inside the weeds. Let it fall until it hangs up in the weeds, and then give the rod an upward wrist snap to get it moving. Use a slow swim-and-drop retrieve, brushing the weeds whenever possible.

Once the jig clears the weeds, swim it slowly back to the boat. Northerns are born followers, and they're liable to grab the minnow at any time. We've had 15 lb. fish splash at the boat, and even had one nail an unattended jig that was hanging over the side of the boat and pull the whole works overboard!

Don't forget—a big pike will often swim right at you. Keep setting the hook and taking up the slack. It's easy to get fooled into thinking you've got a small "hammer-handle" on. Even a 20 pounder will sometimes come in like a lamb and then take off like a lion once it reaches the boat. But if you get a decent hook set and don't give 'em any slack, you'll almost always catch the fish—no matter how big!

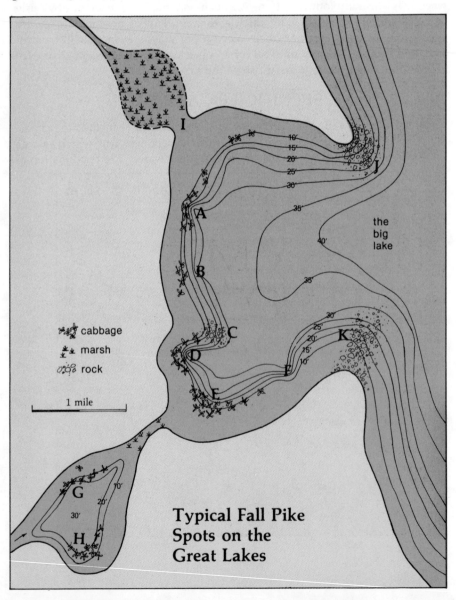

Typical Fall Pike Spots on the Great Lakes

There are basically two characteristics that must be present in a bay of the Great Lakes for it to support a northern pike population. First, it must have a marshy spawning area, such as **Area I**. This is usually found in conjunction with a river. Secondly, the bay must have a flatness to it. A gorge with 80 feet of water and no shallow weedgrowth simply isn't going to support northerns. A bay like this, with a significant amount of water shallower than 15 feet, is a good candidate. Add the spawning sloughs, and you've got a pike hot spot.

Sharp inside turns in a healthy weedline, with immediate access to deep water, are gold mines. Both baitfish and big pike stack into areas like **A and D**. Spots like these may be a mile or two apart, but they're well worth the ride!

Area B, by comparison, is only so-so. The sharp corner lies considerably outside the weedline, and although a few fish may cross the intermediate area, it's only a "maybe." **Area E** is even less desirable—good weeds but only a mild corner and a gradual taper.

Area F features a sharp corner and fast drop-off. Baitfish may stack into such corners like crazy, but because there are no weeds present, it'll probably attract very few pike.

Area C is a rock/gravel point. No weeds—no northerns. It might, however, attract walleyes and smallmouth bass. As a rule of thumb, you almost never catch giant northerns and walleyes from exactly the same spot. They may be separated by 80-100 yards, but they won't be side-by-side. Who says that walleyes and smallmouth aren't smart?

Note the smaller lake at the lower left. It's attached to the big lake by a river. This is a real sleeper. Connected waters like this often draw trophy northerns in from the big lake during the fall. Find the same type of sharp, steep, weedy corner (**Area G**), and you've got a real winner. It also gives you a good place to get out of the wind when the bay is rough. **Area H**, on the other hand, has a slow taper and probably isn't worth the effort.

Areas J and K are too barren to be pike spots, but they're worth discussing. In cold Lake Superior, these would be strictly trout/salmon territory. The other four Great Lakes have much warmer average temperatures, and these spots could also attract walleyes and smallmouth, in addition to seasonal use by trout and salmon. It all depends on the environment. But regardless of where you are, these bays are usually teeming with some species of fish almost all year long!

these three elements—the turn, the weeds, and the drop—are dynamite. Omit one of them and you have a *potential* spot. Omit two and you usually have a poor producer. But put all three together and chances are you have a real winner. The accompanying illustration depicts several typical cold water pike situations you're likely to encounter.

Interestingly enough, the northerns are not always directly *on* the deep weedline, but are often *slightly up* into the weeds. In this instance, a trolling approach along the weedline doesn't do the trick. When they're up inside the weeds, you must go after them—by casting.

In our experience, a jig and minnow combination is the #1 lure for this condition. The water is fairly cold, and the pike don't seem to want to *chase* a crankbait or spinnerbait all that much. Yes, we've caught fish with them, but the overwhelming superiority of the jig and minnow makes it questionable to fish anything else.

The basic rig consists of a ¼-⅜ ounce wedge-shaped, Pow-rr head jighead, wire leader and a 5-8 inch chub. The triangular pointed shape of the jighead slides through sparse weeds with a minimum of hang-ups. The wire leader is a 12-inch section of 38 pound test Berkley Seastrand or Weller Tough Stuff *solid* stainless steel wire, and is very easily constructed by attaching the wire to the jighead with a haywire twist. The other end is a #7, heavy-duty barrel swivel, to minimize line twist and provide an easy tie-on point.

Chubs are definitely your #1 bait if they're available. Simply hook them up once through the bottom jaw and out the top of the head. They're so tough they'll stand up to the punishment of casting far better than a sucker—and infinitely better than a fragile shiner. In fact, if the weeds are sparse, you may be able to hook the chub through the lips and keep it in a live, fish-attracting state for hours.

Quickly scout the edge of the first drop-off with your depth finder, looking for the presence of inside turns, healthy weeds and a sharp drop-off. As we said, two out of three might be a good spot, but find all three together and it's slimin' time!

Position the boat slightly outside the deep edge of the weeds and use your electric motor (or outboard if it's windy) to slowly creep along the edge. Pitch a short cast up *into* the weeds and let the jig sink to the bottom, or until it settles onto a weed stalk. Tighten up the slack, and give the rod a "pop" by snapping your wrists up and back. This will usually clear the jig from the weeds and send it scooting along, swimming and slowly sinking. Take up the slack, and keep your rod tip low so you'll be in position to set the hook.

Be ready at all times. Big pike tend to follow the jig and *then* hit it. The trouble is, they continue swimming *toward* you. It's a real panic trying to set the hook and take up the slack line all at the same time. But you must. Eventually, fish come near the boat, and perhaps under the boat, and then take off like a streak for deep water. It's scary! You never know if it's a junior or a giant until it gets up close.

Either have a dependable drag, or be prepared to backreel like crazy. You *cannot* stop the first run of a big northern no matter how heavy your tackle is. Let it complete the run, and then slowly pump it in again. Be prepared for more runs and other sneaky tricks. A big northern is never in until it's in.

We started out using heavy spinning rods and 14 pound test monofilament line for this style of fishing. It's a real toe-to-toe, wrist-aching battle. We know others who use casting gear and about 17 pound test line. The ultimate pike rig, however, is probably a 7½ foot Flippin' Stik loaded with 20 pound test line. It's very easy to snap the jig free of the weeds with a simple flick of the wrist, and the hook-setting, fish-fighting power is awesome.

We once learned a valuable lesson by experimenting with a spinning rod that was *too stiff*—a super-stiff musky rod blank tied up into a spinning rod. We thought we were being clever. As it turned out, we outsmarted ourselves. The rod was so stiff that it was difficult to keep a distinct bend in the rod on a hooked fish. As we said before, it's sometimes tough to get a good initial hook-set on a fish that swims directly at you. By not keeping a tight enough line, several good fish were able to shake their heads and get enough slack to throw the jig. Our normal 95% hooking ratio suddenly plummeted to 50%. It was quite a shock, since under normal conditions you almost *never* lost a fish using this method properly. We finally went back to lighter tackle and started hooking fish again. Later, the Flippin' Stik became our standard. The moral is, feel free to use a heavy spinning rod, but stay away from the pool-cue variety!

Using this system, we've taken a good number of Great Lakes pike *over* 20 pounds, but are still looking to crack the elusive 30 pound barrier. We know it can be done. And, best of all, there are usually few, if *any*, other fishermen to contend with. That's perhaps the best part of all—being on big fish and having the spots all to yourself. If you're adventuresome, the following areas are excellent places to put this system into action.

GREAT LAKES

LAKE SUPERIOR

LAKE MICHIGAN

LAKE HURON

LAKE ONTARIO

LAKE ERIE

GREAT LAKES PIKE LOCATIONS

With the exception of the shallow western basin of Lake Erie, most of the deep, open water of the Great Lakes is salmon or trout country. However, there are many localized pike populations at the mouths of rivers, and in the shallower waters of the bays, rivers and connecting adjacent small lakes. These areas function as smaller, warm or cool water environments connected to huge, cold water ones. Some of these sections are tiny and provide only a very limited pike fishery; others are quite large, such as: the St. Louis River estuary and Chequamegon Bay of Lake Superior; portions of Green Bay in Lake Michigan; huge Lake St. Clair, and the Detroit and St. Clair Rivers between Lake Huron and Lake Erie; and the Thousand Islands/Bay of Quinte region of Lake Ontario.

Because of their great diversity, and commercial fish exploitation (past and present), the fishing potential of each Great Lakes pike area must be judged on a case-by-case basis. The local habitat (or environment) will determine how numerous a given pike population can become. In some areas, for instance, dams have cut pike off from their spawning sloughs, and pike populations have been severely diminished.

Perhaps the best advice to fishing Great Lakes pike is *not* to be intimidated by what may at first appear to be "unusual" conditions. The fact is, besides the size of the waters, there is nothing very much out of the ordinary involved. Pike relate to humps, points, weedbeds, etc., just like they do in smaller inland waters. The fishing methods are much the same as in inland waters. True, the larger bays are *large*, yet they're no more imposing than fishing big waters like Lake Winnibigoshish in Minnesota or Lake of the Woods in Ontario. In most cases, you can usually use the same types of larger boats you use on inland waters.

The accompanying maps list some of the better-known and documented pike fisheries of the Great Lakes. We've included a brief description of each general area, a note on the general structural conditions and some of the more popular methods used. In most cases, the fishing situations and techniques are commonly used in other waters and are fully described in other chapters of this book.

Most of the areas identified here are at the mouths of rivers. The reason for this is that most pike are taken in and around these areas in spring and fall. However, little work has been done in late spring, summer, and early fall in the lake areas adjacent to these rivers. To date, little is known about pike movement outside the rivers themselves. Only future investigation will un-cover some of the mysteries of where the big pike from each of these "return" areas go, and what they do after they leave the rivers.

LAKE SUPERIOR

Of the five Great Lakes, Lake Superior probably has the least number of pike relative to its overall size. Yet it seems to produce the biggest fish. Where populations have developed, lunkers (sometimes numbers of them) are available.

The general makeup of Lake Superior, with its fast-dropping, granite-walled, very cold (mostly weedless) shorelines is not that hospitable for pike. Most of the north shore (with the exception of the Thunder Bay area) has this kind of makeup, and simply does not provide the proper environment for pike development. Therefore, most of the pike potential occurs in pockets along the south shore.

In some of the bay areas along the south shore where weedgrowth and marsh exist (and offer good spawning and rearing areas), localized populations of very big pike can develop. However, in areas like Chequamegon Bay, development and plain old exploitation have taken their toll, and the pike population is a mere remnant of what it was—or could be. This is true of Thunder Bay and Black Bay as well.

Unlike some of the other Great Lakes, Lake Superior has few connecting smaller lakes. Therefore, most of the pike fisheries are in the backs of large bays which periodically function as warm or cool water environments, as op-posed to strictly very cold ecosystems. It's here that pike are generally found.

Most of the incoming streams and rivers which enter Lake Superior at points other than the bays are narrow, rock-bound, very cold, have little weed-growth, and are very short and shallow (before a falls or a large rapids occurs). These are hardly pike spawning and rearing grounds.

Available and conducive prey (for pike) is also a problem over large areas of Lake Superior—especially for pike in the small and intermediate size ranges. Except for the warmer bay sections, there is generally little select prey for these

smaller fish. Therefore, even if big fish can "hack it" in this harsh environment, so few fish make it to the big size that populations simply don't develop.

Unlike some areas of the other Great Lakes, Superior's pike areas are not
very extensive, and conditions allow fish little opportunity to range very far
from their home grounds. In most cases, five miles or so in each direction is
probably as much as the fish might travel. Nonetheless, some of these bays are
very large, and contain various different pike groups.

The accompanying map lists Lake Superior's major pike areas. There are
probably several "sleepers" in other bay and river mouth areas as well. Fall is
the best time to hunt the lunkers, although big fish are also taken in the Pre-
spawn and Pre-summer Periods. For you fish eaters, Lake Superior pike are
perhaps the finest-eating northerns found anywhere on earth!

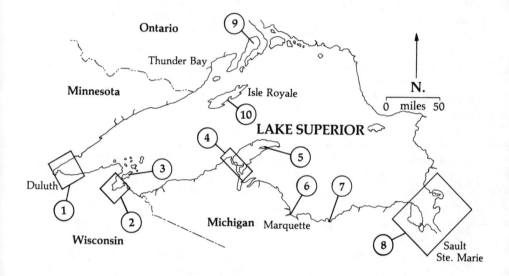

1. St. Louis River/Duluth Harbor/Superior Entryway: A very good, underfished pike opportunity. In early spring, many fish spawn in Pokegama Bay.
In summer, the pike spread out into the lake. A rare, early-summer, big pike
fishery is available. Big fish are often caught off the breakwaters.

2. Chequamegon Bay: It's not what it was in the early days, but there are
still big fish to be had. With the introduction of salmon and trout, pike are
quite ignored, and the big fish population is building.

3. Madeline Island: A limited but totally unexploited big pike fishery.

4. Keweenaw Waterway: A prime big pike fishery. However, a health ad-
visory recommends you not eat any fish from these waters. It's strictly catch
and release.

5. Bete Grise Bay: Limited but unexploited fishing (some real lunkers).

6. Marquette/Dead River/Presque Isle Harbor: Limited fishery.

7. Munising/Au Train Bay: This entire section holds some big pike (and
muskies, too). The opportunities are here for those willing to work for them.

8. Batchawana/Goulais/Tahquamenon Bays: Big pike, and some very large
muskies, too!

9. Thunder/Black/Nipigon Bays: Commercial fishing has taken a big chunk out of this area's potential. However, a fishery does exist, although the real lunkers don't seem to be present. Perhaps the water quality is unfavorable.

10. Isle Royale: A big pike fishery exists here for those in-the-know. You can bring a car and boat to the island via ferry. Plan to do plenty of exploring.

LAKE MICHIGAN

Lake Michigan probably sustains the best overall population of good-sized northern pike of all the Great Lakes. In fact, localized populations have not been as adversely affected by the plagues of damming (that prevent pike from getting to marsh areas), eradication of marsh areas by development, pollution, intense angler exploitation and commercial overharvest (in years past). Lake Michigan also offers the greatest amount of beneficial pike habitat.

Some areas house anything from very limited, but good-sized fish opportunities, to very respectable amounts of good-sized fish. The map is also only meant as a guide to the most probable areas. Sleeper sections also exist.

We do not know the extent of summertime dispersal from the mouths of rivers or marsh areas out into the bays and more distant shoal areas. However, tagged fish have been known to move as much as 15 miles and more from points of capture.

The structural makeup of some of these areas is so diverse and complex that the interested pike angler must actually go to each area, get local maps, do his own reconnaissance and ferret out the best areas for himself. Keep in mind that the best, consistent pike action has been recorded in fall. Big, pre-spawn fish have also been taken in spring, but seldom in numbers.

1. Green Bay: A huge area, but fish of all sizes are here. Many trout anglers trolling along the east shore catch as many pike as trout in fall. Maps and work will pay off.

2. Little and Big Bay de Noc: Historic lunker pike areas. There are good-sized fish, plus some trophies to be had. Again a large area, but work (in fall) with live bait can pay huge dividends.

3. Little and Big Traverse Bay: Not a great pike fishery—but not a bad one either. There are pike at the back ends of the bays.

4. Washington Island: The majority of pike are in and around the areas of Detroit and Jackson harbors. Some big fish can be had here.

5. Mink River/Rowley Bay: Two of the authors have caught several huge pike here in early spring (pre-spawn) trolling for brown trout at ice-out. This is an excellent area that could produce numbers of big pike in fall.

6. Various Creeks and Shoals Between Whitefish Point and Baileys Harbor: These areas put up pike—and some big ones—but in limited numbers and spread out in distance.

7. Sturgeon Bay: The bay supports many small and medium-sized fish, as well as some lunkers. The best lunker time is very early ice-out and fall. Spring is small fish time.

8. Stony Creek: Pike are here in early spring.

9. Ahnapee and Kewaunee Rivers: A significant number of fish spawn in these two rivers in spring. Small and intermediate-sized fish probably stay in the main parts of the rivers all year. However, most larger fish move out to

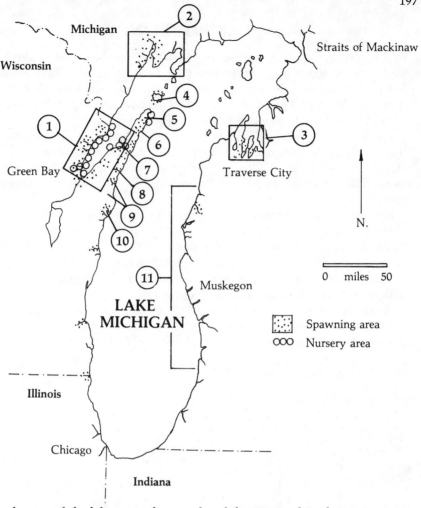

Michigan

Wisconsin

Straits of Mackinaw

Green Bay

Traverse City

N.

0   miles   50

Muskegon

LAKE
MICHIGAN

Spawning area
Nursery area

Illinois

Chicago

Indiana

shoal areas of the lake or to the mouths of the rivers when the waters warm.

10. East and West Twin Rivers: This area has surprisingly overlooked pike potential, and there are lots of intermediate and good-sized pike. Fish stage in the rivers at ice-out. It is very possible that larger-sized fish move to the river mouths or adjacent shoal areas in summer. Extensive fall fishing is yet to be worked to any degree here. Maybe a sleeper.

11. Lower Michigan's Western Coastline: Small lakes connected to the big lake by canals or rivers dot Michigan's west coast, and most attract pike. Some have small and intermediate-sized fish—others a few lunkers. The big fish probably move out into the big lake in summer if the lake, canal or river does not offer cool enough water. Each area must be judged on a case-by-case basis. Some of the better areas are:

A) Manistee River (and lake)
B) Marquette River (and lake)
C) Muskegon Lake (and canal)
D) Grand River (Spring Lake)
E) Macatawa River (and lake)
F) Kalamazoo River (Saugatuck Harbor)

LAKE HURON

For pure numbers of good-sized and lunker northern pike, Lake Huron ranks second to (or maybe even in a close tie for first with) Lake Michigan. While there are not as many different places to fish as in Lake Michigan, the spots that do support pike put out numbers of good-sized fish. With the advent of salmon and trout, pike are indeed underfished.

Like all the Great Lakes, Lake Huron has changed markedly in character in the last 100 years. Destruction of habitat (including pike spawning and rearing areas), lowered water quality and commercial exploitation have all left their mark. Still, northern pike populations persist. In some places, they are even in good (if not great) shape.

Northern pike have never been what could be termed sought-after sport fish in these waters. At best, they are an incidental fish—something caught while fishing for something else. So, the amount of interest is unusually low. This is good news for pike aficionados. In many areas, you have little fishing competition.

The sites listed here report numbers of fish. Naturally, there are other areas with fewer, yet still respectable numbers of fish.

Again, we do not go into any detail. You must do your own scouting for specific areas. Since little information exists, and few persons are willing to divulge their secrets, be prepared to do some exploring on your own.

1. St. Martin's Bay/Les Cheneaux Islands: A decent, big pike fishery exists in this section. Fish in the 20 pound class are there for those willing to work for them. In spring, pike move to the marshes to spawn, but in late spring and summer move out to deeper waters. In fall, as forage fish move back into shallow water, active pike take up positions in deep, green weed beds.

2. Cheboygan River: A small population of fish work this area. They spawn near the mouth of the river and in Duncan Bay. Little is known about summertime big fish location. Some large fish are taken in fall.

3. Calcite Harbor/Grand Lake Outlet: Again, a small, yet fishable population of pike (some of decent size) range this area. In spring, fish spawn in marshy areas and then move out to unknown summer locales. Some good fall opportunities might exist here.

4. Thunder Bay: Some excellent pike spawning conditions still exist here, and the bay hosts a fair resident fishery. The spawning grounds may also attract migrant fish which come in spring, and then move out in summer —perhaps even staying out until next spring. In the past, folks trolling for brown trout with Rapalas have taken big pike in fall.

5. Saginaw Bay: Perhaps Lake Huron's prime pike spot in terms of numbers. Lots of small and intermediate-sized fish can be taken. Although rarely caught in summer, they are taken in fall, and sometimes in spring. Since this is such a large area, exploration is in order.

6. Matchedash Bay: There are pike opportunities near the town of Waubaushene.

7. North Channel: Various bays, cuts and stream mouths offer some pike opportunities. Sections like Bayfield Sound on Manitoulin Island, and the shallow area from Hennepin Island to Serpent Harbor, all support pike. Just how, when and where to catch them is up to the intuitive pike angler.

8. St. Mary's River: See the special section on connecting waters.

LAKE ERIE

By 1850, the once large Lake Erie pike population was already extremely reduced. Ditching and diking of streams drained or halted access to spawning marshes, and cut the pike population to low numbers. The elimination of vegetation due to turbidity and siltation further accelerated the process, and today Lake Erie probably offers the least of all the Great Lakes in terms of a good pike fishery. Yet some hold-out populations still exist.

In very cold environments like Lake Superior, large pike need not wander too far from some of the bays to get away from warm water stress. On the other hand, pike in warmer Lake Erie (especially in the Western Basin) actually migrate long distances to spawn, and then later to feed and find adequate temperatures in the lake itself.

Lake Erie pike do not appear to exhibit the growth potential nor the longevity of the pike in the colder Great Lakes. While certain areas produce numerous 3 to 4 pound fish, pike in the 10, 12, or 14 pound bracket are no longer common.

With all the other fishing opportunities for walleyes, perch, smallmouths and even cold water fish like trout and salmon (in the Eastern Basin), pike take a back seat to other Lake Erie gamefish. In most areas, pike are incidental fish (caught when fishing for something else). However, the following places have the potential to produce more than just a few fish. There are probably some sleeper spots as well.

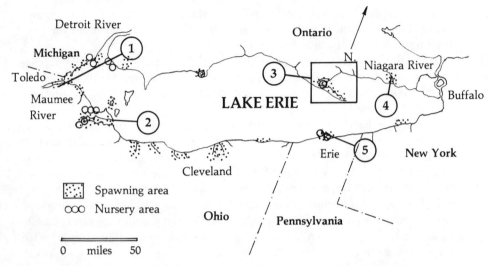

1. **Maumee River:** In the 1800's, huge runs of pike ascended the river to spawn in the Maumee Basin swamps. But as these swamps were blocked and drained, the numbers of fish using this part of the lake declined drastically. Today, only a limited amount of fish use the river. These fish move out into Maumee Bay and into the Western Basin in summer, or utilize the bay area in fall when the main lake cools.

2. **East Harbor:** A resident population still spawns along the south and west shores of the harbor, and fish are caught in the pre-spawn and fall seasons. A 10 pound fish is considered a good one.

3. **Long Point Bay:** This is without question the finest northern pike area in Lake Erie, and for all practical purposes the only one. In the early 1900's, millions of pike spawned in this area. Today, while the numbers are reduced, huge numbers of pike are still here for the taking. It is perhaps under "sport" fished.

The average pike in Long Bay does not fall into the good-sized category. However, there are countless 3 to 7 pound fish, and numerous 7 to 12 pounders. The top-out size appears to be 15 pounds or so, and 20 pound fish are very rare. Like most "quantity" fisheries, the average size ("quality") is low.

Since there are many fish in the small and intermediate size range, the warm water stress factor does not play such a big role here. You can take these fish throughout the summer, as well as in spring, fall and winter. It is a truly underfished area.

4. **Port Maitland (Grand River):** In the early 1900's, huge runs of pike utilized the river, but channelization, bulkheading, riprapping and cleaning of marsh areas have left only a remnant population today.

5. **Presque Isle Bay:** A residual and quite localized pike population operates here. In fact, many of the lagoons function as rearing and nursery areas for

young-of-the-year pike.

While small and intermediate-sized pike can function in the deep and weed-edged portions of the bay after the water warms, most large-sized pike move out to the surrounding shoal areas in summer. There may be a late fall movement back into these bays by bigger fish when the main lake water cools, and many baitfish move back into the bay.

LAKE ONTARIO

If Lake Superior produces the largest northern pike, and Lake Erie the smallest, then Lake Ontario appears to put out the most intermediate-sized fish—those 5- to 12-pounders.

Certain areas of Lake Ontario, like Burlington Bay near Hamilton, Ontario, at one time "swarmed with pike" in early April. But development and water quality problems have vastly reduced the numbers. The same is true of Toronto Bay, whose destruction of marsh areas in the early 1900's caused massive declines in the pike population. On the other hand, pike populations in areas like Chaumont and Henderson Bay, as well as certain waters near the Bay of Quinte, have continued producing pike at a fairly consistent rate.

From what we can tell about pike size from contests and catch records, Lake Ontario pike do not seem to grow to the large proportions they do on Lakes Superior, Michigan and Huron. Indeed, a 20 pound pike would be considered a super lunker.

The physical makeup of Lake Ontario is such that large portions of the northern and southern shoreline, except for the bay-like areas, do not provide good pike habitat. Short, narrow-lip areas, little weedgrowth and upwelling of very cold water all conspire to make life tough for young pike in these unprotected areas.

The areas marked on the map are some of the more productive spots where pike are taken. However, limited amounts of pike exist in just about every bay and river mouth area. A large ice fishery has developed in some bay areas on the eastern end of the lake, and various local derbies and contests take place in the winter months.

1. Burlington Bay: In the early 1900's, this area swarmed with pike in early April, but development and declining water quality now allow only a small resident pike population. Nonetheless, there is a fishery of sorts, and post-spawn and pre-summer fish can be caught.

2. Toronto Harbor: Like Burlington Bay's, Toronto Harbor's pike population (which was large in the late 1800's and early 1900's) has suffered because of development, and today only a few fish exist.

3. Prince Edward County Peninsula: One of the better areas for pike, this whole area supports a fair-to-middlin' pike fishery. Sections near East and West lakes in Wellington Bay, and Wellers Bay near the town of Consecon, are some of the better known waters.

4. Grenadier Island, Chaumont, Black and Henderson Bay Areas: There are lots of fish here. But again, lunkers are few and far between. Pike fishing slackens for the better-sized fish in summer. However, smaller-sized fish can be taken during almost all seasons. More pike are probably taken in winter by ice anglers than at any other time.

Very little innovative fall pike fishing is done here, although some large fish can be taken at this time. Fishing pressure, perhaps, keeps numbers of pike from growing to their possible potential.

5. North Pond Adjacent Areas: Both resident and migrant populations use these marsh-like areas for spawning. The shallows also serve as rearing areas for young-of-the-year fish. In summer, pike spread out along the shoreline from Mexico Point to Stony Point.

6. The Various Bays, Ponds, Cuts and Stream Mouths Along the South Shore: The south shore of Lake Ontario (unlike the north shore) has more of a shallow lip to it and a slower, shallower taper. There are more indentations and sheltered areas where weeds can grow and pike can live. While no sector harbors lots of pike, each of these sheltered areas—like Sodus Bay, the Salmon River mouth, Braddock Bay (a good area) and Irondequoit Bay—all have local populations which move in and out of the shallows and bays, and seasonally use the shoreline as water temperature permits.

GREAT LAKES

CONNECTING WATERS OF THE GREAT LAKES

Between each of the Great Lakes, connecting them as they drain to the sea, are huge river systems and even a huge lake—all of which support pike in varying quantities. In fact, some of these areas are *prime* pike waters.

Because of resultant physical makeup and just plain geography, most of the waters in these sections are shallower or warmer than the "big water," are bounded by marsh, and provide (at least seasonally) some of the very necessary ingredients for pike usage. Some of these sections held countless pike in the past, but because of development no longer support the number of fish they used to. Yet there are pike in some of these waters—at times, lots of them, and sometimes, even lots of lunkers.

The main waterways leading to the Atlantic Ocean are: the St. Mary's River, which connects Lake Superior with Lakes Michigan and Huron (which are at the same level); the St. Clair River, which drains Lake Huron into Lake St. Clair; the Detroit River, which drains Lake St. Clair into Lake Erie; the Niagara River, which flows over Niagara Falls into Lake Ontario; and the St. Lawrence River, which flows to the Atlantic Ocean.

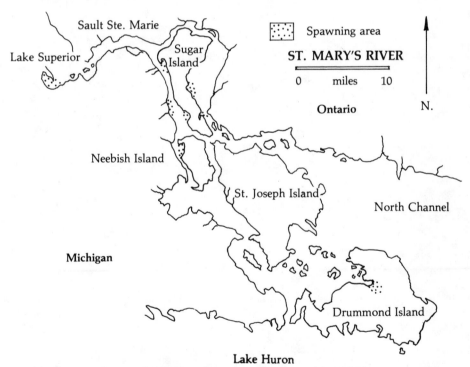

Lake Huron

1. St. Mary's River: The section (actually a part of Lake Huron) under the Sault Ste. Marie locks is historic pike water. It still harbors some good fish. Lunkers in the 20 pound plus bracket can be taken. In spring, spawning takes place in the bays and marshes throughout the river. This section serves as a nursery area for young-of-the-year fish, and a growth area for small and intermediate-sized pike. Large and lunker pike, however, operate differently—as they do in all the other waters.

In spring, the areas around Drummond Island, as well as Waiska, Mosquito, Mark's and Frog Bays all attract pike. Fall fishing can be good for lunkers here. However, some refined methods might have to be used. All in all, it's a good pike area.

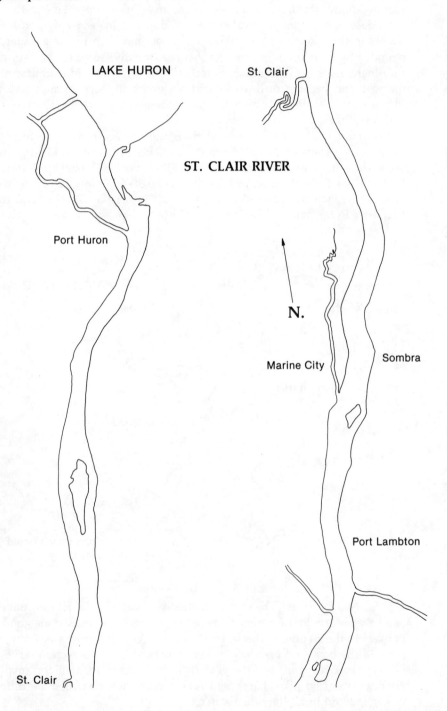

2. St. Clair River: While some resident pike exist in this section, the lack of any extensive "proper" pike habitat precludes any numbers or size of fish from developing.

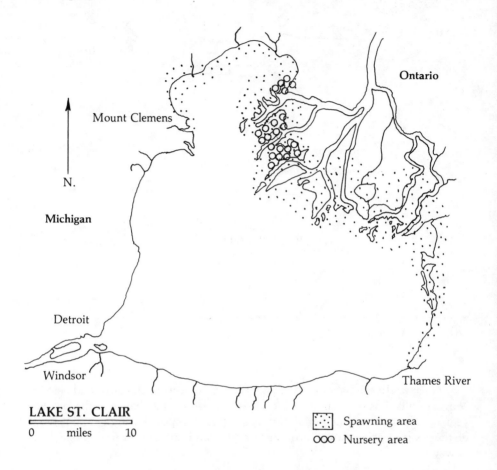

N.

Mount Clemens

Ontario

Michigan

Detroit

Windsor

Thames River

LAKE ST. CLAIR

0   miles   10

⬚ Spawning area

∞∞ Nursery area

3. Lake St. Clair: Huge sections of preferred pike habitat are found here, and very sizeable pike populations have developed. However, with the emphasis on other fish like muskies, walleyes, perch—and even bass—northern pike get very little angler attention. While there are large numbers of small and intermediate-sized pike, there are also some big ones. However, few anglers seem willing to work their way through the smaller fish in order to take the lunkers.

In spring, fish congregate near marshes and the shallows. In summer, the small and intermediate-size fish stay in the weeds, and the big fish seem to disappear. In fall, the few big fish taken usually fall to anglers fishing for something else.

4. Detroit River: Localized resident populations exist, but the overall makeup of the river, with its fast current, developed shorelines, siltation, etc., don't seem conducive to providing any number of big or lunker-sized pike. The Elba Island/Elba Bay area perhaps attracts the major concentrations of pike.

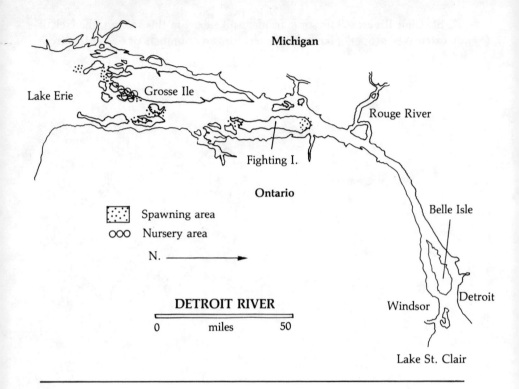

Michigan

Lake Erie

Grosse Ile

Rouge River

Fighting I.

Ontario

Belle Isle

:::: Spawning area

OOO Nursery area

N. ———————▶

DETROIT RIVER

0   miles   50

Windsor

Detroit

Lake St. Clair

5. Niagara River: Never a great pike area, this river, both above and below Niagara Falls, has been subjected to great environmental change in the last 20 years. The northern pike population has suffered, especially in the main stem of the river. Various areas around Grand Island still support some stocks, however.

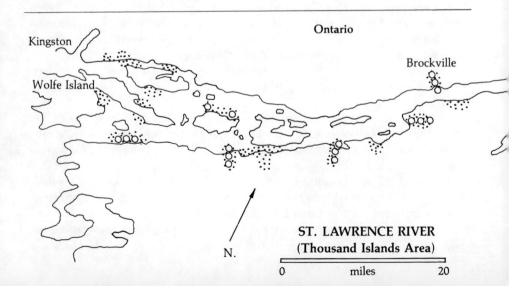

Ontario

Kingston

Brockville

Wolfe Island

N.

ST. LAWRENCE RIVER
(Thousand Islands Area)

0   miles   20

Lake Ontario

NIAGARA RIVER

New York

N.

0   miles   5

Niagara Falls

Grand Island

Ontario

Buffalo

Spawning
area

Lake Erie

6. St. Lawrence River (Thousand Islands Area): With the damming and locking of the river to construct the St. Lawrence Seaway, a reservoir-like situation developed. Just about every marsh and stream has a spawning population of northern pike. Small, intermediate, as well as large fish are here for the taking. The big fish seem to disappear in summer months, only to become active again in fall.

This is a huge section of water, and each specific area must be viewed on a case-by-case basis. However, lots of fish—and many big ones—are here for the taking. Two of the authors who fished the area found it literally "teeming" with pike of all sizes. For those who know how, this is a real opportunity.

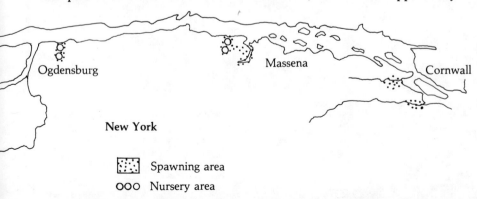

Ogdensburg

Massena

Cornwall

New York

Spawning area

OOO Nursery area

HUNTING & FISHING LIBRARY

Chapter 21

THE DEAD BAIT PHENOMENON

Big northern pike—those rare, 20 pound plus fish—enjoy an eerie mystique. Seldom seen, seldom caught, they *lurk*—somewhere—in the inky depths. Their unknown ways and fiendish appetite are the things legends are born of.

And what an appetite! Forget the stories of pike eating fish half their size. Those are common. More exotic are the tales of the pike devouring muskrats, rats, ducklings, small dogs, weasels, moles, snakes and baby pigs. Pike have even latched onto the noses of foxes, calves and—believe it or not, even mules —as they lowered their heads to drink, only releasing their death-grip after the startled animals hauled them ashore. A meaner, more savage, more vicious creature has never haunted the angling scene!

Squaring off against this underwater eating machine sounds like challenging a dragon to hand-to-hand combat. What weapon would you choose? What bait, lure or tackle could deceive the monster and bring it to bay? How about *dead* bait?

Dead bait? Impossible! The same savage beast that engulfs baby herons and relishes squirrels . . . fall for dead bait? Definitely!

THE BRITISH CONNECTION

Winston Churchill once said that the British and Americans are, "two peoples separated by a common language." They are also two peoples brought together by a common gamefish—the pike! Northern pike are treasured gamefish in the British Isles, and we "colonials" can definitely learn a thing or two about pike fishing from our friends across the sea.

Americans have the edge in sophisticated, artificial lure fishing, but British anglers have developed dead bait fishing to a fine art. In fact, the *majority* of very large British pike are probably taken on dead bait. To understand why this occurs, and how we can benefit from their techniques, it helps to compare British fishing situations to ours.

European pike attain much larger size than their North American cousins.

The reason, apparently, is that European waters have many varieties of soft-finned, high-fat baitfish that grow to a larger size, offering pike efficiently-captured food sources that North American waters lack. Consequently, European pike grow larger.

Biologists theorize that North American pike get "stuck" at a *predation barrier.* Very simply, big pike seem to prefer to eat fish that are 15% to 20% of their size. That's a 5 or 6 pound meal for a 30-pounder! In Europe, they have that option. But in America, they don't. Carp (a European import!) are one of the few American fish that might provide this food requirement. Yet they are seldom plentiful, and are often absent from, North America's best pike waters. Thus, once North American pike reach a certain size, they are unable to switch to a larger food source, because it just isn't available. Instead, they must eat numerous, smaller meals, and therefore can't feed as efficiently. Growth suffers.

Why do muskies grow so large, then? Well, we can only put forth a few theories. Apparently, they do better in warm water, and feed far more efficiently on fish like small walleyes, than northerns do. Lunker pike prefer cooler water than muskies, and may not be able to feed as effectively in the same warm water areas as muskies during the summer months. It appears that their metabolism speeds up too much if they stay in the warm water.

Observations indicate that *lunker* northerns tend to seek out deeper, colder water than muskies during summer. Scuba divers also spot them lying, fairly inactive, in the vicinity of cold water springs. In short, big pike seem to avoid warm water, if possible.

Many of Britain's best trophy pike lakes, by comparison, are cold enough to contain salmon (a prime pike forage), and provide the best combination of

water temperature and an abundance of preferred-size food. Most of Canada's famed cold water pike waters offer far less "ideal" food species. Big Canadian pike top 20 pounds, but 30's are plenty scarce.

Regardless of theory, Europeans have far more opportunity to catch, study and learn about big northerns. And one thing British anglers have learned is that dead bait is very effective for catching big, cold water pike. The bulk of their fishing season spans the cold water months, and dead bait is tailor-made for these conditions.

Britain's famed pike angler, Fred Buller, offered his reasoning for this phenomenon in his book, *"Pike and the Pike Angler."* Fred likened the pike to an African lion: certainly a ferocious and effective predator, but also a top-of-the-line scavenger! And why not? Why shouldn't big pike conserve energy by feeding in the most expedient manner, even if it is by picking up dead fish off the bottom? The answer? There's absolutely no reason they shouldn't!

Fred theorized the following styles of lunker pike feeding behavior:

1) The pike's first preference is to pick up any worthwhile fish or food morsel found dead in its path. Reason: maximum economy of effort.

2) The pike's second preference is to strike at any worthwhile injured or sick fish or food morsel that it chances upon. Reason: assured success with economy of effort.

3) The pike's third preference is to ambush a live food item of *preferred* size (15%-20% of its own weight). Reason: to preclude the need for further effort in the immediate future.

Studies show that small pike begin life almost exclusively as live bait feeders, but progressively depend more on scavenging as they grow larger. Buller theorizes that scavenging provides a *continuous* food supply, which is critical to continue the growth of very large fish. Since pike have an excellent sense of smell to lead them to dead bait, Fred's ideas certainly make sense.

DEAD BAIT RIGS

Now, the rigs: a unique collection of the fisherman's art, sculpted from hooks, wire, swivels and line. We've compiled a gallery of dead bait rigs, foreign and domestic, that cover a wide range of uses. Each has its time and place.

You may not have access to tench or roach as bait, but you certainly should be able to obtain ciscoes or smelt. Smelt are dip-netted all around the Great Lakes each spring, and gillnetters pick up ciscoes each fall from many meso

lakes. If you have to, resort to suckers, although we definitely prefer oily fish like ciscoes or smelt. They set up a scent trail that draws pike like blood draws sharks.

If you're organized, you can pick up extra hooks, install them in a number of baits at home, and pop 'em in the freezer so they'll be all set when you need 'em. Soft fish like ciscoes and smelt stand up to abuse better when they're partially frozen. If you're not organized, at least keep 'em on ice when you're out in the boat, and hook 'em on one at a time.

INSTANT STRIKE RIGS

These dead bait rigs are not designed for repeated casting. Just pitch them out and let them sit. They do, however, provide extremely good hooking success and you don't have to let pike swallow them.

The crux of these rigs is that you can cast them—once—and then they partially disassemble. That solves the problem of having the bait secured firmly enough for casting, but lightly enough for the hooks to pull out of the bait when you set the hook.

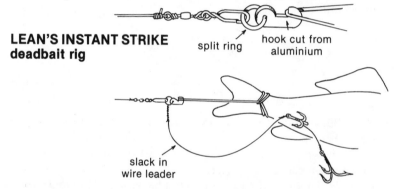

LEAN'S INSTANT STRIKE deadbait rig

split ring

hook cut from aluminium

slack in wire leader

Using the Lean's rig, the weight of the bait rests on a piece of 10-14 pound test line, wrapped around the minnow's tail on one end and resting on a home-made aluminum hook on the other. Once you cast it, the line falls off the aluminum hook, leaving only the braided wire leader *lightly* hooked into the bait.

The Oxford rig accomplishes much the same thing. It uses a stapled piece of paper that holds the line during the cast, but dissolves once it enters the water. Again, the mono line detaches from the swivel, leaving just the wire leader running to the bait.

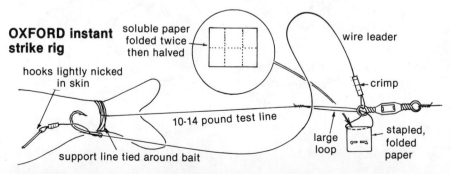

OXFORD instant strike rig

soluble paper folded twice then halved

wire leader

crimp

hooks lightly nicked in skin

10-14 pound test line

large loop

stapled, folded paper

support line tied around bait

SEMI-CASTING RIGS

These rigs hook the baits more firmly, although they're not designed for repeated casting because the soft baitfish will fall apart. They're also easy to set

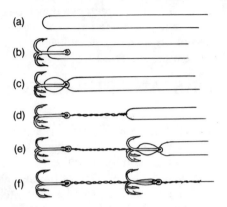

(a)

(b)

(c)

(d)

(e)

(f)

TAYLOR deadbait tackle rig

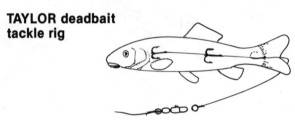

the hook with. Fred Buller doesn't believe in waiting a long time before setting the hook with dead bait, because the fish can sense it's dead and don't wait very long before swallowing it. Hit 'em when they start swimming off, or 30 seconds after they hit, whichever is shorter.

Make a Taylor rig by hand-braiding 27 pound test Sevenstrand braided wire as shown. Add a crimp if you feel it is necessary. Make sure the hooks are spaced to match the size of the bait.

Fred Buller's Universal snap-tackle rig adjusts to the size of your bait by simply wrapping the line around the beaked hook whenever you want it; you don't have to carry different sizes! The wrapped beak hook will hold fairly securely in place.

Buller suggests using fairly small hooks, because you have to rip them out of the bait. His favorite combinations are:

No. 4 Beak with No. 8 treble
No. 2 Beak with No. 6 treble
No. 1 Beak with No. 4 treble

UNIVERSAL snap-tackle rig

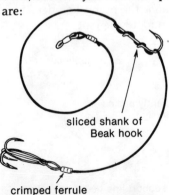

sliced shank of Beak hook

crimped ferrule

BOBBER RIGS

These rigs are frequently used with live bait, although they are also effective with dead bait. We admit a drifting bobber rig covers a wider area than a stationary rig, although a dead bait suspended off the bottom isn't as attractive as

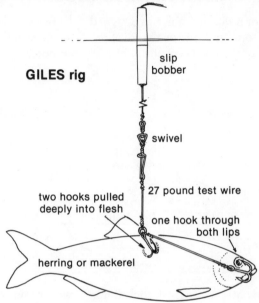

one lying on it. Still, you can use this rig to set a lure, say, 5 feet deep, and then let it drift into the shallows until it stops at the 5 foot level. The bobber will also indicate a strike.

The Giles drifting rig is self-explanatory. However, *balance* is the key! The bait should hang perfectly level in the water, so make sure the top hook is placed to keep the bait perfectly horizontal.

The lasso rig (we'll call it that because we don't know its name) is adjustable

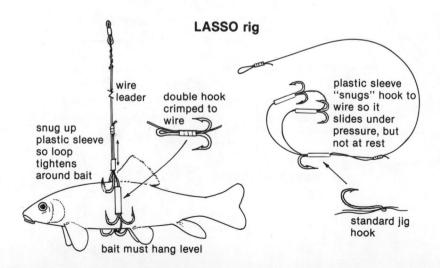

to fit any size minnow. Hook the single hook in the top of the minnow at the balance point, and then tighten the wire loop until the minnow is snugly surrounded. This is an excellent rig for live bait as well.

SHORE FISHING RIGS

These are single- or multiple-hook rigs designed to be fished from shore. The weight is at the bottom, and one or two dropper lines are spaced at intervals above it. The angle of the line keeps the baits near, but not necessarily on, the bottom.

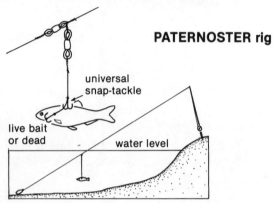

PATERNOSTER rig

universal snap-tackle

live bait or dead

water level

The standing pike paternoster rig is common in Great Britain. Anglers use a sand spike rod holder, like the ones American surfcasters use, to keep the rod tip high and the line tight. The one shown here is rigged with a Universal snap-tackle hooking arrangement.

The Missouri River pike rig is a commercially made set-up, and is available at Missouri River baitshops in both steel leader material and heavy monofilament. Mustad's Universal Double Bait Hook is pressed into the back end of the minnow and out the mouth. Then the tiny clip is attached, securing the bait.

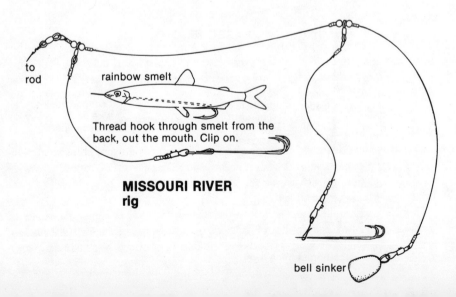

to rod

rainbow smelt

Thread hook through smelt from the back, out the mouth. Clip on.

MISSOURI RIVER rig

bell sinker

ICE FISHING RIGS

The one place American anglers do use dead bait rigs is ice fishing for pike. The suspended, motionless minnow is very attractive to cold water northerns. Remember, these can be fished equally well from a bobber!

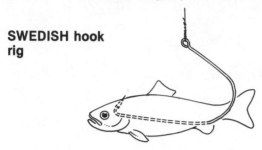

SWEDISH hook rig

The Swedish hook rig is the ice fisherman's standby. Thread the bait onto the hook from back to front, trying to achieve the best balance possible. If you have to, try sticking various-sized nails down the minnow's throat to make it sit *perfectly level* in the water. It makes a big difference.

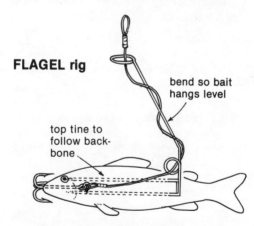

FLAGEL rig

bend so bait hangs level

top tine to follow back- bone

The Flagel rig achieves much the same purpose, but is much easier to balance. Simply bend the wire support shaft open or closed until the bait hangs perfectly level at rest. Flagels are available from the Billy Boy Co., Markesan, Wisconsin.

HEAVY-DUTY CASTING RIGS

These rigs are designed for repeated casting and for natural, lifelike appearance. They work better with tough baits like chubs or suckers, although they'll work OK with more fragile baits. The key is firmly securing the bait to the hook so it doesn't tear apart.

The sucker harness is a commonly-used musky system designed for repeated casting, and does not really fit into our stillfishing approach (although it would work well). The key is hooking the bait up through the head and "sew-

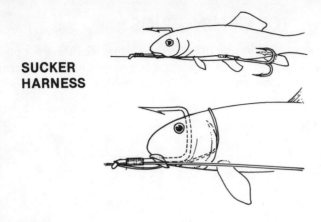

SUCKER HARNESS

ing" the bait securely to the hook with dacron line to take the strain off the sucker's weak skull. Stick a sinker down the throat if you need extra weight to sink the bait.

There are a variety of rigs commercially available. Some have extra hooks on a harness that stretches the length of the body. Hook the tips of the rear hook(s) lightly into the minnow, or hold the harness against the bait with a rubber band. The Weller Company, 2651 Murray Street, Sioux City, Iowa 51111, makes a good harness.

SPRAT WOBBLING rig

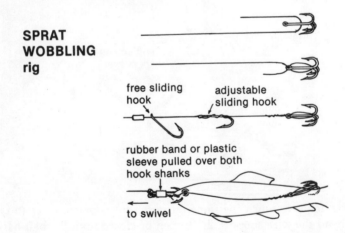

free sliding hook

adjustable sliding hook

rubber band or plastic sleeve pulled over both hook shanks

to swivel

The sprat wobbling dead bait rig is quite ingenius. It has two sliding hooks that combine to lock the head firmly in place. Once adjusted, slide the small plastic sleeve or rubber band over the hooks to prevent them from sliding.

These are just a handful of the many variations you can use with dead bait. There are countless other spinner, jig and trolling combinations in use. However, our topic is stillfishing dead bait, so we won't try to list them all. In any event, don't be afraid to experiment.

New rigs are just waiting to be invented, so use your imagination. Put together a box of component parts, buy some wire, and start fiddling with various combinations. You'll be shocked what you come up with!

Dr. Barry Rickards releases a 32 pound British pike. The size of European pike is unbelievable to many Americans.

Dead Bait Components

Neat things you never knew existed . . .
but now can't live without—
and some old standbys.

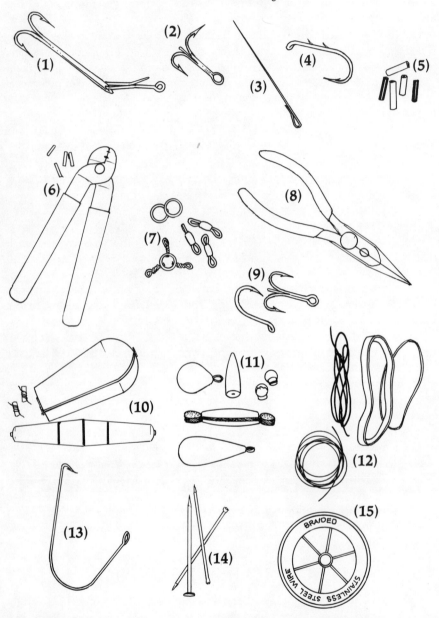

1) **Mustad #9148 Universal Double Bait Hook.** This hook is designed to be threaded through the back of a dead minnow and out the mouth. Then the clip is inserted to attach it to your line. O. Mustad & Son, Inc., Box 838, Auburn, NY 13021.

2) **Bent treble.** You may not find this in American tackle shops, but you can

simply bend one hook of a normal treble to the side. Stick the bent point into the dead bait. When you set the hook, it'll rip out of the minnow easier, helping you bury the hook.

3) **Mustad #7712 Baiting Needle.** This gadget enables you to thread line or wire through the body of a minnow instead of merely wrapping the line around it.

4) **Mustad #92461 Hollow Point Beak Hook.** These "bait holder" hooks work very well for the adjustable-length rigs shown in this chapter. The tiny barbs prevent the twisted wire from slipping too readily.

5) **Plastic sleeves.** These are nothing more than the plastic coating off pieces of electrical wire. Simply strip them off with wire strippers. These sleeves slide over hooks and wire, creating a "snug" fit.

6) **Wire crimping tool and crimps.** These are invaluable for quickly and securely tying up your own wire rigs. Weller Company, 2651 Murray St., Sioux City, IA 51111.

7) **Assorted swivels and split rings.** These make the best tie-ons and junctions. They're available at any tackle store.

8) **Long-nosed pliers/wire cutters.** Don't leave home without 'em! You can't bite off excess wire ends!

9) **Assorted treble and single hooks.** Carry a supply of all sizes and shapes to match the conditions you're faced with. Eagle Claw, Wright & McGill Co., 4245 East 46th Ave., Denver, CO 80216.

10) **Slip bobbers and bobber stops.** Large slip bobbers will help you keep baits off weed- or snag-infested bottoms, and let you use a drifting approach. Plastilite Corp., P.O. Box 12235, Omaha, NE 68112.

11) **Assorted sinkers.** You can never have too many sizes and shapes of sinkers. Always be willing to experiment. Water Gremlin Co., 4370 Otter Lake Road, White Bear Lake, MN 55110.

12) **Rubber bands, string, flexible solid wire.** Use these items to wrap, lasso or hog-tie wire leaders and line *tight against the side* of a dead bait. A sagging harness looks unnatural.

13) **Mustad Swedish Pike Hook.** The "standard" for dead bait fishing through the ice.

14) **Assorted nails.** Use nails to balance Swedish hooks or any dead bait rigs.

15) **Braided wire.** You can use single strand stainless steel wire, but braided wire has much better flexibility for constructing dead bait rigs. The 10-40 pound test range is usually best. Sevenstrand Tackle Corp., 5401 McFadden Ave., Huntington Beach, CA 92649; or Berkley & Company, Inc., Trilene Drive, Spirit Lake, IA 51360.

PLACES TO FISH DEAD BAIT

Think back to what we said earlier about big pike. They're generally caught in cool-to-cold water. Obviously, then, any time you can corner them in a constricted area of cold water, you have an excellent chance of catching them.

Early spring is an excellent time to use this approach. If you've ever seen pike come cruising into their shallow spawning grounds, you'd know why. When the water is very cold, they just barely inch along, hardly moving at all. A fast-retrieved bait will either spook them, or get no response at all. But, place a nice piece of easily-apprehended dead bait right in front of their noses, and the pike might snap it up.

PRE-SPAWN—RESERVOIRS

Some impoundments, like the Missouri River Reservoirs, host excellent numbers of large pike. When these fish move into the back ends of coves to spawn in early spring (40°F water temperature), they're suckers for dead bait.

When pike enter a cove, they can be suspended at nearly any level. But as they progress toward the back end of a cove, it will grow shallower and narrower. Eventually, the fish will encounter the drop-off. When this happens, they will tend to follow it at the level they were suspended, yet still keep heading into the back of the cove. This behavior will eventually lead them into the creek channel that feeds the cove, and they'll follow it up into the cove until they finally reach a point where the water becomes so shallow that they scatter into the back end.

The river channel acts as a *funnel*, and that's where you want to be. Anchor your boat, or take up a position on shore, where you can reach the channel with a cast. Pick an area that's just deep enough so the pike don't scatter—say, 8-10 feet. Pitch a dead bait rig out, sit back and relax. Let the fish come to you. The best fishing generally occurs on warm, sunny afternoons.

PRE-SPAWN—BAYS OFF MAJOR RIVERS

Similar pike behavior occurs in spawning bays off major rivers like the Mississippi. You may not find a creek channel to concentrate fish, though, so pick out the next best thing. Anchor near an area of heavy weedgrowth, preferably a marsh, where the fish will spawn. Place your bait somewhere they must pass. Nothing complicated about that!

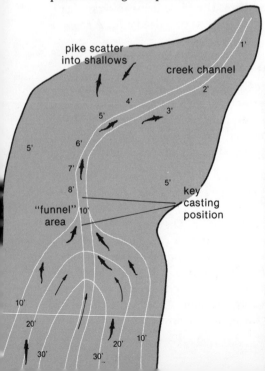

PRE-SPAWN—CREEK MOUTHS

Feeder creeks entering larger rivers, lakes or impoundments are natural pike attractors. Anchor your boat or fish from shore, and soak your dead bait in an eddy or any slack water in the general area. Pike will remain in these areas even after spawning, giving you a good shot at big fish for several weeks.

PRE-SPAWN—INLAND LAKES
AND THE GREAT LAKES

Inlets to spawning bays are "the" place to be. Any time pike have to pass through a channel, it funnels them down into a limited area and you have 'em cornered. Position one or more baits in the center of the channel, and let nature take its course. You'll encounter fish passing in and out of the bays, so you have a double shot at them. This is an exceptional pattern for taking a huge fish on one of the bays of the Great Lakes.

PRE-SPAWN—CANADIAN LAKES

The same principle applies to bays of Canadian lakes, although you may not have a real "funnel" spot. When the fish are way up in the backs of the bays, they're active enough to catch on artificial lures. Thus, only use dead bait during the "off-times" when the fish are fairly inactive.

The key spots are the rocky points at the mouths of the bays. Sit on shore, cast a bait out across the mouth of the bay, and have your lunch. In fact, cast one *way out* into the main lake; if you hit deep water, you might catch a lake trout. They're notorious scavengers, too! Many big Canadian pike are accidentally caught by lake trout anglers using this same system!

POST-SPAWN—NATURAL LAKES

Big northerns will hang in shallow reed patches and disperse into developing weed flats for awhile after they spawn. Fish likely-looking areas with a bobber rig. Your "funnels" are the thickest weed patches; they'll concentrate the fish. This pattern will produce until the water warms enough for the pike to leave the area.

SPRING HOLES—ANYTIME—ANYWHERE

These are the most underfished lunker pike hideouts of all. Trouble is, they're very hard to find. It takes a lot of work with a water thermometer. If you see patches of rotten ice in the winter, go back and check the spots during summer. It could be an indication of springs.

Lakes, rivers, reservoirs—it makes no difference; springs are excellent summer spots in all of them. Anchor and work them patiently. You may find a gold mine.

BIG PIKE WATERS

The biggest North American pike generally come from waters with suspended baitfish like ciscoes or smelt. Bays of the Great Lakes, the Missouri

River, mesotrophic lakes and the Canadian North are your best bets for giant fish. However, these systems will work anywhere pike are found. Only the size of the fish will vary.

We can see it now; some of you are scheming a way to cast a 4 pound carp! *Don't* go bionic! You don't need a giant bait; they're too hard to handle. Stick with something more in the 4-10 ounce range; a bait that's easy to handle, yet big enough to tempt an aquatic monster. That's just what they are, you know. Snakes! Slimes! All teeth and jaws, and packed with a double dose of mean 'n ugly.

Except when you catch 'em. Then they're beautiful!

Chapter 22

BONELESS PIKE FILLETS & FAVORITE RECIPES

In Finland, the northern pike is the number one commercial fish with some 15 million pounds caught and sold annually. In the rest of Europe, the northern ranks on *top* because of its fine eating qualities. In fact, it's been reported that a large pike could sell for twice the price of lamb during the days of Henry VIII.

Surprisingly, Canadians do not value northerns as a food fish. Most of their commercial pike catch is shipped into the United States. However, northern pike are excellent eating, high in protein, but low in fat content. Some people even feel that pike taste better than walleyes or crappies.

The only true complaint rises with the troublesome Y-bones along the lateral line on either side of the body. However, these can be removed while filleting. Two options for this are pictured on the following pages, along with some of our favorite ways of preparing northern pike.

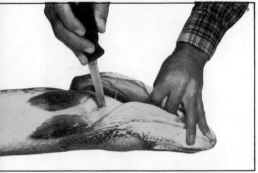

Step 1: Cut into the chest cavity (not the belly cavity) of the fish. Move the blade around to cut the blood vessels. This will bleed the fish and help keep the blood out of the meat.

Step 2: Make an incision behind the gill cover of the pike. Cut all the way down to the backbone.

Step 3: Starting at the bottom, cut straight back over the pectoral fin, pelvic fin and anal pore.

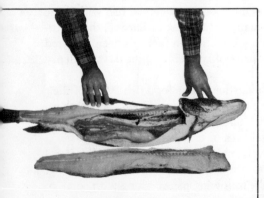

Step 4: Turn the knife towards the tail of the fish. Running the knife as close as possible to the backbone, remove the fillet.

Step 5: Repeat steps 2, 3 and 4 on other side.

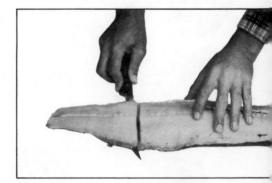

Step 6: Cut straight down and then back, removing the tail section of the fillet. The tail section does not have many bones in it.

Step 7: Continue removing pike pieces in sections shorter than the length of your knife, or of appropriate size for recipes.

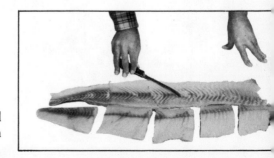

Step 8: The filleted pieces and skin are shown separated. Repeat on other side of fish.

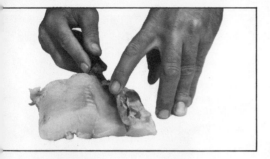

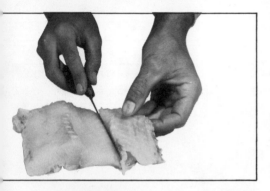

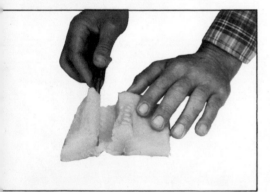

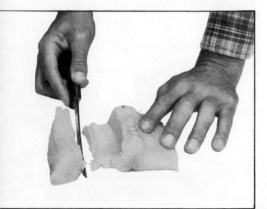

Step 9: Now take each of the sections and remove the rib cage. Begin at the rib cage and cut along and below it.

Step 10: Remove the rib cage and also remove any area of belly fat.

Once the rib cage has been removed, it is time to remove the "Y" bones. The tops of the "Y" bones lie almost in the center of the fillet and then run back. The bottoms of them project into the meat and bend back towards the thickest part of the fillet. Find where the "Y" bones project out of the flesh. You can usually see a line of white bones.

Step 11: Option A — Take the knife and cut straight down until you hit where the "Y" bones start to bend back into the flesh. As you cut straight down and hit the bones, turn the knife and continue to cut along their tops.

Step 12A: You will reach a point where the bones stop. Option A is to cut straight down and remove the top boneless section.

Step 13A: Look for the line that runs through the center of the flesh. It usually corresponds with the lateral line. Insert the knife into that line, cut straight down for about ¼ inch, and then start to cut in toward the top of the fillet. You should be able to feel the bones as you continue to cut beneath the "Y" bones.

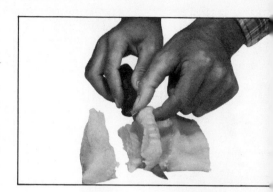

Step 14A: The bones have been removed, leaving two boneless sections, plus the section of "Y" bones which is thrown away.

Step 11: Option B — This option keeps the fillet in one piece, and is advantageous for some recipes. Begin by finding the top of the "Y" bones, and cut straight down until you meet the bones.

Step 12B: Once you meet the bone, turn the knife towards the top of the fillet and cut until you reach the top of the "Y" bones. Stop cutting at this point.

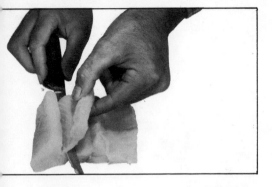

Step 13B: Start another cut on the other side of the bones. Cut straight for about ¼ inch, turn the knife, and you should be able to feel the bones. Cut towards the top of the fillet, keeping the knife just under the "Y" bones.

Step 14B: Continue your cut until you have reached the end of the "Y" bones and remove them from the fillet.

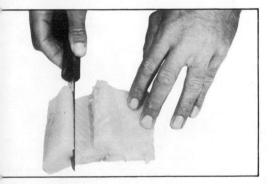

Step 15B: This shows the intact piece of fillet, and the portion containing the "Y" bones to be thrown away.

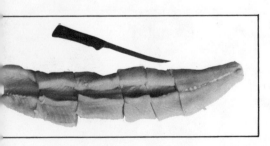

Step 16B: A completed northern pike fillet cut into 6 sections with the "Y" bones removed. There may be a few small bones in the tail section.

Our first two recipes use Old Guide's Secret "Shore Lunch" brand by Sportsman's Recipes for pan frying or deep frying boneless pike fillets.

FOR PAN FRYING:

1. In a cast iron or other heavy skillet, pour cooking oil to a depth of about 1/3 the thickness of your fillets.
2. Heat oil to approximately 350°F (medium heat).
3. Use boneless pike fillets. Fillets should be cool, not cold or frozen.
4. Moisten fish and shake in a plastic bag containing Shore Lunch breading.
5. Fry about 4 minutes, turning once, until golden brown.
6. Drain fish on paper towels.

BEER BATTER
FOR DEEP FRYING:

1. In deep fryer or heavy pan, add 3 to 4 inches of cooking oil.
2. Heat oil to 375°F.
3. In a medium bowl, combine 3/4 box of Shore Lunch batter mix (about 1-1/2 cups) with 8 oz. beer (about 2/3 can), and mix thoroughly. Batter should be thin. Add more beer as batter thickens. NOTE: Water may be substituted for beer, if desired.
4. Cut boneless pike fillets into 3-inch pieces. Fish should be cool, not cold or frozen.
5. Dust fish in a plastic bag filled with remaining Shore Lunch mix. (Important, since this holds the batter to the fish.)
6. Dip fish in batter until coated, and drop carefully into deep fryer.
7. Cook and turn fish until golden brown all over, about 2 to 3 minutes. NOTE: Watch heat to

maintain oil at 360°F-375°F.
8. Drain fish on paper towels.

STOVE TOP DRESSING:

Purchase a small box of Stove Top Dressing or use your favorite homemade dressing. Serves 4.
1. Lightly grease 9" x 9" pan.
2. Prepare dressing according to directions on package. Spread dressing in pan so it is about 1-inch thick.
3. Place boneless pike fillets on top of dressing, allowing 1 piece per serving.
4. Place wedge of lemon on each pike fillet. Sprinkle with parsley, pepper and paprika. You may add some butter if you choose.
Bake 20-25 minutes at 350°F or until the meat flakes.

POOR MAN'S LOBSTER

Deboned pike fillets
3-4 tablespoons salt
Onion slices
Bay leaf
Boiling water
1. Bring water, salt, onions and bay leaf to boil in pan with a strainer.
2. Drop in pike fillets. Again bring water to boil and boil for 3 minutes or less. (Do not overboil, or fish will get mushy and break apart.)
Serve pike fillets with melted butter. Season with salt and pepper.

BACON-SEASONED PIKE

7 pound pike (or larger)
2 onions, sliced
2 carrots, diced
Strips of bacon
Apple, sliced
1. Cut off tail and head. Gut and clean cavity of fish. Scrape off all slime.
2. Stuff carrots and onions into

cavity of fish. Place cavity side down in roasting pan.

3. Alternate strips of bacon and apple slices across back of pike. Bake 2 to 2-1/2 hours at 350°F (depending on size of fish). Fifteen minutes before pike is done, pour barbeque sauce over pike.* Bake remaining 15 minutes. Discard onions and carrots. To serve: Cut down center of fish and remove all backbones. Melt butter, season with salt and pepper and pour over meat.

*Barbeque sauce is optional.

FISH PATTIES

One average size northern
Remove skin. Use food processor or meat grinder with fine blades to break up pike and mix with the following:

1/2-3/4 cup cracker crumbs
1 egg
1/8 teaspoon salt
1/2 teaspoon pepper
1/2 teaspoon minced, dried onions
1/8 teaspoon garlic salt
Corn flake crumbs

Form into patties, dip into one egg (well beaten) and then roll in corn flake crumbs.

Fry in lightly-greased pan at medium heat.

MARY LINDNER'S PICKLED PIKE

(Herring from Northern Pike)*

8 pounds (or less) fish fillets cut into
1/2-inch square cubes.

Place fish cubes in brine of:
4 cups water
1 cup salt
1 tablespoon powdered alum

Let stand 48 hours. Use a plastic, glass or stainless steel container for this. Drain and rinse well. Cover with white vinegar for 24 hours. Drain but don't rinse fish.

Pickling Brine:
3-1/2 cups white sugar
4 cups white vinegar
3 tablespoons pickling spices
10 whole bay leaves
1/2 teaspoon whole peppercorns

Bring this brine to a boil, stirring until sugar is dissolved. Taste it at this point and adjust to your liking. Add more sugar for a sweeter herring, more vinegar for a tautier taste.

Cool brine. Slice 1 lemon and 1 medium onion in slices. Place fish, onion and lemon in jars so they are mixed.

Pour cool brine over fish. Cover tightly and store in refrigerator for at least 3 to 4 weeks. Keep tightly covered and refrigerated after opening. □

*If raw fish have not been frozen for at least 48 hours at 0°F, they should be simmered either in the pickling liquid or in or water for 5 to 10 minutes, or until easily pierced with a fork. This is necessary to kill the broad fish tapeworm, a parasite that may affect humans.

PIKE FISHING.

CONCLUSION

While this book contains a very extensive look at northern pike, the "complete" pike book is still being written. As further research is done on the pike's personality and genetic code, and new angling techniques develop, we add new chapters to our pool of knowledge. In some of the preceding chapters, for example, we advanced theories based on empirical knowledge and observations, with the hope that perhaps some graduate student or DNR biologist might someday carry the ball to the next "down." We expect they will.

Yes, gathering knowledge is a never-ending chore, and we already have a number of new topics which could be added to this book. For example, the ice fishing aspects of fishing for this "coolest of the cool water fish" are so wide in scope that we could not do them justice in a brief chapter or two; instead, we plan to cover them in an upcoming book that is wholly dedicated to the intricate art of ice fishing.

We also want to caution you that the responsibility to use knowledge wisely is essential. When you put this information into practice, you'll take more pike. In the process, you must start practicing catch and release (where applicable). There are bodies of water where you can (and should) keep all the pike you catch, and there are waters where you should release the fish to ensure a harvest in coming years. This books goes a long way in helping you recognize when and when not to keep and eat your catch.

While *PIKE: A Handbook of Strategies* concentrates its efforts on understanding pike, in most cases the pike is the top-of-the-food-chain predator and is seldom the dominant gamefish in any body of water. So pike have a social interaction with other fish like walleyes, bass, trout, etc., as well as a relationship with preyfish like perch, ciscoes, bluegills, etc. Understanding how these fish operate goes hand-in-hand with understanding why a pike does what it does, in a specific body of water, in a given set of circumstances.

To these ends, we encourage you to read our companion books: *WALLEYE WISDOM: A Handbook of Strategies* and *BASS: A Handbook of Strategies*. These studies in fish behavior (and tactics to find and catch them) will help fill in the blanks. This book is the third in a 10-volume, ongoing, classic series intended to introduce fishermen to the whole spectrum of freshwater angling.

By the same token, if you are truly interested in becoming a top-flight fisherman, we urge you to subscribe to our *IN-FISHERMAN* Magazine, the foundation for this knowledge. We offer a free brochure which lists the books and magazines we publish. Simply write to *IN-FISHERMAN*, Box 999, Brainerd, MN 56401 and ask for the free brochure.

And with this, we wish you *good fishing!*

The Pike Fisherman's GLOSSARY

ADAPTATION: The process of getting used to or fitting into a particular set of environmental circumstances.

AGGREGATION: A group of gamefish or prey fish holding in an area, but not moving together in a school. See *school*.

ALGAE: Simple, one cell plants usually having the ability to photosynthesize sunlight into energy. Initial step in a food chain.

ALLEY: Parallel openings between patches of emergent weeds (usually bulrushes), or emergent weeds and the shoreline.

APPETITE MOODS: The three basic attitudes of fish toward feeding. See *positive, neutral and negative feeding moods.*

BACKTROLLING: A system of boat control, simultaneously moving a boat slowly in reverse and using lure or bait presentations (casting or trolling).

BASIC NATURE: A species' inherent makeup or tendencies which determines its niche in an environment.

BASIC NEEDS: The three basic survival requirements of any fish species; namely reproduction, suitable habitat and food. A favorable environment fulfills these needs.

BASIN ZONE: A lake zone. The area lying below the Deep Water Zone, beginning where hard bottom ends and soft bottom begins. This zone includes the deepest water areas.

BIOLOGY: The study of living things.

BITING: The feeding action of a hungry fish. See *striking*.

BOAT CONTROL: Boat use to aid bait or lure presentation. See *backtrolling, controlled drift, front trolling, speedtrolling*.

BOTTOM-BUMPER: A lure or rig which strikes the bottom (i.e. jig).

BOTTOM CONFIGURATION: A locational factor; the relative make-up (shape, size, depth, islands, etc.) of the bottom.

BOTTOM CONTENT: Bottom types in a body of water (rock, sand, gravel, silt, muck, submerged cribs, brush and/or trees, etc.).

BREAK: Any change in otherwise regular terrain.

BREAKLINE: That point in a body of water where there is a definite increase in depth—sudden or gradual—or a change in cover, like a weedline or brushline; edge of channel or hole; where two layers of water meet and differ in temperature, oxygen and/or turbidity; the limit of effective light penetration, etc.

BREAKLINE, SECONDARY: A second or auxilary point of change. For example, a second definite increase in depth after the first drop-off.

BRUSHLINE: The inside or outside edge of a line of brush.

CABBAGE: Any of the pondweeds (Potamogeton); usually attractive to gamefish.

CALENDAR, IN-FISHERMAN: A calendar based on ten identifiable periods of activity for various species of gamefish. These ten periods constitute a *fish cycle.*

CALENDAR PERIOD: Any of the ten periods of fish activity in the IN-FISHERMAN Calendar.

CLEAN BOTTOM: The bottom (usually hard bottom) of a body of water that is free of debris, etc.

CLIMATE: The average weather conditions for a region.

COLD FRONT: The line of impact when cold air forces the warm air upwards. As a cold front moves, cold air beneath is slowed down by contact with the ground, and piles up. This pile of cold air forces warm air up very rapidly, often causing storms. See *post-front.*

COLD WATER PERIOD: A period of the fish cycle which occurs twice—in early spring between the Frozen Water and Pre-spawn Periods, and in late fall between the Turnover and Frozen Water Periods. Most times applied to the fall season.

COMPETITIVE SPECIES: An aspect of *social condition* involving the relationship of species within a body of water, particularly in regard to available food and spawning areas.

CONTROLLED DRIFT: A system of *boat control* using an outboard, electric trolling motor or oars to keep a boat moving along a specific course.

COSMIC CLOCK: The sun's effect on water and local weather factors, such as barometric pressure, wind, cloud cover, seasonal change, etc.

CRANKBAIT: A lipped diving plug.

DEEP WATER ZONE: A lake zone. Hard bottom lying below the first major drop-off and below the open water zone. It ends where soft bottom begins.

DEPTH CONTROL: One of two primary factors in successful bait or lure presentation.

DISSOLVED OXYGEN: (DO). Oxygen chemically bound into water by forces such as wind and plants. It is utilized by fish.

DROP-OFF: A point where there is definite increase in depth.

ECOLOGY: The branch of biology dealing with relations between organisms and their environment.

ECOSYSTEM: A system formed by the interaction of a community of organisms and their surroundings.

ELECTROPHORESIS: A process that can determine the genetic make-up of fish.

EPILIMNION: The warmer layer of water above the *thermocline.*

EROSION: The process by which the surface of the earth is being constantly worn away. The most important elements responsible for erosion are rivers and streams, wind, waves and glaciers.

EUTROPHIC: *A lake classification* or lake type used to describe bodies of water characterized by high levels of nutrients in proportion to their total volume of water.

FANCAST: To make a series of casts systematically covering an area.

FISH CONTACT: Locating fish—usually by catching them. Includes visual observation.

FISH CYCLE: All ten Calendar Periods. See *Calendar*, IN-FISHERMAN.

FISHING PRESSURE: The number of anglers using a body of water.

FLAT: An area characterized by little or no change in depth.

FOOD CHAIN: A step-by-step representation of feeding relationships in a community. Food chains originate with the sun's energy and each link in the chain represents energy transfer. All the food chains in a community make up a food web.

FOOD PRODUCING AREA: Any area that seasonally produces forage for fish.

FRONT TROLLING: A system of *boat control* with the boat moving forward.

FROZEN WATER PERIOD: A period of the fish cycle when a body of water is mostly or completely covered by ice. In southern waters, which rarely freeze, the sustained period of coldest water.

GEOLOGY: The science dealing with the earth's physical history.

HABITAT: The place where a plant or animal species lives.

HARD BOTTOM: Firm bottom areas (sand, clay, rock, gravel, etc.).

HIGH PROTEIN FORAGE: High-fat content, soft-rayed forage species such as ciscoes and whitefish.

HOLDING STATION: Any specific position regardless of depth where fish spend much of their time.

HYPOED LAKE: A body of water stocked with a species of fish to bolster its natural fishery.

HYPOLIMNION: The colder layer of water below the *thermocline*.

IMPOUNDMENT: A confined area where water accumulates, usually the result of damming a river. See *reservoir*.

INFILLING: The process by which higher surrounding terrain tends to fill in lower terrain.

INSIDE EDGE (OF WEEDS): A line of weeds between the shoreline and the weedline. See *outside edge* (of weeds).

JUNK WEEDS: Any type of weed usually not attractive to gamefish.

LAKE CLASSIFICATIONS: Broad categories of lake types; oligotrophic (infertile), mesotrophic (fertile), eutrophic (very fertile).

LAKE MODIFICATION FORCES: Forces such as ice action, wave action, erosion, etc., which change bodies of water.

LAKE TYPE: A group of bodies of water whose characteristics are similar enough to one another that they can be approached from an angling standpoint in much the same manner. See *lake classifications*.

LAKE ZONES: Four designated IN-FISHERMAN water zones: *shallow water, open water, deep water and basin zones*.

LIMNOLOGY: The study of the biological, chemical, geographical and physical features of bodies of water.

LITTORAL ZONE: Shallow water zone.

LOCAL WEATHER FACTORS: The prevailing weather conditions affecting the day-to-day locational patterns of a fish species.

LOCATIONAL PATTERN: Where, why and how a species positions itself to take advantage of its surroundings.

LOOSE ACTION PLUG: A lure whose side-to-side movements are wide and distinct.

MARL: Deposits of sand, clay and silt with a high concentration of shells (calcium carbonate).

MESOTROPHIC: *Lake classification* used to describe fertile bodies of water between the late-stage *oligotrophic* and early-stage *eutrophic* classifications.

MIGRATION: The movement of fish from one area to another. Migrations generally occur on a seasonal basis, from one set of distinct environmental conditions to another, such as from winter habitat toward spawning areas. They would not be confused with *movements*.

MORAINE: A mass of rocks, sand, etc., deposited by a glacier.

MOVEMENT: The locational shift of fish from one area to another, generally on a daily or even hourly basis. Also can refer to fish changing from a neutral to a positive feeding mood, with fish shifting only a few feet from a resting to an advantageous feeding position. A *directional* movement is one which is made from one specific area to another specific area, usually at a fast rate of speed. A *random* movement is the slow milling activity made within a specific area.

NEGATIVE FEEDING MOOD: An *appetite mood* in which the attitude of fish is negative toward biting. Fish also are said to be inactive.

NEUTRAL FEEDING MOOD: An *appetite mood*. The attitude of fish which are not actively feeding but could be tempted through refined presentation. See *striking*.

NICHE: Based on a species' characteristics, and depending on competing species, an organism assumes a particular role and a set of physical surroundings within an ecosystem.

NURSERY AREA: Areas where fish species are reared to the fingerling stage.

OLIGOTROPHIC: *Lake classification* used to describe bodies of water characterized by low amounts of nutrients in proportion to their total volume of water. Infertile.

OPEN WATER ZONE: A lake zone. The upper water layer from the outside edge of the first major drop-off down to the deep water zone.

OUTSIDE EDGE (OF WEEDS): The *weedline*. The outside edge of a line of weeds.

PATTERN: Any consistently reoccurring locational/presentational situation.

PHOTOSYNTHESIS: Green plants have chlorophyll which allows them to synthesize organic compounds from water and carbon dioxide using the sun's energy. This is called photosynthesis, and produces oxygen.

POPULATION DENSITY: The number of individuals occupying a certain area. For example, the number of bass per acre.

POSITIVE FEEDING MOOD: An *appetite mood*. The attitude of fish which are actively feeding.

POST-FRONT: That period after a weather front. Usually used in reference to a cold front when the atmosphere becomes clear and bright, and is accompanied by strong winds and a significant drop in temperature.

POST-SPAWN PERIOD: The period immediately following spawning characterized by poor fishing because fish are recuperating and relocating.

POST-SUMMER PERIOD: A period of the fish cycle following the Summer Period. It can mean about a week or more of terrific fishing.

PRECAMBRIAN SHIELD: The Canadian Shield. A geological rock formation covering much of eastern and central Canada and some of the north central U.S.A.

PREDATOR: An organism which feeds on another.

PREDATOR/PREY RELATIONSHIP: An interrelationship between a species and an accessible and suitable forage.

PREFERRED FOOD: Food or forage best suited to a species' basic needs.

PRE-SPAWN PERIOD: The period of the fish cycle immediately before spawning when fish position themselves near their spawning grounds.

PRE-SUMMER PERIOD: The period of the fish cycle immediately following post-spawn. Fish mood is often positive, but fish establish a wide variety of patterns.

REEDS: Bulrushes or rushes.

RESERVOIR: Impoundment. A place where water is collected and stored.

RIG: A fishing boat; the hook, snell and other terminal tackle for live bait fishing; assembling tackle.

SADDLE: A site where a structural element narrows before widening again.

SCHOOL (OF FISH): A number of fish of the same or similar species grouped together and moving as a unit to benefit from the defensive and/or feeding advantages associated with coordinated activity.

SHALLOW WATER ZONE: *A lake zone.* The area out to the first major drop-off.

SHIELD WATER: Body of water located on the Precambrian or Canadian Shield. Specifically, a body of water in an area where the basin and surrounding terrain has had their nutrient-producing rock and sediment layers eroded away by glaciers.

SLICK: A sand or clay bar, point or drop-off devoid of weeds, brush, rock or boulders, etc.; a section of calm surface water in a river.

SOFT BOTTOM: Bottoms (silt, mud, muck, marl, etc.) which are not hard.

SOCIAL CONDITION: One of three elements helping to determine a species' locational pattern. It includes population density, food availability, and competitive species and how these interrelate.

SNAKETROLLING: A system of *boat control* in which a lure or bait is trolled in a weaving manner to cover a wide area and a range of depth levels.

SPAWN PERIOD: A brief period of the fish cycle directly linked to seasonal progression and a range of suitable temperatures. When a species reproduces.

SPECIES: A group of closely-related organisms which can produce offspring.

SPEED CONTROL: One of two primary factors in bait or lure presentation. The other is depth.

SPEEDTROLLING: A system of *boat control* in which a lure is trolled behind a boat moving at fast speed.

SPOOKING: Frightening or "turning off" one or more fish.

STRAGGLERS: Fish lingering apart from others of their species after a movement.

STRIKING: An involuntary reflex action prompted by a bait or lure. Fish are made to bite. See *biting.*

STRUCTURAL CONDITION: One of three elements helping to determine a species' locational patterns. It includes bottom configuration, bottom content, water characteristics, vegetation types and water exchange rate.

STRUCTURAL ELEMENT: Most any natural or man-made, physical features in a body of water. See *bottom configuration.*

SUMMER PERIOD: A period of the fish cycle when fish generally hold to patterns established during the last part of the Summer Peak Period.

SUMMER PEAK PERIOD: A short period of the fish cycle which begins after the first hot spell that remains for several days and nights. Fish begin establishing summer patterns at the latter portion of this period.

SUSPENDED FISH: Fish which are hovering considerably above the bottom in open water.

TAPER: An area that slopes toward deeper water.

THERMOCLINE: The center area of temperature stratification in a body of water. Specifically, the division between the epilimnion and hypolimnion. Temperature changes very quickly.

TIGHT ACTION PLUG: A lure whose side-to-side movements are short and distinct.

TOPWATER PLUG: A floating lure designed for use on the water's surface.

TOTAL ENVIRONMENT: The body of water a species lives in, and any outside stimuli influencing it.

TRANSITION (BOTTOM): The point where one type of bottom material changes to another.

TRIGGER: One of eight lures or bait characteristics designed to stimulate positive responses from fish (action, color, size, shape, scent, sound, vibration, texture). Triggers appeal to the sensory organs of a species.

TURNOVER PERIOD: A very brief period of the fish cycle when some lakes or reservoirs are in turmoil. A mixing or "turning over" of the water takes place as cold water on the surface settles and warmer water from below rises. This turnover homogenizes lakes that have thermoclined (layered according to water temperature) in summer and reoxygenates the water.

TWO-STORY LAKE: A body of water in which warm water species inhabit the upper portion while cold water species inhabit the deeper portion.

WATER CHARACTERISTICS: The characteristics of a body of water, usually referred to in terms of mineral content (soft, few minerals; medium, some minerals; hard, many minerals). The amount of minerals determines fertility.

WATER EXCHANGE RATE: The rate at which water enters or leaves a body of water.

WORKING METHOD: An aspect of presentation consisting of triggers, controls, gear selection and technique.

British pike expert Fred Buller's book Pike **and the** Pike Angler *is available from the* IN-FISHERMAN, *P.O. Box 999, Brainerd, MN 56401.*

Dutchman Jan Eggers has been fishing since boyhood and has always been intrigued by the pike. Eggers is greatly interested in the big pike records of the world.

An old-time pike stringer from central Minnesota.

A true brace of lunker European pike.

A prime example of a summer-stressed pike caught by Ron Lindner. Notice the sunken stomach.

Dave Csanda with a modern day catch of Great Lakes pike.